The Poetics
of the Occasion

The Poetics
of the Occasion

Mallarmé and the Poetry
of Circumstance

Marian Zwerling Sugano

Stanford University Press
Stanford, California
1992

Stanford University Press
Stanford, California

© 1992 by the Board of Trustees of the
Leland Stanford Junior University

Printed in the United States of America

CIP data are at the end of the book

For Tom
because *things tend to work out*

Acknowledgments

It would be virtually impossible to acknowledge all the intellectual and personal debts I have incurred in the years since I began this project. I would like first of all to thank Leo Bersani, whose stirring seminars at Berkeley gave me the inspiration and the courage to write on Mallarmé, and without whose encouragement this book would not exist. I owe a great deal as well to Bonnie Isaac, whose intelligence and generosity contributed immeasurably to my work, and to Robert Alter, for his sensitive reading of the manuscript. Special thanks go to the friends and colleagues who helped me refine the ideas that eventually worked their way into this book, especially Caroline Newman, for her insights and friendship, Jean Andrews, and Jorge Duany. I thank Hélène Vilavella for her revision of the Mallarmé translations. To Helen Tartar, the accomplished editor at Stanford University Press, I offer thanks both for her enthusiasm and for her intelligent direction.

An abbreviated version of Chapter 5 entitled " 'L'objet tu': Reconceptualizing the Literary and Sculptural Art Object" appeared in vol. 23 (1988) of *Pacific Coast Philology*, the annual publication of the Philological Association of the Pacific Coast, and is used here with the kind permission of Caroline Locher, the Executive Director of PAPC.

I wish to express my gratitude to François Chapon, Conservateur en chef de la Bibliothèque Littéraire Jacques Doucet in Paris, as well as to Conservateurs Mme Nicole Prévot and Mlle Jacqueline Zacchi, for the kind and generous assistance they gave me in my research and in helping me to secure the photographs of Mallarmé's "manuscripts" of the *Vers de circonstance*.

I must finally express my greatest debt, which is to my family: to my father and Susi, who always believed in me; to Danny and Helen, from whom I learn more every day; and to my husband Tom, who gave me the freedom to pursue my goals in my own way and at my own rate, who brought computers into my life and made them work for me, and to whose love and ingenuity I dedicate this book.

M. Z. S.

Contents

A Note to the Reader

For convenience the texts and translations of the long poems discussed here are provided in the Appendix. Sonnets and shorter poems appear in the text. Except where otherwise noted, the French texts follow the Pléiade edition of Mallarmé's *Œuvres complètes* (1945). All references to this volume are cited as *O.c.*

All translations from Mallarmé and from other French sources are my own, except where noted otherwise. The translations are for the most part literal ones, and they are provided to give nonreaders of French access to this book. The difficulties of all translation, and particularly of the translation of Mallarmé's idiosyncratic syntax and the multiple levels of meanings present in both his poetry and prose, have been amply documented. The long process of translating Mallarmé has been, to say the least, a humbling one, and I am enormously grateful to the many translators who have gone before me whose work I was able to consult: Paul Auster, Keith Bosley, Brian Coffey, Robert Cohn, Bradford Cook, Ursula Franklin, Roger Fry, Rosemary Lloyd, and C. F. MacIntyre.

The Poetics
of the Occasion

Introduction:
Mallarmé and the Occasional Mode

The difference between the historian and the poet is not that the
historian employs prose and the poet verse . . . rather . . . the one
tells of things that have been and the other of such things as
might be. —Aristotle, *Poetics*

In historiography the prosaic element [lies] especially in the fact that
. . . its actual form ha[s] to appear accompanied in many ways by
relative circumstances, clustered with accidents, and sullied by
arbitrariness, although the historian ha[s] no right to transform this
form of reality which [is] precisely in conformity with what immedi-
ately and actually happened. The task of this transformation is one to
which poetry is chiefly called if in its material it treads on the
ground of historical description. In this case it has to search out the
inmost kernel and meaning of an event, an action, a national
character, a prominent historical individual, but it has to strip away
the accidents that play their part around them, and the indifferent
accessories of what happened, the purely relative circumstances and
traits of character, and put in their place things through which the
inner substance of the thing at issue can clearly shine.
—Hegel, *Aesthetics*

There is, admittedly, a degree of circumlocution involved in
calling attention to the opposition between historiography and po-
etry in order to point up the moment at which the two come together
in an ideal scene of encounter. For Aristotle as for Hegel, a poetry
that treats of "real events" serves as an arena for the contradictory
claims of historian and poet. But my tactics will no doubt regain cred-
ibility as it becomes clear that the point of designating this scene of
encounter is precisely to mark its borderline positioning between his-
tory and poetry, between fact and fiction, between the circumstantial

and the essential. Such is the case for occasional poetry, which, implicitly in Aristotle, explicitly in Hegel, becomes a critical placeholder in their attempts to elucidate the nature of poetry.

For Aristotle poetry "is a more philosophical and a higher thing than history, in that poetry tends rather to express the universal, history rather the particular fact. A universal is: The sort of thing that (in the circumstances) a certain kind of person will say or do either probably or necessarily, which in fact is the universal that poetry aims for" (*Poetics* 9.54). In direct opposition to Plato, who wished to banish poets from the Republic because of their lack of adherence to the truth, Aristotle hailed the poet as an adept prevaricator, a "maker of plots" rather than a chronicler of actions. This did not mean, however, that the poet was forbidden the imitation of historical or contemporary events: "So even if on occasion he takes real events as the subject of a poem, he is none the less a poet, since nothing prevents some of the things that have actually happened from being of the sort that might probably or possibly happen" (9.54). Thus a poetry treating real, particular events comes to occupy a peripheral position within the domain of the properly poetic.

Hegel converts what for Aristotle is the marginal case into an imperative. Riding on centuries of misconstrued anti-Aristotelian sentiment and numerous defenses and apologies for the value and legitimacy of a poetry divorced from history, Hegel agrees with Aristotle that "in poetry it is only the poetical, not something outside poetry, which must rule as the determining and executed end" (*Aesthetics* 995), but then immediately counters this affirmation:

But, conversely, the art of poetry should not seek to maintain an absolutely isolated position in the real world, but must, as itself living, enter into the midst of life. . . . Poetry's living connection with the real world and its occurrences in public and private affairs is revealed most amply in the so-called *pièces d'occasion*. If this description were given a wider sense, we could use it as a name for nearly all poetic works: but if we take it in the proper and narrower sense we have to restrict it to productions owing their origin to some single present event and expressly devoted to its exaltation, embellishment, commemoration, etc. But by such entanglement with life poetry seems again to fall into a position of dependence, and for this reason it has often been proposed to assign to the whole sphere of *pièces d'occasion* an inferior value although to some extent, especially in lyric poetry, the most famous works belong to this class. (995–96)

Hegel's seesawing discourse is indicative of the kind of difficulties one encounters in trying to situate the occasional poem in critical discourse. Within the space of the paragraphs that introduce the discussion of occasional poetry in the *Aesthetics*, he first asserts the absolute autonomy and independence of the poetic, next warns against its isolation from the real world, and then decries its "position of dependence" and "entanglement with life." Poetry must be autonomous but not insular, independent and yet not self-sufficient. Hegel's definition of occasional verse is no less contradictory; he hesitates between the narrowly defined and the all-inclusive. And finally, as to value, the occasional poem would seem in some sense to evidence both poetry's greatest potential and its most inferior productions, its most famous works and its moments least worthy of inscription.

Although Aristotle's idea of a poetry that takes real events as its subject cannot simply be equated with Hegel's notion of the occasional poem, two points remain unequivocal: (1) From antiquity through the early nineteenth century a marginal area was designated as lying between the properly historical and the properly poetic; that is, a poetry that cannot be defined by exclusivity (i.e., neither history nor poetry) but rather by its inclusiveness—at once history *and* poetry. (2) This kind of text holds a special fascination for the critical imagination because of its elusive, dual nature, and yet has had an anomalous status in the history of literary criticism. Given the historical ambiguity and potential power of the occasional poem, one would expect it to enjoy a position of consequence in contemporary theory and criticism. Indeed, in the light of the controversy generated by recent revelations concerning Paul de Man's engagement with society, his comments written over a decade ago about literature's representation of the real are particularly noteworthy:

The spirit of the times is not blowing in the direction of formalist and intrinsic criticism. We may no longer be hearing too much about relevance but we keep hearing a great deal about reference, about the nonverbal "outside" to which language refers, by which it is conditioned and upon which it acts. The stress falls not so much on the fictional status of literature—a property now perhaps somewhat too easily taken for granted—but on the interplay between these fictions and categories that are said to partake of reality, such as the self, man, society, "the artist, his culture and the human community" as one critic puts it. Hence the emphasis on hybrid texts considered to be partly literary and partly referential. (*Allegories* 3)

But in point of fact, in spite of its undeniably "hybrid" nature, occasional literature per se is practically nonexistent as a topic in current literary criticism. With the exception of a small number of articles on Renaissance and eighteenth-century poets,[1] contemporary critics and theorists have not as yet directly confronted the problematics of the occasional.

How can we account, then, for what appears to be a conspicuous neglect of occasional poetry in an age "beyond formalism" that actively seeks, in accordance with our sense of a "highly respectable moral imperative . . . to reconcile the internal, formal, private structures of literary language with their external, referential, and public acts" (de Man, *Allegories* 3)? Hegel has already furnished one plausible answer in alluding to the "inferior value" often assigned to the occasional poem. Even the term itself now bears a stigma. (It is perhaps worth noting in this regard that Hegel's translator felt compelled to substitute the more eloquent French "pièce d'occasion" for our less fortunate English term, "occasional poem.") The juxtaposition of "occasion" with "poetry" has come to have something of an oxymoronic flavor to the extent that we have so thoroughly assimilated and still so insufficiently moved beyond the New Critical doctrine of the poem as autonomous object, or in more recent parlance, as self-sufficient text.

As we have seen, Hegel attributes occasional poetry's lack of prestige to an "entanglement" (*Verflechtung*) with life by which it seems to fall into a position of "dependence" (*Abhängigkeit*). The choice of terminology is telling in that it conjures up images of hopelessly inextricable relations on one hand and a moral, philosophical inferiority and parasitism on the other. But if "life" and the poetic had come to be so antithetical in Hegel's day, and if a poetry directed at, circumscribed by, and limited to the "exaltation, embellishment, [or] commemoration" of a contemporary event was inevitably precluded from claims to distinction, this certainly had not always been the case. A brief historical sketch, an outline of the changing reception of occasional poetry, will perhaps help us to understand better its present situation.

But such a history, let me stress at the outset, will be necessarily a one-sided one, distorting the rather eclectic nature of the phenomena of the occasional into a convenient narrative. A more representative history of occasional verse would indeed be a schizophrenic one. On one hand it would have to trace, from classical to modern times, the body of "serious" poetry written for special occasions such as memorial pieces composed in honor of royalty or aristocratic patrons, sonnets or odes commemorating state occasions or historic events, epithalamiums, funeral elegies, and the like. Such a history would include the great works of Western literature from Pindar and Horace to Ronsard, Jonson, Milton, Goethe, Yeats, and Mallarmé, as will be our purpose to show. This history would necessarily take into account the long-standing tradition of the court poet and poet laureate and would cover the details of the institution of patronage in antiquity and the Renaissance. It would be a history of public poetry, a history of the victors and the monuments, imposing or mediocre, erected in verse to them.

And yet a parallel history could be told revealing the other face of the occasional: verse written in a lighter vein, not for the public at large but for a private circle of friends or lovers, a poetry commemorating birthdays, containing invitations, expressing condolences, offering gifts, and so on. Clearly, however, these two histories could not be entirely distinct given the important historical transformation of the notions of "public" and "private" and the fact that this second body of poetry, composed of what we might call trivial verse, has often found its way into anthologies and has been monumentalized along with the rest. Any attempt at a clear binary alignment of descriptive and evaluative terms is doomed to failure.

In Ancient Greece occasional works were classified by Menander and taught as types of epideictic oration, and such forms remained essentially the same until the late seventeenth century. As O. B. Hardison, Jr., has shown, the notion of a rhetoric of praise or blame is essential for understanding the function of poetry in the Renaissance:

During the Renaissance . . . occasional literature was highly valued. Poets and critics agreed that literature had an important social mission. The great forms like epic and drama dealt with legendary or historical figures and produced generalized patterns for emulation or admonition. The occasional forms dealt with contemporary events and living (or recently living) figures. They were particularly suited to arousing patriotism, stimulating interest in specific institutions or events, teaching admiration for a particular ruler, or demonstrating the existence of virtue in the society in which the reader actually lived. (108)

This conception of literature as predominantly didactic, as a form whose productions must contribute to the edification of society and the individual, helps us see exactly what was at stake in the polemics that raged in the historical space encompassed by my opening epigraphs. Obviously, if poetry's mission is to instruct, it must not run too far afield from accurate historical representation. Occasional poetry, in particular, must invest heavily in, as Hegel said, "what immediately and actually happened," and the poet's efforts "to search out the inmost kernel and meaning of an event" are necessarily predetermined by prevailing moral and ethical considerations (994).

A succinct account of the evolution of the relationship between literature and society in the Western world can be found in "The Reader in History: The Changing Shape of Literary Response" by Jane P. Tompkins. Offered as an epilogue to her critical anthology on reader-response theory, the article contrasts two fundamentally different approaches to the text, one characterizing the classical period through the eighteenth century, and one that distinguishes the major critical movements of the modern period. Although her purposes lie elsewhere, and she never mentions the term "occasional literature" itself, Tompkins provides the best introduction in current criticism to a historical and theoretical consideration of occasional verse. She distinguishes between the classical concept of language as action, as a force acting on the world, and the modern concept of language as signification, as a series of signs to be deciphered. In antiquity, it is the fact that poetry is a political force that explains Plato's banishment of the poet: "Only someone who accorded poetic language the highest degree of power in determining human action and behavior could regard poets as dangerous enough to exile" (204). This concept of language as a performative is crucial to my consideration of occasional literature and will be developed in detail in Chapter 2.

The essentially political character of patronage as an institution is perhaps the single most important aspect of Renaissance poetry. Very few writers regarded literature as their chief pursuit; it was rather the means to an extraliterary end (Sheavyn 19). Even for lawyers and doctors, the writing of poetry was a socially acceptable way of seeking professional advancement (Leighton 349). The existence of the courtier and aspiring poet was a precarious one, subject to the changes of political fortune, and competition for favor at court was polite but fierce. Typically, a poet would dedicate various versions of his work to a number of potential patrons in the hope of securing recognition and remuneration. Poetry was written to commemorate the daily occurrences as well as the more significant events in the patron's life, and, consequently, a great deal of the verse composed was little more than servile flattery.

The profuse production of courtiers and hopeful social climbers testifies to the validity of Tompkins's description of Renaissance poetry as "public relations": "In addition to being regarded as an inculcator of civic virtue, poetry becomes . . . a source of financial support, a form of social protection, a means of procuring a comfortable job, an instrument of socialization, a move in a complicated social game, or even a direct vehicle of courtship" (208). Tompkins notes that in the Renaissance "a literary work is not so much an object, therefore, as a unit of force whose power is exerted on the world in a particular direction" (204). Her contrast of Renaissance and modernist attitudes toward literature is instructive:

[In the Renaissance,] literature exists in order to serve its clientele and is subject to the audience's judgement. In the modern period, on the other hand, the work is not written for a known constituency, nor is it intended to have such well defined results. . . . The work is not a gesture in a social situation, or an ideal model for human behavior, but an interplay of formal and thematic properties to be penetrated by the critic's mind. The imputation that a poem might break out of its self-containment and perform a service would disqualify it immediately from consideration as a work of art. The first requirement of a work of art in the twentieth century is that it should *do* nothing. (210)

That the Renaissance poem was indisputably intended to *do* (and not simply *be*) is evident in J. W. Saunders's account of the Tudor court. The ideal courtier, according to Castiglione's *Il libro del cortegiano*, the most influential of the sixteenth-century handbooks of courtesy, was expected to be something of a poet in addition to his other accomplishments. Poetry was the means by which social intercourse and court affairs were conducted:

Within the Court circle it was used to grace and comment on virtually every happening in life, from birth to death, and [from] the presentation of a Christmas gift to the launching of a war. It was the agent of flattery, of ego-titillation, of love-making, and of condolence. It was the means whereby the Courtier discussed experience and pondered the approach of death. Sir

Henry Wotton said that Robert Devereux used to *think* in verse—to "evaporate his thoughts in a sonnet" was the common way. (Saunders 151)

What Saunders's description provides is a notion of the poetic as a quotidian, social discourse, a form of written conversation, almost a thinking aloud in verse. Such poetry might be described as casual and characterized by its adaptability and availability to the caprice of circumstance. At the peak of its efflorescence it was a generalized, pervasive phenomenon, the dominant form of polite social discourse.

Gradually, however, throughout the seventeenth and eighteenth centuries, political and social conditions metamorphosed so completely that the patronage system and, consequently, the institution of occasional literature were irrevocably transformed. The erosion of the monarchy and the degradation of the court changed the function and social significance of the occasions formerly celebrated in poetry, thereby altering the very foundations of literary endeavor. By the end of the eighteenth century the genre of occasional poetry had fallen into disrepute for many reasons: the sheer proliferation of undistinguished verse celebrating persons and occasions of dubious importance, the growing sense that the occasional poet was little more than a literate schemer in pursuit of social advancement or financial remuneration, an increasing conviction that writing prompted by objective rather than subjective stimuli was no more than literary prostitution, the widening perception that the occasional poem was a private piece whose public or representative significance was diminished, and economic factors such as, in Germany, the gradual decline of the printed funeral oration (Leighton 355). Though occasional poetry continued to be written, it was more and more viewed as an inferior mode of literary creation.

Goethe, who had written and been censured for his share of unmemorable court verse, almost single-handedly dealt occasional poetry its deathblow when, in one of his conversations with Eckermann, he said:

The world is so great and rich, and life so full of variety, that you can never want occasions for poems. But they must all be occasional poems; that is to say, reality must give both impulse and material for their production. A particular case becomes universal and poetic by the very circumstance that it is treated by a poet. All my poems are occasional poems, suggested by real life, and having therein a firm foundation. I attach no value to poems snatched out of the air. (18)

Whether this declaration is read as elevating occasional poetry to the rank of "true" poetry, or as simply conflating the two by abolishing the specificity of the occasion, Goethe so enlarged the notion of the occasion as to render it meaningless, and the future usefulness of the term "occasional literature" as a descriptive category was largely diminished.

By the nineteenth century the patronage system was extinct. "From this moment on," writes Bertrand Bronson of the first generation of literature conceived and conditioned by its commercial purpose and mode of existence, "gradually but increasingly there develops a race of authors who write to an indefinite body of readers, personally undifferentiated and unknown, who accept this separation as a primary condition of their creative activity and address their public invisibly through the curtain, opaque and impersonal, of print" (302). The personalized social context that governed and nourished occasional literature in its heyday was lost in the opacity of print.

The patronage system was replaced by two parallel institutions, one economic and one psychological. The reading public became the new financial patron of the poet, and he became dependent on public taste for his financial security. But unlike the sixteenth-century patron who offered his courtier not only money but also living quarters, educational opportunities, constant work, protection against calumny and piracy, and above all the genuine encouragement that could only arise from a shared interest in literature (Thomson 274), the nineteenth-century public was remote and impersonal. Gradually, with the development of the notion of the *poète maudit*, the gifted poet accursed by but dependent on his powerful but envious contemporaries, the public came to be perceived as hostile. In a sense, the nineteenth-century poet reproduced within himself the notion of the patron. And thus a new phenomenon arose, the financial independence of the poet and his professionalization as a man of letters. This newfound independence had, of course, enormous repercussions for the kinds of occasions that were to be celebrated in poetry. Except in the case of the poet laureate, affairs of state were no longer automatically to be memorialized in verse. The impetus to write occasional poetry was no longer predominantly external but internal, and consequently, the notion of the occasion became so blurred as to be confused with mere lyric impulse. Many of Wordsworth's titles, for instance, would seem to point to the circumstances of his writing, but in actuality are no more than an arbitrary point of departure for a composition that soon exceeds its occasion: "Lines Composed a Few Miles Above Tintern Abbey On Revisiting the Banks of the Wye During a Tour, July 13, 1798," "Sonnets Composed upon Westminster Bridge, September 3, 1802," or even more ambiguously, "Elegiac Stanzas Suggested by a Picture of Peele Castle, in a Storm, Painted by Sir George Beaumont."

Hegel's attribution of the "inferior value" of occasional verse to its "entanglement with life" thus would seem to be in consonance with the metamorphosis of the relationship of literature and society from classical times through the last century. But it must be remembered that Hegel's purpose was not only descriptive but prescriptive as well; that the *Aesthetics* functions not only as a critical reflection on art but also as a rather protracted *art poétique*. He proposes the following to assure that poetry's necessary involvement with life does not result in an entanglement:

Therefore the question arises: In what way can poetry still preserve its independence even when there is this conflict with its given subject-matter? Simply by not treating and presenting the external given occasion as an essential end, and itself only as a means to that, but instead by assimilating the essence of that actual fact and forming and shaping it by the freedom and the right of the imagination. In that event poetry is not the occasion and its accompaniment; but that essence is the *external* occasion; it is the stimulus which makes the poet abandon himself to his deeper penetration of the event and his clearer way of formulating it. In this way he creates from his own resources what without his aid we would not have become conscious of previously in this free way in the actual event directly presented to us. (996)

For Hegel, then, the resolution of the problem posed by occasional literature is to be achieved by means of a fusion of dualities to reach a higher level of consciousness: what appears to be the "external given" occasion must be formed and shaped by the poetic imagination to arrive at a newly found, essential rendition of the actual event. Inner and outer, means and end coalesce in a vertical loss of self: the poet "abandon[s] himself to his deeper penetration of the event." Hegel's choice of vocabulary here is telling, especially when we juxtapose it to that in our epigraph. Occasions are necessary but undesirable elements in the process of poetry making: they are "relative circumstances," and "indifferent accessories" that "sull[y] by arbitrariness" the properly poetic. They are "accidents" that must be "strip[ped] away" so that the "inmost kernel," the "inner substance," can be reached. For Hegel, the poetic is clearly not a surface effect, but rather, a poetry of depth.

Aristotle's belief that poetry expresses the universal, and history the particular fact is but an earlier version of the recurrent essential/contingent metaphor of our philosophical tradition that Hegel exploits here. The construction and employment of such binary systems have enormous implications for occasional literature. They point up a fundamental paradox that pervades the very notion of occasional poetry, especially as an aesthetics of value is applied. The best occasional poetry, as both Aristotle and Hegel give us to understand, is that which denies its status as such. The scandal of occasional literature is that it is most highly considered when it eschews its own defining status. C. M. Bowra, in his book on political poetry, a topic that significantly intersects with the occasional, patently and unabashedly reiterates the paradox: "The distillation of an essential poetry from transitory occasions gains by the omission of a reference to the actual shape of the occasions themselves" (77). The message is clear but unsettling: occasional poetry best addresses its circumstances by not addressing them at all.

This paradox is most explicit in modern poetics, although to some extent it underlies the entire tradition of occasional literature. In the introduction to their anthology of modern American poets, Sanders, Nelson, and Rosenthal speak to the problem of the occasional in terms of the modernist obsession with "pure" poetry. They tame the paradox of occasional literature considerably, only to give voice to a more astounding contradiction:

An interesting feature of the whole movement of modern poetry has been that, while from its beginnings it has appeared to struggle toward the kind of "purity" we associate with, say, Imagism—that is, a freedom from sentimentality and rhetoric and an assertion of intensity itself, whether of emotion or sensation, as a value independent of political, religious, or moral considerations—it has nevertheless been steeped in the dominant issues of the period. As a result, our poetry, despite its high aesthetic standards, has been profoundly, even violently, involved in the intellectual and social struggles of the age. The most successful poetry has been that which could transcend those struggles not so much by ignoring them as by remaining art even while wrestling with them. (10)

The implication, of course, is that "art" is antithetical to the "intellectual and social struggles" of our time, and, by extrapolation, that occasional literature can only be art by evidencing a degree of self-contortion (witness the metaphorical registers of the actions that must be performed to this end: *transcendence* [Sanders et al.], *distillation* [Bowra], and *assimilation* and *penetration* [Hegel]). Such is the principle underlying the formalist perspective that emphasizes the self-referentiality of the text. In all these formulations the text is seen as passive, having a capacity only to mirror its occasions. But is this the only way to conceive of the relationship between a poem and its circumstances?

Edward Said would answer with an emphatic negative. Instead, he proposes to call the text's way of engaging the world its "worldliness": "Most critics will subscribe to the notion that every literary text is in some way burdened with its occasion, with the plain empirical realities from which it emerged" (35). Said denounces literary theory as it is practiced in the American academy today in that it has

for the most part isolated textuality from the circumstances, the events, the physical senses that made it possible and render it intelligible as the result of human work. . . . My position is that texts are worldly, to some degree they are events, and, even when they appear to deny it, they are nevertheless a part of the social world, human life, and of course the historical moments in which they are located and interpreted. (4)

Actually, as it is no doubt already clear, Said's proposition is in part a repetition and embellishment of what I have described above as the view predominating from classical times through the eighteenth century, the concept of language and literature as action, as forces acting on the world. However, in spite of recent attempts to move significantly beyond formalism and beyond interpretation, a workable critical approach to occasional poetry has yet to be elaborated. Said himself has shown that the condition of the text is such that it explicitly compels attention toward the world even as its casting as fiction or poetry forcefully compels us away from it, bringing us into a self-reflecting discourse that shuns its worldly circumstances (45–46). The opposing forces are not, however, separable: they function simultaneously, and cannot be dealt with singly. All hybrid texts, and especially occasional poems, are susceptible to the contradictory claims of and to world and text.

The crucial question facing occasional literature is therefore that with which we began, the fundamental issue that Aristotle and

Hegel sought to illuminate. What *is* poetry's relationship to its occasion? Does poetry imitate it? Merely complement or report it? Recreate it? Create a parallel occasion? Supplant it? Does poetry compensate for it, creating the occasion where history neglected or failed to? Or is poetry rather constitutive of the occasion it appears to describe? If, as Said suggests, poetry itself is an event, how then does it interact with its context? How does language confront the world, and, specifically, how do poetic texts make and reflect their occasions?

The prevailing conception of occasional poetry suggests that there is a (usually, though not necessarily prior) external and independent event that is represented in the poem, and that the two moments, text and pre-text, can be clearly distinguished. The nature of their relationship would seem to have been straightforward in, for example, the seventeenth century, when poems were commissioned to commemorate an event or composed by a poet to initiate one. But even here it is difficult to ascertain what in the poem relates specifically to the circumstance, and what exceeds it. It would be difficult to find a writer whose poetry is more "frankly occasional"[2] than Ben Jonson's, and yet a recent article on his occasional works seeks to account for the "prevailing but ultimately misleading sense of many readers that his poems commemorate or respond directly to events that transpire in the public or political world" (Kamholtz 78). Kamholtz further claims that "Jonson's occasional poems seem to float free of the occasions that may have inspired them, and he omits or abbreviates many, if not all, of the typical descriptive and prescriptive elements" (80). Although to some extent it could be granted that such criticism imposes a twentieth-century reading on Renaissance literature, the example demonstrates to what degree the distinctly progressive historical narrative I outlined above for occasional poetry must be set off against the unnarratable history of poetry's link to the occasion. The latter would show that poetry's relation to its circumstances is a more or less constant swerving away from or incompatibility to occasion. It becomes clear that any simple conception of the relationship between the event and the poem in occasional poetry is necessarily deluded, and that the phrase "occasioned by" is perhaps more complex and more interesting than occasional verse has been credited for.

Indeed, a poem may be "occasioned by" specific circumstances and yet not exhibit any direct thematic relationship to the occasion itself. The question becomes as follows: if the text is not in some way imitative of the occasion, how can we call it occasional? The fundamental difference between occasional and other poetry may lie less in the way it relates to the occasion than in how the reader's strategies must be varied to deal with it. What does it mean to read a poem within the context of its occasion? To what degree can it or should it be divorced from that occasion? To what extent does or should the occasional origin of a poem condition its critical reception? To pose such questions is to take up the most fundamental problems of contemporary theoretical thought that opposes the autonomous and the referential, the textual and the worldly.

Clearly, these questions cannot be explored without reference to a specific body of poetry. I have selected for this purpose the occasional poetry of a modern rather than a Renaissance poet in order to confront the problem in its most complex form. Mallarmé's notorious dismissals of the real world, combined with his early critics' willingness to ignore the occasional nature of his work, radically problematize the question of the relationship between circumstance and writing in his poetry.

The decision to study occasional poetry by focusing on the work of Stéphane Mallarmé may in some quarters still be met with skepticism. By now it has become a cliché of literary history to place him at the nexus of that rupture in the nineteenth century in which language becomes increasingly divorced from reality and is seen as turning in upon itself. A century of criticism has sedulously fostered a version of Mallarmé as the paragon of ivory-tower poets. Because of his youthful essay, "L'Art pour tous" ("Art for All"), in which he urges poets to adopt "une langue immaculée—des formules hiératiques dont l'étude aride aveugle le profane et aiguillonne le patient fatal" ("an immaculate language—hieratic formulas whose arid study blinds the profane and spurs on the fatally resolute") and the now notorious verse, "Donner un sens plus pur aux mots de la tribu" (*O.c.* 70) ("To give a purer meaning to the words of the tribe"), Mallarmé has acquired the seemingly unshakeable reputation of high priest of self-reflexive literature. Statements such as "Au fond je considère l'époque contemporaine comme un interrègne pour le poëte qui n'a point à s'y mêler" (*O.c.* 664) ("Basically I consider that for the poet,

our times are an interregnum in which he should not get involved")
and "[le] poëte . . . est un grève devant la société" (*O.c.* 870) ("the
poet is on strike before society") are frequently quoted as evidence of
Mallarmé's apolitical stance and social apathy.

In fact, however (as Jacques Scherer pointed out as early as 1957
in his introduction to the fragments of Mallarmé's *Le Livre* [9]), with
few exceptions, all of Mallarmé's works after 1873 manifest a rein-
vestment in the world subsequent to the metaphysical crises of the
1860's and the years of silence that followed. The poetry and prose
of this prolific period are all occasional, written largely in perfor-
mance of his role of *homme de lettres* and *maître* of the young sym-
bolists. In addition to the "Tombeaux" poems, the toasts, and certain
of the "Eventails," which are considered among the "serious" poems,
he wrote the *Vers de circonstance* (address quatrains, gift poems on
candied fruits, on Easter eggs, on small stones gathered at Honfleur,
on jugs of Calvados), as well as translations, dedications, theater re-
views, a women's journal, a study of the English language, and various
other commissioned journalistic or celebratory pieces. The "Biblio-
graphie" that Mallarmé appended to the Deman edition of his *Poésies*
is a meticulous recording of the circumstances for which the majority
of the poems were composed. It attests to his rather peculiar insis-
tence on their occasional nature (at least from "Toast funèbre" on)
that is only further dramatized by his postfixing this rather curious and
ambiguous note: "Tant de minutie témoigne, inutilement peut-être,
de quelque déférence aux scoliastes futurs" (*O.c.* 78) ("Such atten-
tion paid to detail evinces, uselessly, perhaps, a certain deference to
future scholiasts"). Mallarmé here addresses his future public in of-
fering his poetic occasions for scrutiny and at the same time under-
mines the usefulness of such annotations.

But concomitant with this compelling attention to the world is an
increasingly hermetic language. The later works evidence a ceaseless
gesturing toward the world, staging a democratic, desolemnizing free
circulation of poetry, and yet the bulk of this writing is precisely his
most difficult, the most intractably obscure. It is as if at the very mo-
ment of turning toward the world, Mallarmé turns away from it. Syn-
tax becomes increasingly unrecognizable as the desire for communi-
cation intensifies. How can we reconcile such radical sociability with
its recalcitrant hermeticism?

Furthermore, the bulk of the late poetry is ostensibly rather friv-

Stéphane Mallarmé, from a lithograph of an 1892 drawing by James Whistler (Bibliothèque Littéraire Jacques Doucet). In thanking Whistler Mallarmé wrote: "Ce portrait est une merveille, la seule chose qui ait été jamais faite d'après moi, et je m'y souris." ("This portrait is a marvel, it is the only one that has truly caught my likeness, and I'm much pleased by it.") Mallarmé accompanied his gift to Whistler of the first numbered copy of *Vers et Prose* with this distich:

> Whistler
> selon qui je défie
> Les siècles, en lithographie.

> Whistler
> according to whom I defy
> The centuries, in a lithograph.

olous verse; its themes, when identifiable, are seemingly inconsequential. There would appear to be a violation of literary decorum posed by the disproportion between occasion and utterance. Here the problematics of occasional poetry become increasingly complex: the gulf between formal difficulty and anecdotal modesty futher exacerbates the question of the relationship between the circumstance that occasions poetry and the act of writing that celebrates circumstance. This, then, becomes the justification for placing Mallarmé at the core of my investigation: the problem of occasional poetry is precisely most interesting where it is most difficult.

Historically, Mallarmé's situation is an intriguing one in that the very hermeticism of the late poetry and prose obscured the fact that the works were occasional. But even when exegetes reached a more or less coherent consensus as to the origins and "subjects" of the major poems, there was a reluctance to admit that such abstract and irregular syntax had been put to the service of a trivial thematics. After decades of critical negligence or abuse, when Mallarmé's reputation as one of the great poets of nineteenth-century France was finally established, it would have been counterproductive to insist on the circumstantial nature of the serious texts.

Today, however, Mallarmé's prominence is so thoroughly unassailable and the attribution of mastery to him so totalizing that a reconsideration of his poetic output is in order. The industry of exegesis that dominated Mallarmé scholarship from 1940 through 1970 and the wave of structuralist and poststructuralist attention that followed, finding in Mallarmé a precursor of the revolution in poetic language, is now giving way to another level of criticism that is not blind to the actual nature of his production. Virginia A. La Charité has called attention to the fact that Mallarmé's reputation rests on an exceedingly slim eighty-six of the over 1,600 pages in the Pléiade edition ("Mallarmé" 173). I believe that his so-called minor works now deserve critical attention to the extent that they illustrate the poetics of another Mallarmé, not the "intellectual inhibited by the white sheet of paper which he was too fastidious to violate" (Brereton 282) featured in traditional literary histories, but the other Mallarmé, the Parisian Maître, host of the "Mardistes," the poet of a civil, public language, a discourse at once domestic and obscure, Mallarmé the loquacious, the occasional poet.[3]

My purpose, then, is twofold. By exploring the occasional verse of a poet who took the problematics of the occasion as the specific occasion of his writing, I wish to rehabilitate such writing for critical study; not by proclaiming its high seriousness, but instead by insisting on its casual, amenable, public nature. Those who have written on occasional literature in the past have often felt compelled to preface their work with apologies and to justify their straying into the fringes of the literary canon by stressing the potential of their material to clarify the relationship of poetry and society. But the wit and graciousness of this criticism make manifest a kind of reveling in what has been cast aside as second-rate work, a delectation in addressing the marginal. I would hope to evidence that same delight, all the while insisting that in a poetics of the occasion, traditional oppositions such as center/margin become skewed and break down.

And second, I hope to come to a better understanding of Mallarmé in the light of what he actually wrote, rather than in terms of the work projected in his correspondence and prose articles. Each of my chapters highlights one particular aspect of occasional poetry through an investigation of one or more of Mallarmé's texts. In Chapter 1 I examine the poetry of Mallarmé's crisis period, "Ses purs ongles," "Ouverture ancienne d'Hérodiade," and "L'Après-midi d'un faune," which can be seen as attempts at exploring the nature and limits of the occasion as pre-text, and its relationship to the occasion of the writing itself. But my findings here suggest that the specificity of occasional literature cannot be determined solely in terms of the relationship between the inter- and extratextual. In Chapter 2 I therefore attempt to bring the problem within another focus by considering the rhetorical status of the occasional text, juxtaposing it with recent work on the performative. In "Toast funèbre," the emphasis is less on a descriptive, constative "portrayal" of the dead poet Gautier than on the now of the poetic occasion, the act of celebrating him in verse. In the poem, which inaugurates Mallarmé's career as occasional poet, he appears to be performing a kind of deconstruction of the performative as he celebrates the occasion of his own awakening to occasion.

Chapter 3 is pivotal in that it provides textual examples for the theoretical questions posed above and provides the foundation on which the new poetics of writing can be established. Here the problem of poetic language as constative or performative is reformulated in terms of two texts from the 1880's, "Prose pour des Esseintes" and the prose poem "La Déclaration foraine." The texts are similar in that they can be read both thematically and functionally as allegories of the situation of the occasional text, providing two possible models for conceiving the relationship between text and world.

In Chapters 4 and 5 I shift my emphasis from a theoretical question about poetic representation to the writing of the occasion itself. I explore the two poles of occasional poetry, the monumental and the trivial. The first is examined in the light of the monuments Mallarmé actually erected, his "Tombeaux" poems. Moving from the traditional tribute to Poe to the unconventional mobility of the Verlaine "Tombeau," I show how Mallarmé displaced conventional notions of representation as immobilization to move toward a more mobile, trivial form of writing. Finally, using Mallarmé's *carte de visite* (calling card) as a working model opposed to the monument, I suggest that it is the textual performance of the *Vers de circonstance* that may ultimately be his most radical undertaking as a writer.

Chapter One

Between World and Text:
"Ses purs ongles," "Ouverture ancienne
d'Hérodiade," and "L'Après-midi d'un faune"

The occasion is the delicate, almost invisible, web in which the fruit
hangs. Insofar, therefore, as it sometimes seems as if the occasion
were the essential element, this is in general a misunderstanding, for
normally it is but a particular side of it.　—Kierkegaard, *Either/Or*

> The poem is the cry of its occasion,
> Part of the res itself and not about it.
> —Wallace Stevens,
> "An Ordinary Evening
> in New Haven"

In its simplest form occasional literature presupposes two ele-
ments: an occasion and its textual inscription. Traditionally, the oc-
casion is conceived of according to a philosophical hierarchy that
places it, as an extratextual origin, temporally prior to and logically
causal of the poetry it inspires. The occasional poem is then viewed
as an aftereffect, an imitation or representation of the original oc-
casion. In its most typical gesture, occasional literature seeks to re-
capture the world within its textual confines.

Using Mallarmé's poetry as a site of confrontation, I hope to dem-
onstrate the shortcomings of such unproblematized notions of mi-
mesis and representation. Throughout this book I reformulate the
question, re-posing it from the different perspectives suggested by
those Mallarméan texts that most acutely engage the problem of lit-
erature and its contexts. My elaboration of a more adequate poetics
of the occasion begins with the poems of Mallarmé's crisis period, the
notorious "nights of Tournon," an interval of intellectual and aes-
thetic questioning that reached the proportions of a philosophical

suicide. Viewed within this perspective, the poems of the 1860's, although not occasional in any conventional sense, can be read as attempts at exploring the nature and limits of the occasion as pre-text and its relationship to the occasion of writing itself.

By means of a number of shared thematic and representational concerns, "Ses purs ongles," "Ouverture ancienne d'Hérodiade," and "L'Après-midi d'un faune" all participate in a speculative inquiry that might be described in its broadest terms as the exploration of the problem of duality. In these poems the relationship of occasion to text is but a subset of a more general problematics of oppositional poles such as single/dual, outside/inside, male/female, or same/different, matched pairs that inhabit all the texts but manifest themselves, as I shall show in greater detail, most prominently in one or the other. I read the early poems as confronting these questions in strikingly similar metaphorical terms: each displays a series of thematic and formal constructs that attack the problem of representation in terms of a double valency of the object as both container and contained.

From the "cinerary amphora," the "empty parlour," the "mirror," the "frame," or the unfathomable "ptyx" of "Ses purs ongles" to the "basin/pool" or the "cinerary tower/pale mausoleum" of the "Ouverture ancienne" to the "empty cluster" of the "Faune," we have repeated attempts to fashion an answer to the larger question of how the world "gets into" the text and how the text "contains" the world. In each of the three poems there is a seeing, speaking subject (the poetic persona/Master in the "Sonnet," the Nurse of "Hérodiade," and the Faun) who must be viewed as the origin of the discourse about the relationship of world to text.[1] In each case the "seer" (literally, one who sees) must deal with the questionable ontological status of the objects that are taken on in its utterances, ranging from the seemingly present golden frame of the mirror in the sonnet or the empty bed in the "Ouverture," to the myriad figures of absence that paradoxically "populate" the three texts: the "nixie . . . defunct nude in the mirror," the "Master [who] went to draw tears from the Styx," Hérodiade/Dawn, the "beautiful bird" who has escaped the "weighty tomb," or the nymphs of "L'Après-midi." In the three poems the seer's obsessive attention to the world amounts to a voyeurism: that kind of fixed attention to anything necessarily imbues it with eroticism and converts the simple business of looking into an activity bordering on the pornographic.[2]

In "Ses purs ongles" and "Hérodiade" the voyeuristic aspects of perception are enhanced by our inability to pinpoint the location of the spectator's eye: does it peep in through a window at the two capricious interiors (and here one is reminded of Baudelaire's "Les Fenêtres": "Il n'est pas d'objet plus profond, plus mystérieux, plus fécond, plus ténébreux, plus éblouissant qu'une fenêtre éclairée d'une chandelle" [288]) ("There is no object more profound, more mysterious, more fecund, more darkly captivating, more dazzling than a window illuminated by a candle") or does the "regard" come from within the room itself?[3] In either case, in the two poems what we do *not* have is a mere description or word imitation of a room whose objects can be identified as present or absent; we are not simply asserting positivities or even negativities. Nor, I believe, are we witness to a privileged moment of glimpsing objects on the threshold of their disappearance, as they are transformed from presence to their "presque disparition vibratoire" ("vibratory near disappearance"). The conventional mimetic model outlined above depends on a conception of textual representation as imitation of objects or events fully present to themselves. But what we have in these early poems of Mallarmé is an already problematized notion of mimesis: the rooms of the "Sonnet en yx" or the "Ouverture" are already a kind of theatrical stage that does not exist prior to its linguistic formulation. Rather, its "existence" is coeval with its "description" in writing. The objects within are just as "real," but more important, just as "unreal" as the text that evokes them. They are, in fact, textual artifacts, inhabiting a limbo, materializations of the space in between world and text.

In fact, I will argue that both "Ses purs ongles" and the "Ouverture ancienne" are in some sense texts *about* the profusion of objects; that is, in both poems, but particularly in the latter, Mallarmé explores the conjunction of the real and the textual by straining the reader's ability to draw one to one correspondences between textual signs and extratextual referents. The texts operate by proliferating references to worldly objects and then withdrawing them. The reader is confronted with an array of objects that are constantly being reshuffled, reordered, and revised, creating a mobile corridor between sign and signified. The effect is a dizzying disorientation that leads to an infinite rewriting and rereading ending in a bizarrely mobile stasis.

In "L'Après-midi d'un faune" the question of the correspondence between the real and the textual becomes the principal thematic concern as the problem of representation shifts from the object to the temporality of the event. Rather than focusing on the ontological status of an amphora or the "ptyx" and its textual description, in the "Faune" the text moves the present/absent figure into time and hence, into a questioning about its anecdotal and narrative status. Here we are concerned not only with the existence or nonexistence of the nymphs but with the "story" of the Faun's involvement with them. Whereas in "Ses purs ongles" and "Hérodiade" the questioning involves a problematized duality of world and text, in the "Faune" a third category arises, that of dream or fantasy, which mediates between the two. The result is particularly rich in its effect on the container/contained problem, for it expands it, multiplying considerably the number of possible framings. Not only can the world be seen as both contained in and containing the text, but the world is contained in dream, which is then contained by the text, and conversely, text contains dream, which contains the real. The "Faune" suggests, ultimately, the untenability of a model of representation that rests on polar opposites of inter- and extratextual, for each term itself can be seen as already both container and contained. Finally, all may be read, according to the poem's last image of the Faun as a vast receptacle of the world ("and how I love / To open my mouth to the efficacious star of wines!"), which itself is swallowed up in its own textual fabulation ("in the forgetting of blasphemy") as nothing more than "false / Confusions between itself [the surrounding beauty] and our credulous song"; that is, as modulations of the uniformity of art: that "sonorous, vain, and monotonous line."

Sonnet

Ses purs ongles très haut dédiant leur onyx,
L'Angoisse, ce minuit, soutient, lampadophore,
Maint rêve vespéral brûlé par le Phénix
Que ne recueille pas de cinéraire amphore

Sur les crédences, au salon vide: nul ptyx,   5
Aboli bibelot d'inanité sonore,
(Car le Maître est allé puiser des pleurs au Styx
Avec ce seul objet dont le Néant s'honore).

Mais proche la croisée au nord vacante, un or
Agonise selon peut-être le décor   10
Des licornes ruant du feu contre une nixe,

Elle, défunte nue en le miroir, encor
Que, dans l'oubli fermé par le cadre, se fixe
De scintillations sitôt le septuor.

Sonnet

Her pure nails very high dedicating their onyx,
Anguish, this midnight, holds up, torchlike,
Many a vesperal dream burned by the Phoenix
That no cinerary amphora gathers.

On the credenzas, in the empty parlour: no ptyx   5
Abolished knick-knack of sonorous inanity
(For the Master went to draw tears from the Styx
Using this sole object with which Nothingness
    adorns itself).

But near the vacant window in the north, a gold
Is dying perhaps according to the decor   10
Of unicorns hurling fire at a nixie,

She, defunct nude/cloud in the mirror, although
In the oblivion contained by the frame, is fixed
By scintillations at once the septet.

I begin with "Ses purs ongles" in spite of the fact that even the first version of the text (1868) is chronologically subsequent to "Hérodiade" (begun 1864), because from my perspective it functions as something of a pedagogical exercise, a rather didactic version of conceiving the relationship between the world and the text. Despite the poem's obvious difficulty, there is in the sonnet an almost too neat framework constructed with the thematics of the container/contained at its core. In a sense the poem's numerous containers function somewhat too predictably as showcases for the display of their respective objects, and, conversely, the objects as the raison d'être for their containers.

The first stanza, for instance, is dominated by the image of the "cinerary amphora" that is constituted as a container precisely insofar as it does *not* gather the ashes burned by the Phoenix. The myth of the Phoenix sets in motion the infinitely recurring emptiness at the core of the container that nevertheless features the cinerary remains of "many a vesperal dream." Thus the hollowness of the container brings referentiality back into the text at both the thematic and for-

mal levels: we read by forcing (even if only temporarily) the enig-
matic word containers into pointing to worldly objects. The difficulty
of the first two verses,

> Ses purs ongles très haut dédiant leur onyx,
> L'Angoisse, ce minuit, soutient, lampadophore,

> Her pure nails very high dedicating their onyx,
> Anguish, this midnight, holds up, torchlike,

has led commentators to proffer any number of objects by way of ex-
plaining the opaqueness of the vocabulary and syntax. Ellen Burt, for
example, sees in them a "statue of Anguish holding her hands up to
the heavens [that] is reminiscent of Atlas who bears the universe on
his broad shoulders" (64). For my own part I have occasionally
amused myself by reading the gleaming pure fingernails as a sort of
container holding up ("soutient") Anguish as a mythical and hyper-
bolic representation of the poet's troubled head, as in this letter Mal-
larmé wrote to François Coppée in December 1866:

Plus que jamais, il y a quelques minutes, j'étais accablé par la Province. La
tête dans les mains, je m'attristais, quand des trompettes, éclatant à mes car-
reaux, me traversèrent et secouèrent de mes yeux une vieille larme, amassée
par bien des heures ordinaires, de tracas étrangers à l'Angoisse, de bêtise.
(*Correspondance* 1:233)[4]

More than ever, a few minutes ago, I was overcome by provincial life. My
head in my hands, I was feeling sad, when trumpets, blaring forth at my
window pane, traversed me and shook loose an old tear from my eyes, caused
by many ordinary hours, by petty preoccupations foreign to Anguish, by stu-
pidity.

The first stanza is then itself "contained" by the second in that its
various objects are placed "within" (or at least, in relationship to)
the empty room:

> Sur les crédences, au salon vide: nul ptyx,
> Aboli bibelot d'inanité sonore,
> (Car le Maître est allé puiser des pleurs au Styx
> Avec ce seul objet dont le Néant s'honore).

> On the credenzas, in the empty parlour: no ptyx
> Abolished knick-knack of sonorous inanity

(For the Master went to draw tears from the Styx
Using this sole object with which Nothingness adorns itself).

Although, referentially speaking, the room may be the largest container thus far mentioned in the poem, it is the "ptyx" that has been universally read by critics as the master container, for being a word in no language and having, consequently, no single worldly referent, it opens itself to all referents. This receptivity is made even clearer when read in conjunction with the verse in the sonnet's first version that appeared in apposition to "no ptyx": "Insolite vaisseau d'inanité sonore" ("Incongruous vessel of sonorous inanity"). The incongruous vessel, absent object in an empty room, which nevertheless functions as self-adornment for Nothingness, is absent precisely in its function as container capable of retrieving tears from the river of death. Like the parenthetical expression that explains its absence, it is neither quite there nor not there, but somehow in between. On the formal level the parentheses themselves also function as a container, marking out the text proper from that which stands outside it, but nevertheless (or better said, because of this) provides a key to it. The Maître, yet another master figure, is contained within the parentheses, but is notwithstanding, as a metaphor for the poet, he who contains the entirety of the poem within him. The double valency of the full gamut of objects in the sonnet would seem to be so pervasive as to fall into a self-annihilating redundancy.

How exactly is this effect achieved? In a July 1868 letter to Henri Cazalis, Mallarmé had described the first version of the sonnet, entitled "Sonnet allégorique de lui-même" ("Self-Allegorical Sonnet"), as an exercise in self-reflexive language:

J'extrais ce sonnet, auquel j'avais une fois songé cet été, d'une étude projetée sur *la Parole*: il est inverse, je veux dire que le sens, s'il en a un (mais je me consolerais du contraire grâce à la dose de poésie qu'il renferme, ce me semble) est évoqué par un mirage interne des mots mêmes. En se laissant aller à le murmurer plusieurs fois, on éprouve une sensation assez cabalistique. (*Correspondance* 1:278)

I extract this sonnet, which I thought about once this summer, from a projected study of *the Word*: it is inverted, by that I mean to say that its meaning, if there is one (but I would console myself of the contrary thanks to the dose of poetry that it seems to me it contains), is evoked by an internal mirage created by the words themselves. When one indulges oneself in murmuring it several times, one experiences a rather cabalistic sensation.

The desertion of the Maître thus can be seen as a highly dramatic way of illustrating what Mallarmé elsewhere termed a necessary condition for creating a work of pure poetry: "la disparition élocutoire du poëte" ("the elocutionary disappearance of the poet"). In order for the poem to attain the status of a "sonnet nul et se réfléchissant de toutes les façons" ("null sonnet self-reflecting in all possible ways") (same letter to Cazalis, *Correspondance* 1:279), the figure of the poet must disappear, allowing words to express nothing but themselves: "ils s'allument de reflets réciproques comme une virtuelle traînée de feux sur des pierreries, remplaçant la respiration perceptible en l'ancien souffle lyrique ou la direction personnelle enthousiaste de la phrase" (*O.c.* 366) ("they kindle each other with reciprocal reflections like a virtual trail of fire on precious stones, thereby replacing the perceptible respiration characteristic of the old lyric gesture or the personal enthusiastic shaping of the phrase"). The earlier form of the sonnet accomplishes this adequately in its version of the quatrain I have just been discussing:

> Sur des consoles, en le noir Salon: nul ptyx,
> Insolite vaisseau d'inanité sonore,
> Car le Maître est allé puiser l'eau du Styx
> Avec tous ses objets dont le Rêve s'honore.

> On consoles, in the black Parlour: no ptyx,
> Incongruous vessel of sonorous inanity,
> For the Master went to draw water from the Styx
> With all his objects with which Dream adorns itself.

Here the Maître clearly has left the room, but what he takes with him is only a quantity of ambiguous objects whose relation to the rest of the sonnet remains unspecified. The definitive version of the poem amply heightens the irony of the Maître's abandonment by relegating him to a figure doubly absented from the poem (both referentially, having left the room, and grammatically, by reducing his exile to a glossing comment within parentheses).[5] Furthermore, in the final version what the Maître takes with him is the master container itself, the "nul ptyx," the "sole object with which Nothingness adorns itself." He figuratively empties out the quatrain, removing the one object it has labored to produce. This operation is echoed at the structural level in that the introduction of the parentheses enclosing the sonnet's middle verses (six lines precede them, six lines follow) similarly creates a void at the formal center of the poem. The container/contained problematic modulates to a metaphorics of framing as the parenthetical expression itself becomes reified as an "object" framed in by the symmetrically aligned outer verses.

In the two tercets the frame then moves from an external decorative construct to its own objectification. In the first, the frame emerges gradually from a dying golden gleaming to take on a certain materiality: it becomes the site of the confrontation of fabulous beings, unicorns and a nixie, which in turn frame "fire," the now identified "dying gold." The clash of genders represented by the combat of the male unicorns and the female nixie only repeats and enhances the problematics of duality I have been exploring in the poem. Here the alternating masculine and feminine rhymes of the sonnet become allegorized as duelling creatures (in the quatrains, rhymes in -yx or -ix alternate with rhymes in -ore, but in the tercets the genders are switched: masculine -or alternates with the now feminine -ixe).

In the space between the first and second tercets the nixie appears to undergo a profound transformation. If in the first tercet she seems to be "alive" and "located" on the frame, in the second she has suffered a pronominal death and moved into the space framed (no longer "a nixie," she is now "She, defunct nude in the mirror"). But whether the "défunte nue" is a naked dead female or a defunct cloud, she/it is blotted out by the "oblivion contained by the frame" and replaced by a cosmic mirroring of nature, the scintillation of the Great Bear constellation. To the degree that it reflects the vastness of the heavens, this final framing frames nothing at all, much as the "ptyx," fully open to all meanings, ends up showing the arbitrariness of meaning itself.

I opened my discussion of "Ses purs ongles" by calling it a rather propaedeutic exercise in conceiving the relationship between the world and the text. This contradicts, of course, the bulk of scholarly exegesis of the sonnet that has taken its cue from Mallarmé's self-commentary that the poem's meaning, if it has one, is evoked "by an internal mirage created by the words themselves." Many recent interpretations have been considerably more interested in exploring the nonreferential aspects of the text than in establishing its commitment to the world. Michael Riffaterre, in fact, uses the sonnet as one of the building blocks of his "semiotics of poetry," which proposes itself as offering an alternative to poetic mimesis. Speaking of the second quatrain of the sonnet, Riffaterre calls it "an exercise in verbal exercise" and argues that:

Turn where we may, the picture of reality is erased, so that these varied but repetitious cancellations add up to the one significance so ringingly proclaimed by the title of the sonnet's first version: "Sonnet allégorique de soi-même" . . . a text referring to its own shape, absolute form. It takes the whole sonnet to unroll the description and to annul it, point by point. The destruction of the mimesis, or its obverse, the creation of the semiosis, is thus exactly coextensive with the text: it is the text. (*Semiotics* 19)

For Riffaterre, the process at work in the sonnet is a "mechanism of mimesis cancellation" (17). Although I find his discussion of the poem compelling, I would argue that what is actually at work in "Ses purs ongles" would best be characterized as a mechanism of mimesis "deferral" or "suspension" rather than "cancellation." Paul de Man's admonition concerning Karlheinz Stierle's interpretation of another poem, the "Tombeau" for Verlaine, is valid for all of Mallarmé's poetry:

It is important [to admit] the persistent presence, in the poetry, of levels of meaning that remain representational. . . . Only after all possible representational meanings have been exhausted can one begin to ask if and by what these meanings have been replaced. . . . Up to a very advanced point, not reached in this poem and perhaps never reached at all, Mallarmé remains a representational poet as he remains in fact a poet of the self, however impersonal, disincarnated and ironical this self may become. . . . Poetry does not give up its mimetic function and its dependence on the fiction of a self that easily and at such little cost. (*Blindness* 181–82)

Let us return to the second quatrain of the sonnet in order to attempt to put this problematization of representation into perspective. "On the credenzas" sets up a series of presuppositions. As we read, we begin to produce a "pre-text," which then must be put into relation with the first quatrain. "In the empty parlour" finally gives us a locale for the drama of anguish and the burning Phoenix, as well as the credenzas. The various objects so far mentioned would seem to fit into the frame of the salon. But the fact that the salon is empty thwarts these attempts at forming a coherent representational picture. That the colon indicates that the "nul ptyx" (a double negation, since we know the ptyx is nothing and it itself is "nul") is nevertheless on the credenzas seems only to throw us into utter confusion; clearly, this is not a mimetic description of a typical nineteenth-century bourgeois salon. The next verse, "Aboli bibelot d'inanité sonore" ("Abolished knick-knack of sonorous inanity"), placed in apposition to "nul ptyx" would seem to be overly redundant. Already "abolished" in that it is "nul," the "ptyx" is described as a "bibelot," which would seem once again to place us back into the frame of the bourgeois interior. The phrase "inanité sonore" is the first for which it is nearly impossible to construct, even temporarily, a coherent referent (although the sonorous inanity has been read as coming from the "ptyx," construed as a conch shell, which when held to the ear produces the "inane" roar of the ocean).

The sheer tautology of "Aboli bibelot d'inanité sonore" should make it clear that a mimetic reading, though constantly being reinvoked throughout the reading process, is insufficient. The systematic negation of the description (*empty* parlour, *no* ptyx, *abolished* knick-knack) and, in the next two verses, the affirmation that the Maître has removed the (already absent?) ptyx does not *cancel* mimesis; rather, it seems to *reinforce* our recourse to referentiality by offering an abundance of what appear to be mutually exclusive mimetic accounts. The text seems to create an agitation that proliferates rather than denies its ties to the world. But at the same time, there is plainly an aspect of self-referentiality that forces itself upon our consideration. "Inanité sonore" seems less to point to the world than to the text itself, and especially to "aboli bibelot," whose repetitious vowels (o, i) and consonants (b, l) seduce us to some extent away from mimesis and toward the materiality of the text itself as a pattern of redundant sounds.

But for all this, the text does not therefore disintegrate into a senseless babble of indecipherable reverberations. Its musicality, I would argue, works on yet another level to interact with its mimetic gesturing. The referential absence of the "ptyx" is itself supplemented by the very real phonic presence of the "aboli bibelot." Extratextual and intertextual references do not efface each other, but rather work in tandem. The inane sonority of "aboli bibelot" restores the "presence" of the object in the very act of asserting its absence. The two forces work to make tangible the space between the world and the text as a zone of interactivity.

The same sort of interaction between referential abolition and formal reinstatement occurs in the "Ouverture ancienne d'Hérodiade." The most striking instance is one that closely parallels the functioning of the "aboli bibelot." In the opening stanza the Nurse offers the following as part of her description of the waterfront tower of the princess (lines 9–11):

> Pas de clapotement! L'eau morne se résigne,
> Que ne visite plus la plume ni le cygne
> Inoubliable
>
> No splashing! The mournful water is resigned,
> That neither the feather nor the unforgettable swan still visit

Here the denial of the splashing of water and the anthropomorphic assertion of its submission is energetically complemented by onomatopoetic evidence to the contrary: through its insistence on stop consonant phonemes (p/d/k/p/t), "Pas de clapotement!" makes audible the very rippling noises it referentially negates.

In the context of the first stanza this reinstatement is tinged with a certain irony. The text seems, in fact, so bent on its own destruction that it appears to achieve a stability only through a constant repetition and reinscription of negativity. As Riffaterre claimed for "Ses purs ongles," nearly every object evoked in the opening stanza is marked with a zero index. The very first word is "Abolie": by the time the modifier can be attached to its noun, which grammatically is the "Aurore" of the fourth verse, the lingering resonance of "Abolie" has worked toward abolishing the mention of each object in the preceding verses. Curiously, it even gestures toward abolishing the "aboli" of the second verse, which itself "abolishes" the "bassin."

The Nurse's vision of the "cinerary and sacrificial tower" (the "master container," in the terms of my discussion above of "Ses purs ongles") seems "contaminated" by Hérodiade's absence from it. Her description registers a series of details that appear to empty themselves out or, at least, mark them as deathlike. In the first stanza alone, the "wing" of the first verse is "ghastly," the "gold" that fills the room is "naked," the escaped bird's (at once Hérodiade's and the dawn's) plumage is "vain" and "black," the "lands" are "fallen" and "sad," the water is "mournful," resigned, and unvisited. The water reflects something, but it is only abandonment. There is a torch, but it is extinguished. It is autumn, the season of fallen things, the swan's head is "grieved," and there is a star, but it is "Antérieure, qui ne scintilla jamais" ("Anterior, that never twinkled").

In one sense, of course, we may understand this kind of writing as an exceptionally poetic and therefore hyperbolic way of rendering the simple fact of the Nurse's anxiety in discovering that Hérodiade is missing. But there is more. The repetition of scenes of abolishment and moribundity is matched and perhaps outdone by repetitions on at least three other levels.[6] Thematically, a number of the items that draw the Nurse's attention are, like the "cinerary tower" itself, containers. In the first stanza the tower is itself evoked three other times, each weighed down by a gloomy qualifier: the "weighty tomb," "the manor of fallen and sad lands," and the "pale mausoleum." There are a number of other containers mentioned, each of which registers what I will call (for lack of an exact terminology) a series of parallel contours. The shapes carved out by the items are all vertical constructs that trail in their respective receptacles: the "aile affreuse dans les larmes / Du bassin" ("ghastly wing in the tears / Of the basin"), the "eau morne . . . / Que ne visite plus la plume ni le cygne" ("mournful water . . . / That neither the feather nor the swan still visit"), and the water that "reflète l'abandon / De l'automne éteignant en elle son brandon" ("reflects the abandonment / Of the autumn extinguishing its torch in it"). In the final verses of the second stanza these same images are twice called back, by the flowers whose stalks steep in a glass and, in a move that brings us back to the very first line of the "Ouverture," by the Dawn once again dragging its wings in tears (lines 33, 35–37):

> Une touffe de fleurs parjures à la lune . . .
>
> De qui le long regret et les tiges de qui
> Trempent en un seul verre à l'éclat alangui.
> Une Aurore traînait ses ailes dans les larmes!
>
> A bunch of flowers unfaithful to the moon . . .
>
> Of which the long regret and the stems of which
> Steep in a single glass of languid lustre.
> A Dawn dragged its wings in the tears!

The repetition of this image of vertical constructs trailing in containers of water seems important to me in that it restages several aspects of the problem of duality in the text. It is as if, by proliferating these parallel images of duality, Mallarmé were thereby suggesting that the same image could be used to describe everything. First, the repeated construct sets up the sexual tenor of "Hérodiade" in the thinly veiled metaphorical terms of inserting phallic-like objects (the wing, the torch, the flower stalks) in vessels of water, symbols of feminine receptivity. The starkness of the images represents the threat that John the Baptist presents for Hérodiade, while at the same time suggesting, by way of the extinguished firebrand and the "languid luster" of the flowers, the very real challenge of conquering the virgin princess.

This modulation of same and different is perfectly rendered by the image of the flower or wing stuck in a glass. If we conceive of it in terms of the flower stalk, half in, half out of the water, we get a picture of the kind of optical illusion produced by refraction whereby a wave of light is bent as it passes from one medium to another of different density. If we can imagine the surface of the water as a mirror, the whole of the image functions as a figure of an inexact reflection and the stalk, viewed from the side, appears broken. This is a representation of repetition, of course, but of repetition with a difference, precisely the "a-symmetrical pressures," or the "ontological sliding" that Leo Bersani has so deftly described in his detailed discussion of "Hérodiade" (*Death* 10–12). Instances of partial repetition are set up as foils for the exact repetitions that litter the text (the reiterations of the sounds "or" and "b" and "p" in the first stanza, the *rime riche* of the couplets, and the mention of reflecting verbs and mirrorlike surfaces throughout "Hérodiade"). The term "ouverture" itself suggests a kind of a priori repetition, in that a musical overture, like a preface to a book, often contains the melodic lines that will later be developed in the composition. Repetition, in fact, takes on a life of its own in the "Ouverture ancienne." Witness the following lines (30, 35, and 47–49) taken from the second and third stanzas, in which I have highlighted the repetitions in italics:

> Un *arôme* qui porte, ô roses! un *arôme*,
>
> *De qui* le long regret et les tiges *de qui*

Désespéré monter *le vieil éclat voilé*
S'élève: (ô quel lointain en ces appels celé!)
Le vieil éclat voilé du vermeil insolite

An *aroma* that carries, O roses! *an aroma*,

Of which the long regret and the stems *of which*

To rise, desperate, *the old veiled brilliance*,
It rises: (O how far off in these calls hidden!)
The old veiled brilliance of an unusual vermilion

Words become containers for other words by means of reduplication. In the first verse cited, the roses referentially carry the aroma, but syntactically, the aroma contains the roses. This problematic of a reversibility of the possessive is neatly illustrated by the repetition in the second verse of *de qui*. And in the third case, we have yet another instance of parentheses as both container and contained. Here it ties in with a thematics of hiding and veiling. The old veiled brilliance frames the parenthetical interjection, which names itself in that it is a kind of linguistic distance (a stretch of words) doubly hidden, that is, in between the bursts of veiled brilliance and within that, in parentheses. This framing reveals the strategy of the fold or "pli," so often repeated in the "Ouverture." The object seems to be abolished but is actually only veiled, hidden among the profusion of repetitions in which it is ensconced.

The figure of the "pli" reiterates and therefore reopens the question of the status of the representation of reality in Mallarmé's early texts. The fold demonstrates a certain invalidity in the investigation of duality I have been conducting. The fold, of course, is that which appears to be double but is in fact both single and double. As Derrida has amply demonstrated, the fold erases the difference between the inside and the outside making the one contiguous with the other. The "pli" is "out of itself, in itself, at once its own outside and its own inside; between the outside and the inside making the outside enter the inside and turning back the antre or the other upon its surface" ("Double Session" 229). The fold is a corrupt container: it contains without fully enclosing, allowing the inside to be discernible from the outside but nevertheless a part of it. Translated into the terms that most concern me, that is, the problem of text and occasion, the "pli" re-poses the question of whether language can in some way *contain* an extralinguistic reality and vice versa. In the vocabulary proposed in the epigraphs with which I opened this chapter, we must ask, with Kierkegaard, whether the occasion is the web in which the fruit hangs; or whether, as Stevens claims, it is productive of the "thing" itself.

The "Ouverture ancienne" seems to offer its own comment on the question. If it is clear that the world is in the text in the sense that any description can be said to envelop its object, it becomes increasingly evident that the text is just as surely in the world. The Nurse is ostensibly the speaker of the "incantation" that is the "ouverture." As the origin of the voice that provides the description of the room that Hérodiade has abandoned, she is at once the figure in the text of the writer of the description and of the "reader" of the empty tower room. Her incantation, the "hymn of questioning verses," attempts to take account of the world as the other. But by the logic of the "pli," neither she as origin of the voice of incantation nor her hymn of asking verses can be differentiated from their objects. The Nurse, in fact, assumes the figure of the prophet in the text by contiguity. As in a Matisse painting (for example, *Harmony in Red*, or *Red Room*) where the wallpaper pattern is the same as the tablecloth pattern and the floor shares the same hue, thus bringing the foreground into an intimate relationship with the background, the Nurse is associated with sybils not only through a proposed metaphor, but by metonymy. Upon the folds of the room's tapestries are woven the images of sybils, which by a strange contagion also reside on the Nurse's dress (lines 23–27):

> Et sa tapisserie, au lustre nacré, plis
> Inutiles avec les yeux ensevelis
> De sibylles offrant leur ongle vieil aux Mages.
> Une d'elles, avec un passé de ramages
> Sur ma robe blanchie en l'ivoire fermé

> And its tapestry, pearly lustred, useless
> Folds with the buried eyes
> Of sybils offering their aged fingernail to the Magi.
> One of them, with a past of floral patterns
> On my bleached dress closed in ivory

By her own simile, in fact, the Nurse is already a "text" ("Scène," *O.c.* 45):

> Pardon! l'âge effaçait, reine, votre défense
> De mon esprit pâli comme un vieux livre ou noir
>
> Pardon! Age erased, queen, your command
> From my mind blurred like an old book, or black

Her attempt to take account of the world strangely converts the world into a lack of signs: Hérodiade's unslept-in bed becomes a "bed of vellum pages" which can only be read as unreadable: "Qui des rêves par plis n'a plus le cher grimoire" ("Which no longer has the cherished writing of folded dreams").

In like fashion her hymn, having struggled for recognition ("Une voix, du passé longue évocation, / Est-ce la mienne prête à l'incantation?"), also loses the ability to distinguish itself from its object (lines 52–57):

> Elle, encore, l'antienne aux versets demandeurs,
> A l'heure d'agonie et de luttes funèbres!
> Et, force du silence et des noires ténèbres
> Tout rentre également en l'ancien passé,
> Fatidique, vaincu, monotone, lassé
> Comme l'eau des bassins anciens se résigne.
>
> It, still, the hymn of questioning verses,
> At the hour of agony and of funereal struggles!
> And, by dint of the silence and the black darkness
> All returns equally to the ancient past
> Fateful, vanquished, monotonous, weary,
> As the water of ancient basins grows resigned.

This return to an origin from which it never quite separated is further reinforced by the final line of the stanza: its evocation of the "eau des bassins anciens [qui] se résigne" "returns" to the opening of the "Ouverture," citing verses 2 and 9, which had already staged the basin and the resigned "mournful water."

Thus the text's incessant repetition occurs at all levels, thematic, phonic, and formal; it even finds itself repeated in the world and as such dissolves into a network of self-reflecting features. This account of the "Ouverture" seems satisfactory in that the Nurse's song does not merely describe a preexisting room; rather, as incantation, her description is cotemporal with the tower, room, birds, wings, tapestries, basins, water clock, tapers, swans, and lakes that are evoked. Like the recurring folds of the tapestry or the "plis jaunes de la pensée" ("yellow folds of thought") that in turn are like the repeating patterns of holes and folds in lacework ("Par les trous anciens et par les plis roidis / Percés selon le rythme et les dentelles pures" "Through the ancient holes and the stiffened folds / Pierced according to the rhythm and the pure lacework"), the text is not "about" anything except its ceaseless self-generation of objects. At a certain level the text resembles the Nurse's view of the room as a framing container of odd trimmings and paraphernalia: "La chambre singulière en un cadre, attirail / De siècle belliqueux, orfèvrerie éteinte" ("The strange room in a frame, trappings / Of a bellicose century, lustreless gold ware"). In the description of the room as framed, the Nurse's vantage point seems to switch to the outside, as she looks in at the very space of representation. Within this space, the profusion of objects, the reduplication of folds *is* itself the message. Incongruously, there is an intense surfeit of language here, all in the service of describing the absence of Hérodiade from her "empty" room, which is then "filled" by language just as "Pas de clapotement" reinstates the lapping of water it dismisses.

If we are to move closer to a poetics of the occasion, we must shift the problem of representation from description to narration. With "L'Après-midi d'un faune," Mallarmé's embracing of the occasion seems to have followed this path. For all the commotion of language in "Ses purs ongles" and the "Ouverture ancienne," the texts share this feature: an absence of anecdote. In "L'Après-midi" Mallarmé shifts his attention from the ontological status of the object to that of the event. This is complicated by the fact that the narrational sequence in question is a sexual event. Here Mallarmé moves from a problematics of denomination (naming the object as instituting its presence, bringing about its absence, or catching it in transition between the two) to involving the object in copulation; that is, linking it in a syntactic sequence to a subject by means of a verb. The question then is not only, Did the nymphs exist? but also, What is the status of the Faun's story and of the account of his attempts to represent it in art? Thus anecdote enters the text at two levels: in a purportedly past mode, as the memory/fantasy/dream sequence of his

possession of the nymphs, and in his present-tense attempts to re-
capture that experience.

This division delineates the formal structuring of the poem.[7] I read
the sections doubly set off from the main text in quotation marks and
in italics as the Faun's narrative recounting of his afternoon's adven-
tures, whether real or imagined. It is only in the definitive version of
the text that Mallarmé so strikingly differentiated this narrative from
the rest; the previous version, "Improvisation d'un faune" ("Impro-
visation of a Faun"), provides a slightly different arrangement con-
tained within quotation marks, but no contrast between roman and
italic print. The narration functions as the pre-text for the poem, the
specific circumstances that occasion it. The double marking, I would
argue, constitutes the narration as a kind of textual "object" featured
by the rest of the poem, contained within its borders and framed
by it.

The framing text, principally in present tense, never quite consti-
tutes itself as a narrative,[8] though I believe it achieves a certain an-
ecdotal status in that it is a staging or mise-en-scène of the Faun's
attempts to deal with his adventures with the nymphs. The question
of the ontological status of this ravishing becomes the explicit the-
matic concern of the passages in roman type by providing a forum for
the airing of the Faun's doubts. Unlike the eye that sees the room in
"Ses purs ongles," and to a degree never achieved by the Nurse in the
"Ouverture," the problem of representation moves here from one of
world versus text to an intertextuality between mutually competing
fictions.

The staging of the Faun's questioning introduces a third term into
the problem of poetic representation. Whereas up until now we have
been exploring the space between world and text in terms of their
interaction, in the "Faune" a third and mediating term is introduced:
fantasy or dream. The first question that presents itself in the framing
stanzas is thus: Was the afternoon with the nymphs a dream or real-
ity? A thematics of proof versus doubt is set up as a means toward
resolving this conflict. As proof, the Faun offers the physical remain-
der of the experience, the "presence" that lingers in the air as re-
minder: "Si clair, / Leur incarnat léger, qu'il voltige dans l'air" ("So
clear, / Their light rosiness, that it hovers in the air"). There is also
the impression of a kiss, "ce doux rien par leur lèvre ébruité" ("this
sweet nothing by their lips made known"), and the mysterious bite

that appears on his breast: "Mon sein, vierge de preuve, atteste une morsure / Mystérieuse, due à quelque auguste dent" ("My breast, virgin of proof, attests a bite / Mysterious, due to some august tooth"). But each of these "proofs" is undermined in the very act of its enunciation. Each reality is proffered and withdrawn in an operation similar to (though hardly as radical as) that described above in both the sonnet and the "Ouverture": the nymphs' "rosiness" is qualified as "light"; the "proof" of their kiss is a nonproof, "this sweet nothing"; and the bite on the Faun is both mysterious and credited to the uncreditable *"quelque* auguste dent" (*"some* august tooth") (emphasis added). Moreover, we must ask how it is possible to reconcile the proof of the bite ("Mon sein . . . atteste une morsure") with the phrase that intervenes between the mark and its ground: "Mon sein, *vierge de preuve*, atteste une morsure" ("My breast, *virgin of proof*, attests a bite"; emphasis added). The distinction between proof and doubt becomes increasingly unclear, closing, to some extent, the gap between the real and fantasy, between world and dream.

Doubt and proof are linked, in fact, early on in the poem, in the second stanza:

> Aimai-je un rêve?
> Mon doute, amas de nuit ancienne, s'achève
> En maint rameau subtil, qui demeuré les vrais
> Bois mêmes, prouve, hélas! que bien seul je m'offrais
> Pour triomphe la faute idéale de roses.

> Did I love a dream?
> My doubt, accumulation of a former night, ends up
> As many a subtle branch, that having remained the true
> Woods themselves, proves, alas! that I offered myself alone
> For triumph the ideal sin of roses.

The lines are usually read as showing the termination of the Faun's doubt (and the unreality of the nymphs) by means of the still-present woods. But as Hans-Jost Frey has shown in his analysis of the passage, this would indicate rather poor reasoning on the part of the Faun, since the "present absence" of the nymphs "does not contradict their past presence" ("Tree" 45). I would argue, in fact, that the verses go considerably further than simply pointing out the illogicality of the Faun's reasoning. Mallarmé's poetic concatenation, it seems to me, offers a statement less about the reality of the nymphs than about an intimacy between doubt and proof, between dream and reality. The figure is one of doubt reified, ending up as ("s'achève en") subtle branches, which then become transformed into "les vrais bois mêmes" ("the true woods themselves"). Through the metaphor of the tree, doubt would seem to be transformed (materially) into reality.

Whether one would then argue that the doubt is "proven" as real (i.e., that the doubt was justified, and the nymphs were not real) or that doubt is transformed into reality (and thus, doubt abolished, the nymphs were real) still remains unclear. But this question, I sense, is finally less important than the powerful image of the coalescing of doubt and reality. The interesting issue raised is not the duality of dream and world, but their unity. The distinctions between life and fantasy fall away, and the Faun will realize that he can be equally satisfied by "real" nymphs or by the creatures of his imagination. What matters is the attempt at representation, the Faun's persistence in accounting for his experience in art.

The importance accorded to the order of representation can be seen in a brief analysis of the rewriting of the poem's first line through its three principal versions. The first, the "Monologue d'un faune," makes a tripartite division in the line, presenting three stages in the Faun's conception of his experience (O.c. 1450):

> J'avais des Nymphes!
>   Est-ce un songe?
>   Non: le clair

> I had some Nymphs!
>   Is it a dream?
>   No: the clear

First, their existence is affirmed: "J'avais des Nymphes!" But then, doubt is introduced: "Est-ce un songe?" Finally, doubt is discarded for/by proof: "Non: le clair." This first line suggests that the doubt/proof controversy is the center of the poem. In the second version, the "Improvisation d'un faune," the doubt/proof question is displaced into the stanzas that follow, and the Faun's desire is foregrounded: "Ces Nymphes, je les veux émerveiller!" ("These Nymphs, I want to astonish them!"). In the definitive version, the accent on desire remains, "Ces nymphes, je les *veux*" ("These nymphs, I *want* them"; emphasis added), and is now syntactically connected to a verb that combines all the possible nuances of re-presentation: "Ces nymphes, je les veux perpétuer" ("These nymphs, I want to perpetuate them"). "Perpétuer" signifies at once a sexual procreation, the lingering of a dream, the continuance of a reality, the (re-)creation of art, and the perpetuation of a desire to desire, without privileging any one of them.

Perpetuation thus becomes the Faun's principal preoccupation, and the framing anecdote can be read as the account of the succession of the Faun's attempts to find a suitable means for prolonging his pleasures and immortalizing his experience. There are a number of artistic measures more or less fleetingly adopted and discarded: the music produced by his flute; the passing reference to a material or verbal "painting" ("et par d'idolâtres peintures, / A leur ombre enlever encore des ceintures" ["and by idolatrous paintings, / (I will) lift still more girdles from their shadow"]); and the more fully implemented verbal and poetic representation activated by the recitation of the narrative in italics ("Moi, de ma rumeur fier, je vais parler longtemps / Des déesses" ["I, proud of my noise, I will speak for a long while / Of the goddesses"]); and the (equally?) invented account of his appropriation of Venus ("Je tiens la reine!" ["I hold the queen!"], etc.).

The principal metaphor for artistic representation here is once again the image of the container/contained. The Faun brags that he will speak of/paint the nymphs by lifting still more girdles from their shadow ("A leur ombre enlever encore des ceintures"). The removal registers simultaneously on at least two levels: as a sexual image, an unveiling; and as a revelation of plot, a laying bare of the story of the ravishing of the nymphs. The whole of this action is compared to the "ravishing" of grapes, itself a metaphor for artistic appropriation (lines 54–61):

> Moi, de ma rumeur fier, je vais parler longtemps
> Des déesses; et par d'idolâtres peintures,
> A leur ombre enlever encore des ceintures:
> Ainsi, quand des raisins j'ai sucé la clarté,
> Pour bannir un regret par ma feinte écarté,
> Rieur, j'élève au ciel d'été la grappe vide
> Et, soufflant dans ses peaux lumineuses, avide
> D'ivresse, jusqu'au soir je regarde au travers.
>
> I, proud of my noise, I will speak for a long while
> Of the goddesses; and by idolatrous paintings,

[I will] lift still more girdles from their shadow:
Thus, when from the grapes I have sucked the brightness,
In order to banish a regret put aside by my pretense,
Laughing, I raise to the summer sky the empty cluster
And, blowing in its luminous skins, avid
For drunkenness, I gaze through them until evening.

The colon and the "Ainsi" ("Thus") that follows it in the fourth verse cited doubly mark the simile: representing the nymphs is like sucking the clarity out of grapes, which itself describes what Paul de Man has disparaged as "the metaphorical model of literature as a kind of box that separates an inside from an outside, and the reader or critic as the person who opens the lid in order to release in the open what was secreted but inaccessible inside" (*Allegories* 5). As both reader and writer, the Faun must perform the extraction of an essence in order to release concealed truths, an operation familiar in literary history since well before Rabelais, who ridiculed it in the prologue to *Gargantua* ("by diligent reading and frequent meditation, you must break the bone and lick out the substantial marrow" [38]), and ironized in Henry James's "Figure in the Carpet": "Vereker's secret . . . the general intention of his books: the string the pearls were strung on, the buried treasure" (313). But the Faun's gesture thwarts that model by showing that the "inside" of the grape, its "clarity," is no different from its "outside," for the skin itself then becomes that which clarifies the world through the Faun's "regard." And the "real" pleasures of the grape can be easily substituted for by his artistic creations: the grape skins are filled with diverse memories ("regonflons des SOUVENIRS divers") that themselves become containers to be seen through.

Artistic perpetuation seems to involve, then, an erasure of dualities, the modulation of the problematics we have been discussing into the "sonore, vaine et monotone ligne" ("sonorous, vain, and monotonous line"). The irresolution of dualities is denounced in the text as the untenability of the two nymphs, and by the association of crime with such divisions ("*Mon crime, c'est d'avoir . . . / divisé la touffe échevelée / De baisers que les dieux gardaient si bien mêlée*" and "*ce mal d'être deux*" ["My crime, is to have . . . / divided the dishevelled tuft / With kisses, that the gods kept so well entangled" and "this hurt of being two"]). The final image of the Faun is a singular vision of a vast receptacle open to the heavens: "et comme j'aime / Ouvrir ma bouche à l'astre efficace des vins!" ("and how I love / To open my mouth to the efficacious star of wines!"). As both source and container of his adventures, he is both the writer of his poem and the written.

The last line, "Couple, adieu; je vais voir l'ombre que tu devins" ("Couple, adieu: I will see the shadow that you became"), with its unusual conjunction of verb tenses, present and past, and its insistence on seeing/creating representations, thus brings us back to the poem's opening as it reinscribes the importance of "perpétuer." "Je vais voir l'ombre" is the both active and passive registering of experience; the Faun will read and write his story perpetually, resolving the question of the difference between text and world into an artistic performance. The "Faune" suggests that the occasion lies neither wholly outside the text nor entirely within it, and that we must shift our attention from a view of art as mimesis to one of art as performance in order to move closer to an understanding of the literary occasion.

Chapter Two

Occasion and the Performative:
"Toast funèbre"

For some years we have been realizing more and more clearly that the
occasion of an utterance matters seriously, and that the words used
are to some extent to be "explained" by the "context" in which they
are designed to be or have actually been spoken in a linguistic
interchange.   —Austin, *How to Do Things with Words*

As I have shown in the previous chapter, the specificity of the
occasional text cannot be determined uniquely in terms of the con-
junction between the inter- and extratextual. The relationship be-
tween text and occasion is more nuanced and complex: the occasion
is neither simply inside nor outside the poem, nor can it be wholly
identified with or separated from it.

If the inside/outside metaphor that governs a constative view of
language is unable to provide a satisfactory model for framing the
question of the occasional text, perhaps a consideration of its rhe-
torical status will bring the problem within a more productive focus.
The occasional poem would seem to be largely performative in that
the act of writing accomplishes the celebration, memorialization, or
salutation named in the text. Much of Mallarmé's late poetry, the
toasts, the "Tombeaux," the "Hommages," and the address quatrains
entitled *Les Loisirs de la poste*, could in fact be rephrased as what Aus-
tin, in his exposition of a theory of speech acts, *How to Do Things
with Words*, called "pure" or "explicit" performatives: I toast you, I
memorialize you, I salute you, I address you, and so on.[1] The occa-
sional text goes beyond a mere description or representation of an
occasion to *effectuate* an act in language: it is itself an occasion in (and
of) words.

If, however, the occasional poem as a whole seems to function as
a performative, Mallarmé's *Poésies* themselves contain no explicit

performative utterances.[2] This is perhaps not surprising when we consider that the explicit performative is defined as an act that is "*at the moment of uttering being done by the person uttering*" (Austin 60), which in turn implies that in verbal utterances[3] the first person singular present tense must be used. Mallarmé's avoidance of the conjugated verb has been well documented.[4] In *L'Expression littéraire dans l'œuvre de Mallarmé*, Jacques Scherer notes that "far from according an important role to the verb, Mallarmé seeks by all means, even the most indirect, to limit its use and reduce its functions" (105–6). He finds that where verbs are not simply omitted or replaced by nouns or adjectives, Mallarmé employs forms "that express action in its most attenuated, most vague form. . . . Thus he prefers to use the non-personal forms of the verb, the participle and the infinitive" (110).

In spite of the predominance of participles and infinitives, utterances that *approximate* the performative can be found in three poems thematically related by the performance of a greeting or "salut."[5] In two of these, although the performative force is unmistakable, the utterance falls short of the requirements for an explicit performative in that the locus and origin of the action are not immediately discernible. The late (1893) poem entitled "Salut," which Mallarmé placed at the head of the (otherwise more or less chronological) collection precisely because of its phatic and inaugural impact, provides a good example of his avoidance of the conjugated verb (*O.c.* 27):

> Rien, cette écume, vierge vers
> A ne désigner que la coupe; . . .
>
> Une ivresse belle m'engage
> Sans craindre même son tangage
> De porter debout ce salut
>
> Nothing, this foam, Virgin verse
> Only to designate the cup/cut; . . .
>
> A lovely inebriation induces me
> Without fearing even its pitching
> To offer upright this toast

In the "Bibliographie" compiled for the Deman edition of the *Poésies*, Mallarmé described the occasion of the composition of the poem as follows: "ce Sonnet, en levant le verre, récemment, à un Banquet de *la Plume*, avec l'honneur d'y présider" (*O. c.* 77) ("this Sonnet, in raising the glass, recently at a Banquet of *La Plume*, with the honor of presiding there"). In spite of the oblique reference and ellipsis of the subject and personal verb in the gloss itself (the correct French locution for toasting is "en levant *mon* verre"; Mallarmé deforms the expression to avoid the possessive pronoun), it is only with this account of the poem's occasion that it becomes clear that it is the speaker, reduced to a possessive and object pronoun ("ô *mes* divers / Amis" and "Une ivresse belle *m*'engage" ["O *my* diverse / Friends" and "A lovely inebriation induces *me*"] [emphasis added]), who performs the "salut" that precipitates out of the conjuncture of the infinitives "désigner," "craindre," "porter," and the third person "engage." Similarly, in the octosyllabic sonnet "Au seul souci de voyager" (1898), the toast is offered through an impersonal verbal phrase: "Ce salut soit le messager / Du temps, cap que ta poupe double" (*O. c.* 72) ("Let this salutation be the messenger / Of time, cape that your poop rounds"). Here the subject is entirely effaced, drowned out in the "salut" which comes dangerously close to disintegration in the cacophony of initial consonant sounds (k/k/t/p/d). The thrust of the subjunctive is endowed with a performative-like force analogous to that of the *fiat lux*. In a curious kind of doubling-up implicated by the literal meaning of the verb "doubler," the verses endow Emile Benveniste's notion of the self-referentiality of the performative with a new dimension. According to Benveniste the performative refers "to a reality that it itself constitutes by the fact that it is actually uttered in conditions that make it an act. The act is thus identical with the utterance of the act. The signified is identical to the referent" (236). Here the act is identical not only with its utterance but also with the "utterer": the "salut" is at once the enunciation of the message, the message itself, and the messenger.

It is in "Toast funèbre," Mallarmé's "tombeau" composed for the death of Théophile Gautier, that we find the locution that in all of Mallarmé's *Poésies* most closely resembles an explicit performative. The verse "J'offre ma coupe vide où souffre un monstre d'or!" ("I offer my empty cup where suffers a golden monster!") would appear to be the performative moment par excellence to the extent that it conflates the orders of language and event: "J'offre ma coupe" is at once the extratextual moment of proposing the toast, the actual situation of the composition of the text, the fictional situation of utterance, the moment of "performing" the text (reading it aloud or publishing it), and the projected moment of encounter with the reader.[6] The "coupe" functions in at least two distinct but related semantic registers, that of the funerary *toast* (note the related terms that confirm and enlarge this reading: "salut," "libation," "rite," "notre fête") and that within the convention of poetic *elegy* ("chanter l'absence du poëte," "ce beau monument l'enferme tout entier," "la gloire ardente du métier" ["to sing the absence of the poet," "this beautiful monument encloses him altogether," "the ardent glory of our profession"]). The "coupe" thus acquires a variety of signifieds beyond the champagne glass: it is also the poem itself and the "lieu de porphyre" ("place of porphyry"), the (poetic and stone) monument. Similarly, the gesture of raising or offering the cup is at once the proposing of the toast, the writing of the poem, and the rising (ascension) of Gautier in (or and) his monument (note the poem's closing lines: "Afin que . . . / Surgisse . . . / Le sépulcre solide où gît tout ce qui nuit, / Et l'avare silence et la massive nuit" ["In order that . . . / Rise up . . . / The solid sepulcher in which lies all that blights, / Both the avaricious silence and the massive night"]).

However, for a poem that purports to sing the praises of the dead poet Gautier, there appear to be an inordinate number of references to the fictional or poetic situation of enunciation and to the occasion of the celebration itself. The emphasis would seem to lie less on Gautier than on the now of the poetic occasion, on Mallarmé's own performance of the act of monumentalization. References to the speaker abound (highlighted here in italics): "*J'*offre *ma* coupe"; "Ton apparition neva pas *me* suffire"; "*J'*ai méprisé l'horreur lucide d'une larme"; "sourd même à *mon* vers sacré" ("*I* offer *my* cup"; "Your apparition will not suffice *me*"; "*I* scorned the lucid horror of a tear"; "deaf even to *my* sacred verse"). Some of the personal references are, it would seem, all too conspicuously emphatic, even occurring twice in a line: "Car *je* t'ai mis, *moi-même*, en un lieu de porphyre"; "Et l'*on* ignore mal, élu pour *notre* fête"; "*Moi*, de votre désir soucieux, *je* veux voir" ("For *I* put you, *myself*, in a place of porphyry"; "And *we* cannot ignore, chosen for *our* celebration"; "*I*, solicitous of your desire, *I* want to see").

This seemingly displaced insistence is not the only vaguely subversive element in the poem. Early in 1873 Mallarmé had written to Coppée describing the plans for "Toast" as follows:

Commençant par *O toi qui* . . . et finissant par une rime masculine, je veux chanter en rimes plates une des qualités glorieuses de Gautier: le don mystérieux de voir avec les yeux (ôter mystérieux). Je chanterai le *voyant* qui, placé dans ce monde, l'a regardé, ce que l'on ne fait pas. (*Correspondance* 2:37)

Beginning with *O you who* and ending with a masculine rhyme, I want to sing in rhymed couplets one of the glorious qualities of Gautier: the mysterious gift of seeing with the eyes (omit mysterious). I will sing the *seer* who, placed in this world, looked at it, which isn't done.

The projected poem was, therefore, to begin with a most conventional apostrophe to the dead poet. As Jonathan Culler has shown in his appealing article on this trope, apostrophe works by disrupting "the circuit of communication, by raising questions about who is the addressee" (*Pursuit* 135). With the apostrophe to Gautier, Mallarmé's addressing his readers is circumvented by the direct appeal to the dead poet. The speaker calls on Gautier *as if* he desired to enter into dialogue with him, as if the urgency of the vocative could recall him from the grave. But the subsequent verses not only deny the status of the opening line but also underscore its hollowness. The apostrophe becomes an empty address in that Mallarmé makes it clear that Gautier's apparition is not being sought: "*Ton apparition ne va pas me suffire*"; "*Le rite est pour les mains d'éteindre le flambeau* / Contre *le fer épais des portes du tombeau*"; "ce beau monument *l'enferme tout entier*" ("*Your apparition will not suffice me*"; "The rite is for hands to *put out the torch* / Against *the thick iron of the gates of the tomb*"; "this beautiful monument *encloses him altogether*") (emphasis added). Neither Gautier's "mysterious gift of seeing with the eyes" nor his poetic voice is expected to survive his biological death or the ritual of his burial. Indeed, Gautier's two preeminent gifts as a poet, his capacities as both singer and seer, are negated three times throughout the poem in a series of chiasmi that would appear definitively to cancel the possibility of his future poetic occasions. If we read the "quelqu'un de ces passants" as referring to Gautier, as several exegetes have done,[7] the insistence on the absence of his poetic voice and gift of sight seems almost excessive, as is prominently underscored (by italics) in lines 23, 53, and 56:

> Quelqu'un de ces passants, fier, *aveugle* et *muet*,
>
> One of those passing, proud, *blind*, and *mute*,

> De n'*ouvrir pas les yeux sacrés* et de *se taire*,
>
> Not to *open his sacred eyes* and to *be silent*,
>
> Et l'*avare silence* et la *massive nuit*.
>
> Both the *avaricious silence* and the *massive night*.

Even if we were to argue that Gautier, the "Maître" named in line 32, displays all of his poetic talents precisely through his gifts of sight and his inimitable voice, as in lines 32–35:

> Le Maître, *par un œil profond*, a sur ses pas,
> Apaisé de l'éden l'inquiète merveille
> Dont le frisson final, *dans sa voix seule*, éveille
> Pour la Rose et le Lys le mystère d'un nom. (emphasis added)
>
> The Master, *through a profound eye*, has in his wake,
> Appeased the restless marvel of Eden
> Whose final quiver, *in his voice alone*, awakens
> For the Rose and the Lily the mystery of a name.

we would still have to take into account the absoluteness of the negation that then immediately follows (lines 36–38):

> Est-il de ce destin rien qui demeure, non?[8]
> O vous tous, oubliez une croyance sombre.
> Le splendide génie éternel n'a pas d'ombre.
>
> Is there of this destiny nothing that remains, no?
> O you all, forget a somber belief.
> The splendid eternal genius has no shadow.

Rather than simply singing the absence of the poet in the manner of the traditional homage ("notre fête / Très simple de chanter l'absence du poëte" ["our very simple / Celebration to sing the absence of the poet"]), or in pleading for his reappearance, the poem appears to accent the now and forevermore continued absence of his sight and voice. The next lines immediately shift the focus of attention from Gautier as "Le Maître" to Mallarmé himself and to his own sight and voice: "Moi, de votre désir soucieux, je veux voir, / . . . / Survivre . . . / Une agitation solennelle par l'air / De paroles" ("I, solicitous of your desire, I want to see, / . . . / Survive . . . / A solemn agitation through the air / Of words"). In effect, Mallarmé buries Gautier in a plethora of references to the occasion of his own emerging poetic voice. Indeed, to the degree that the poem functions as a statement of Mallarmé's own *art poétique* it is necessary for Gautier's voice to be silenced or simply drowned out. The resoundingly emphatic "Moi . . . je veux voir" has itself a certain performative impact in the poem to the extent that "je *veux voir* . . . une agitation solennelle . . . de paroles" in fact functions as an equivalent to "je *fais* une agitation" ("I *produce* an agitation"). The expression of desire for the solemn agitation of words (this is, of course, the figure for the poetic act centered in that portion of the poem that most explicitly functions as *art poétique*) that is voiced by the poet thus creates that very agitation. The utterance is, therefore, as Benveniste would say, coexistent with the event itself.

Let us return to the question of the poem's opening and to the discrepancy between Mallarmé's projected and actual apostrophes. We are now in a position to discern a logic for Mallarmé's rearrangement of the syntax. The shift from the grammatically orthodox original first verse (as indicated in the letter quoted above), "O toi qui" ("O you who"), to its final dislocated form, "O de notre bonheur, toi, le fatal emblème" ("O of our happiness, you, the fatal emblem"), yields the fortuitous juxtaposition of "O de" or "ode," the poetic category etymologically derived from the Greek for singing or chanting, whose definitions neatly characterize Mallarmé's own poetic effort. The ode is "a lyric poem . . . typically addressed to some person or thing and usually characterized by lofty feeling, elaborate form, and dignified style" (*Webster's New World Dictionary*, 2d ed.) that is "frequently the vehicle for public utterance on state occasions, as, for example, a ruler's birthday, accession, funeral, the unveiling or dedication of some imposing memorial or public work" (*Princeton Encyclopedia* 585). The change from "O toi qui" to "O de" can thus be read as a shift from the importance of the address outward to the metatextual level; that is, from the circumstances of Gautier's death to Mallarmé's own poem, precisely in order to underscore the occasion of writing itself. As Culler has shown, it is exactly this "crucial though paradoxical fact" that governs the apostrophe as trope. The "figure which seems to establish relations between the self and the other can in fact be read as an act of radical interiorization and solipsism" (*Pursuit* 146). The logic of the apostrophe is such that "invocation is a figure of vocation" (*Pursuit* 142) so that in choosing to dislocate the conventional apostrophe Mallarmé doubly calls attention to himself as poet.

This reordering of priorities should make us suspect that Mallarmé's performative commitments lie elsewhere than with Gautier and that, in fact, he may be celebrating as well the occasion of his own awakening to occasion (see Noulet's statement: "Out of a poem of circumstance, he will make the poem of his conviction" [6]). "Toast funèbre" is chronologically significant in that the poem marks the end of the notorious "nights of Tournon" crisis period. In writing "Toast funèbre," Mallarmé emerges from an interval of poetic silence that lasted six years (1867–73). The poem represents Mallarmé's reentry into the poetic community and the beginnings of his acceptance of the role of Maître of the Symbolists that he will assume just over a decade later. With few exceptions, the poems written after "Toast" are all occasional.

Let us now consider the performativity of the verse from "Toast funèbre" in some detail. "J'offre ma coupe vide où souffre un monstre d'or!" ("I offer my empty cup where suffers a golden monster!") is one of the most debated lines in all of Mallarmé's poetry, both because of the incongruity of the "coupe vide" and the obscurity of the "monstre d'or." I would agree with Patricia Parker that "none of the glosses so far suggested for [this line and the preceding one, "Ne crois pas qu'au magique espoir du corridor"] seem . . . to be very helpful. Indeed it is possible that the images were chosen at least partly to raise the question of referentiality itself, a possibility the famous anecdote about the 'monstre d'or' amply illustrates" (173; see my discussion of this anecdote below). Indeed, when we apply a kind of slow-motion scrutiny to the verse in its context, focusing on the "J'offre ma coupe" as speech act, the line yields some very paradoxical readings.

With the enunciation of "J'offre ma coupe" and the various resonances of "coupe" it activates, it would appear that not one but at least three performatives are set in play: the toast is performed, the poem is written, the monument is consecrated, and thus, the celebration is accomplished. Or are they? One more syllable is needed to fill out the hemistich before its own "coupe" is executed: "J'offre ma coupe *vide*" ("I offer my *empty* cup"). Is the act performed if the cup (the champagne glass, the sincerity of the toast, the inscription of the poem, or the inscription on the monument) is empty or void? Does the empty cup make for a "failed communication"? Would it be an infelicity in Austin's terms if the bottle of champagne used to christen a ship were empty? Austin's careful attempts to enumerate

the many possible forms and types of infelicities can only get us so far
in trying to answer such questions. Let us continue reading the verse
in context (lines 3–4):

> *Ne crois pas* qu'au magique espoir du corridor
> J'offre ma coupe vide

> *Do not believe* that to the magic hope of the corridor
> I offer my empty cup

Is the cup offered? Are we to read "Do not believe that I offer it to
the 'magique espoir du corridor,'" or does the negative govern the
entire couplet, "Do not believe that I offer it at all"? Again, the con-
ventions of reading poetry allow us to construe the syntax with a cer-
tain degree of liberty. If we grant that the cup is offered, but then
subordinate the performative "J'offre ma coupe" to the syntax of the
previous line, "Do not believe that in this particular hope I offer my
cup," is the performative robbed of its force? To rephrase it in more
orthodox Austinian terms: "Do not believe that I bet you $20." Do
we have a bet?

> *Salut de la démence et libation blême,*
> Ne crois pas qu'au magique espoir du corridor
> J'offre ma coupe vide

> *Greeting of madness and pale libation,*
> Do not believe that to the magic hope of the corridor
> I offer my empty cup

In strict grammatical terms the first verse here (line 2) ought to
function in apposition to the performance of the "salut" itself, "J'offre
ma coupe vide." But I have already shown that it is questionable
whether the "salut" actually constitutes itself as a genuine act, and
thus it is hardly surprising that the verse dangles expectantly near the
opening of the poem, unable to attach itself to a suitable substantive.
Perhaps, however, it is this very deficiency that is being toasted here
in that the "salut de la démence" may indeed refer to the inherent
"démence du salut"; that is, the "madness" of the toast as act that
both is and is not performed. The lack of proper place for this verse
and the insecurity of knowledge about the status of the toast itself are
underscored in its contrast to the absolute certitude displayed in the
statement made in line 6: "Car je t'ai mis, moi-même, en un lieu de

porphyre" ("For I put you, myself, in a place of porphyry"). Gautier's physical remains are confidently disposed of, though his lingering spiritual and literary traces continue to be problematic (lines 2–4).

> Salut de la démence et libation blême,
> Ne crois pas qu'au magique espoir du corridor
> J'offre ma coupe vide *où souffre un monstre d'or!*

> Greeting of madness and pale libation,
> Do not believe that to the magic hope of the corridor
> I offer my empty cup *where suffers a golden monster!*

If, indeed, the cup is empty, why is there a "monstre d'or" in it, or even on it? What is the golden monstrosity? Can we read it as the very subversion of the speech act itself? The celebration is described as "our very simple celebration to sing the absence of the poet." Certainly to sing one's praises could constitute a performative. But what happens when the act is transformed into singing one's absence? A parallel scenario is played out later in the poem in lines 26–31. Emptiness and empty language come together as the "Vaste gouffre" ("Vast abyss") is carried into a mass of fog "Par l'irascible vent des mots qu'il n'a pas dits" ("By the irascible wind of words he has not spoken"). The wind of words not spoken would seem to prefigure the truncated dialogue that follows in which nothingness, the "néant," and the "Homme aboli de jadis" ("Man abolished of yore") throw words into a void (lines 29–31):

> "Souvenirs d'horizons, qu'est-ce, ô toi, que la Terre?"
> Hurle ce songe; et, voix dont la clarté s'altère,
> L'espace a pour jouet le cri: "Je ne sais pas!"

> "Memories of horizons, what, O thou, is Earth?"
> This dream cries out; and, voice whose clarity fades,
> Space has as its plaything the cry: "I do not know!"

When we recall the suppression of Gautier's voice discussed above, it becomes clear that the poem features a number of attempted but unsuccessful speech acts. In what way can we connect the offering of the empty cup and the singing of an absence to an aesthetic of a performance of the void, which may indeed be the suffering of the "monstre d'or"? For Austin the speech act is defined in terms of failure; that is, the capacity for misfiring is essential to the notion of the performative. But whether we ought to read "Toast" as exhibiting a performance of the void, or as a voiding of the performative, is yet to be determined.

Before I attempt an answer, I'd like to redirect my scrutiny of the verse in question, "J'offre ma coupe vide où souffre un monstre d'or!" For the above discussion I deliberately set aside the problem of the rhetorical status of the line in order to discuss the problematics of its performative impact. But the perception of that impact depends on reading the verse as the equivalent of "I toast [you]" or "I drink [to you]," which, not being entirely self-evident, requires a certain interpretive effort. Taken literally, "I offer my cup [champagne glass, goblet, chalice]" is grammatically sound but, semantically, borders on the nonsensical. It carries no performative force. We might conclude, then, that the verse is constative on a literal level and performative on a figural level. But even in a figural sense, "I offer my cup" can only be understood to the extent that "J'offre ma coupe" *leans on* the conventional idiomatic expression meaning to toast, literally, "I raise my glass," "Je lève mon verre." What is gained (or lost) by retaining the syntactical structure and making the vertical or metaphorical substitutions of "offre" for "lève" and "coupe" for "verre"?

Perhaps the example of another, more famous literary idiom will be instructive. Proust's account of the affair of Swann and Odette might be read by an overeager linguist as the rise and fall of the idiom "faire cattleya" ("to do a cattleya"). To use the expression, as Swann does, to mean "to make love," depends on specific linguistic and symbolic conventions established in the novel. The illicit substitution of other flowers ("faire chrysanthème," for example) could only be understood if considered as parasitic on or parodic of the Proustian idiom. As Derrida has shown, the logic of the parasite is analogous to that of the supplement or the parergon, and is "not a logic of distinction or of opposition. . . . A parasite is neither the same as nor different from that which it parasites" ("Limited Inc" 239). It is rather that which blurs the boundaries between the two, in this case between the literal and the idiomatic. Strictly speaking, "J'offre ma coupe" is neither literally nor rhetorically correct; in neither case does the construing of the phrase offer a totally satisfactory reading. We are compelled to provide the necessary semantic and linguistic apparatus to make the phrase meaningful, but the construction nevertheless remains in a kind of aporia. The interstitial status of the verse in question is in fact parallel to the situation of the occasional poem, as I shall show below.

The fact that "J'offre ma coupe" leans on the idiom "Je lève mon verre" would seem to suggest, by the very "insufficiency" and dependency of the construction itself, that the idiom represents a "fullness." But, as Benveniste has shown in his critique of Austin, locutions such as *I welcome you* and *I apologize* cannot be given as conclusive proof for the notion of the performative because social life has made them so trite: "Since they have fallen to the rank of simple formulae, they must be brought back to their original sense in order for them to regain their performative function" (234). Rather than to consider performatives that have fallen into disuse or to reanimate them with fresh contexts of usage, Benveniste declares it is preferable to choose performatives in full use for his analysis. However, as Barbara Johnson has noted in support of Austin, "Benveniste's attempt to exclude 'simple formulas' like 'je m'excuse' and 'bonjour' from consideration as 'live' performatives is doomed by the very nature of 'living' language itself. . . . The illocutionary force of an utterance is subject to the same kind of temporal fading and conventionalizing that produces 'dead' metaphors and clichés" (*Critical Difference* 65).

Let us take Johnson's critique one step further. The performative itself depends on a certain conventionality. Austin insists on this point throughout *How to Do Things with Words* and Benveniste likewise states that "A performative utterance . . . has existence only as an act of authority" and that such acts are "first and always utterances made by those to whom the right to utter them belongs" (236). Acts of authority, of course, can only be performed by those institutionally and conventionally empowered to produce them. A performative is therefore a conventional utterance; to a certain degree its most full moment is precisely when it is lexically empty. The performative works because it is well oiled; the paths of meaning have been established and well trodden. The exclusion of a locution as performative on the grounds that it is trite (as in Benveniste) is thus something of a contradiction in terms.

The whole question of convention is of course crucial to any discussion of "Toast funèbre." The poem's conventionality on both the level of language and its adherence to certain literary institutions has often been remarked. Alphonse Lemerre deliberately placed the collection of poems composed for Gautier within the context of literary conventions when he explained in his note to the reader that prefaces *Le Tombeau de Théophile Gautier* that the practice of the "tombeau" dates back to the sixteenth century: "We thought of dedicating to the memory of this Master a literary Monument revived from those Elegies that the Poets of the 16th century raised to their illustrious Dead" (Lemerre i–ii). Patricia Parker rightly notes that when Mallarmé's contribution is read together with the other poems in Lemerre's collection,

> it immediately loses some of its uniqueness. Its principal images—"le néant," "le couchant," "monument," "gloire," "flambeau"—are the fundamental and platitudinous stuff of the funerary tribute, and Mallarmé's contribution seems little more than a skilled manipulation of requisite themes. In the experience of reading "Toast funèbre," however, this perception of the original context is a necessary and critical moment. For it is precisely this quality of deliberate *banalité*, or reduction, which shapes the poem's major strategies. "Toast funèbre" is a poem which places itslf within a context self-consciously official and "circonstanciel" and demands to be read within a frame of highly conventionalized *topoi*, or dead letters. (167)

This framework, it seems to me, provides an infinitely more accommodating structure for dealing with the text. Indeed, its functioning as a monument depends on the very "deadness" of the cemetery from which it arises. "Toast funèbre" is an official poem; its tone is solemn, resonant, at times even declamatory. It is clearly one of Mallarmé's most blatant examples of "rhetoric" in its worst sense, what is often termed "empty rhetoric." In fact, there is a multilevel play on "fullness" and "emptiness" throughout the poem. In addition to its rhetorical resonances, the formal structures of the text seem to be determined to some degree by the repetition of the empty vessel image (the "coupe vide") at two other key moments. As Alexander Fischler has noted, Mallarmé recalls the image at least twice again, as the "grand calice clair" ("great white calyx"), the lily that can be filled with a name by the Poet, and, by analogy, in the closing lines as "le sépulcre solide" (310). If at the beginning of the poem the sepulcher was undoubtedly full of Gautier's remains ("Car je t'ai mis, moi-même, en un lieu de porphyre"), by the end the "matter" contained is significantly less weighty (lines 55–56):

> Le sépulcre solide où gît tout ce qui nuit,
> Et l'avare silence et la massive nuit.

> The solid sepulcher in which lies all that blights,
> Both the avaricious silence and the massive night.

In spite of the nominal and adjectival evidence to the contrary ("solid," "all," "avaricious," and "massive"), the sepulcher is "filled" with only the vague, the murky, and the insubstantial: "all that blights," "silence," and "night." Even the unexpected *rime riche* of the final couplet moves away from monumentality and toward trivial wordplay. At the thematic level, the poem seems to abound in still other evocations of the contours of vague containers: the vacant "corridor" (line 3), the "vain walls" (line 20), the "vague shroud" (line 24), "space" that plays with the cry "I do not know!" (line 31), and the "diaphanous look" that isolates and immortalizes the flowers (line 45).

Mallarmé's poem is not of course explicitly *about* concepts of fullness and emptiness, but certainly this metaphoric overlay can help us to understand the larger questions that traverse it. There is a play on the linguistic level between the poem's empty rhetoric and Mallarmé's attempts to rehabilitate the trite expression that threatens it. This, in fact, is one way in which the famous line from another poem, "Le Tombeau d'Edgar Poe," "Donner un sens plus pur aux mots de la tribu" ("To give a purer meaning to the words of the tribe"), has been interpreted. Echoing Rémy de Gourmont, Gardner Davies suggests that part of the obscurity of Mallarmé's texts results from his desire to avoid clichés: "This preoccupation, which does not illuminate the depths of Mallarméan obscurity, nevertheless explains certain unusual phrasings, inversions of normal word order, insertions or ellipses." (*"Tombeaux"* 226).[9] To return to the question posed above, then, about what is gained by the substitution of "J'offre ma coupe" for the lexically empty "Je lève mon verre," we may answer the following: the move to achieve a kind of syllepsis in which the same expression may be read both literally and figuratively can be seen as an attempt to revitalize the performative gesture and give it full expression by choosing a nonconventional locution. However, this gesture, like that of the "pure poet" (line 49), is double-edged; it is both "humble et large." Mallarmé's act is imbued with a massive irony: he fills the voided expression with the empty cup, the "coupe vide."[10]

The full/empty metaphor recalls and may help clarify the issues raised in Chapter 1 about whether language can in some way *contain* an extralinguistic reality. To the extent that this poses the question of the referent in language, the problematic of occasional poetry is in a sense analogous to that of the performative and may profit extensively by the juxtapositioning of the two. As Shoshana Felman has written in *The Literary Speech Act*, "what . . . is important to see . . . is not so much the reintroduction of the referent in the performative, but rather the *change* of the *status* of the referent as such" (a change Felman sees as converging with the change in status of the referent in psychoanalysis) (75). Within a more traditional philosophical view of language as constative, language is "a *statement* of the real, a . . . reflection of the referent or its mimetic representation" (Felman 76). The referent exists outside of language and is prior to it. This is precisely the conventional view of the occasion in its relationship to literature.

Barbara Johnson has shown how the relationship of the referent to language is altered when conceived in terms of the performative utterance that, in naming the act it performs (saying "I toast you" *is* the act of toasting you), is self-referential: "If a performative utterance is originally a self-referential speech act, its production is simultaneously the production of a new referent into the world" and thus language can be seen to "refer only to its own referring to itself in the act of referring" (57). Felman elaborates this same notion without, however, becoming engulfed in the *mise en abyme*:

The referent is itself produced by language as its own *effect.* . . . This means that between language and referent there is no longer a simple opposition (nor is there identity, on the other hand): language makes itself part of what it refers to (without, however, being all that it refers to). Referential knowledge of language is not knowledge *about* reality (about a separate and distinct entity), but knowledge that *has to do with reality*, that acts within reality, since it is itself—at least in part—what this reality is made of. The referent is no longer simply a preexisting *substance*, but an *act*, that is, a dynamic movement of modification of reality. (77)

The relationship of occasion and text may be seen in an analogous manner. If we regard the text itself *as* an event, not *about* an event (cf. Said's statement, quoted in my Introduction, "Texts are worldly, to some degree they are events, and, even when they appear to deny it, they are nevertheless a part of the social world, human life, and of course the historical moments in which they are located and interpreted" [4]), then the occasion lies, at least partially, in the production of the text, simultaneous with or posterior to it.

What exactly would this mean? In my preliminary thinking on this subject, it seemed as if the change in the relationship between text and occasion could be conceived in historical terms. That is, from the (let's say) sixteenth through eighteenth centuries, when poems were commissioned by the nobility to commemorate an occasion, the task of the poet could be seen as "reproducing" the real world event in the order of language. But modern poems such as Pound's "In a Station of the Metro" or Apollinaire's "Lundi rue Christine" make very different demands on the reader's ability to construct the relationship of circumstance to writing. In both the Pound and Apollinaire poems the occasion would seem to be "located" not *prior to* the writing but somehow *in the writing itself*.

In both texts, the title plays a decisive role in the poem's functioning. Austin had shown that titles such as Manifesto, Act, Proclamation, or even the subheading "A Novel" may enact a certain performative force (I proclaim that, I move that, etc.). The question of the title as performative in the Apollinaire and the Pound poems is extremely complex, however, for to posit an "I" that would be able to take sole responsibility for the poem as speech act would be to negate the theoretical impact of the experiments in impersonal construction that underlie the poems. Nevertheless, as Derrida has written in three deceptively simple but perceptive questions that he never quite answers in "Limited Inc," we may well ask: "What is a title anyway? Is it a normal speech act? Can one imagine a sequence without a title?" (226). For "Lundi rue Christine" it is precisely the title that identifies the seemingly disconnected phrases *as* a sequence. The title functions to frame the text, identifying the occasion it gives rise to: bits of conversation overheard in a café or bistro at a "specific" time ("lundi") and "specific" place (Christine Street). Like the title of an abstract painting that serves to orient our perceptions, or the title given to a Duchamp readymade (for example, the French window dubbed *Fresh Widow* or the snow shovel christened *In Advance of the Broken Arm*), it is at the juncture of title and text that the "occasion" is born. The title does not serve to affirm the existence of an event that preexists the text (in contrast to, say, Yeats's "September 1913"), but rather to give a performance of the event itself. Apollinaire's poem is a collage of overheard snatches of conversation (and this much already involves a number of inferences that cannot necessarily be sustained, such as a [single?] ear that overhears the voices rather than a writer who composes them) that outside the poem have no logical connections and only can be persuaded to yield significations (the plural is deliberate) in their juxtaposition within the frame of the artistic event. As such, the pieces "represent" nothing; they merely "present" their sonorous disparity.

"Lundi rue Christine" is antinarrational in that the framed "sequence" never develops as such, never achieves a logical concatenation. In narratological terms, no "récit" could ever be (re)constructed from the "discours." Conversation continually erupts only to trail off and begin anew with no retention or development of subject. The "event" or "occasion" lies precisely in the poem's lack of cohesion, although ultimately, I would suppose one would have to argue, the series of fragments and ruptures achieves a certain unity as a statement about modernist discourse.

Pound's "In a Station of the Metro," that exemplary Imagist poem, is likewise constructed paratactically, by the juxtaposition and not the subordination of one image to another. Again, the "occasion" does not preexist the poem, but instead arises *in* it, *out* of it, out of the very relationships created between its three phrases (title, first verse, and second verse). This perhaps accounts for the abundance and prominence of prepositions in the poem; of its twenty words, five are prepositions. "Positioning" is central to the poetic occasion whose place is named in the title.[11] "*In* a station of the metro" sets the stage for the apparition of "faces *in* the crowd." The initial preposition forms the outermost frame of the text into which the faces are interjected, which themselves are seen as *in* the crowd. A series of Chinese boxes is set up, each framing the next and each related to the preceding and the following by the unstated simile. The faces, by a magnificent poetic leap, stand against the murky outlines of the crowd just like petals on a wet, black bough. The poem, complete with title, links the banality of modern life with the quiet wonder of nature by means of an "apparition," at once a mere appearance and a religious experience. In the critical parlance of the Modernists the "occasion" produced can be termed an "epiphany" or, less spectacularly, the result of a mental rather than speech act (Kenner notes that "the mind that found 'petals on a wet, black bough' had been active [and for more than a year on that poem, off and on]. The 'plot' of the poem is that mind's activity, fetching some new thing into the field of consciousness" [186]).

Thus the referential leaps made in these poems (from conversational fragments to poetic whole, from faces to petals to a metapoetical statement about poetic artifice) produce the occasions of the poems, which are not merely identical to the poems themselves. The occasion is a by-product in the very spatial sense of the word "by," produced to the side of the text but not wholly conterminous with it. There is a remainder whose production is likewise essential to the production of the occasion, but not eclipsed by it. How can we account for this remainder? Felman's critique of the performative is again useful. After noting the importance of the "dialogic situation" to the question of the referent in performative language (as in psychoanalysis), a fact we will return to below, she sides with Austin against Benveniste concerning the referential status of the performative.

For Benveniste, the performative is entirely self-referential, perfectly specular, producing a perfect *symmetry* between meaning and reference. Felman comments:

This reasoning is not without relevance, and yet it draws false implications from Austin's thought. The performative is indeed self-referential, but for Austin this does not mean that it refers to an exhaustive specularity or to a perfect symmetry between statement and enunciation. On the contrary, it is from *asymmetry* that Austin's thought proceeds, from the *excess* of utterance with respect to statement, from "force of utterance" as a—referential—residue of statement and meaning. . . . In the final analysis, the performative has the property of subverting the alternative, the opposition, between referentiality and self-referentiality. If the language of the performative refers to itself, produces itself as its own reference, this language effect is nonetheless an action, an action that exceeds language and modifies the real: self-referentiality is neither perfectly symmetrical nor exhaustively specular, but produces a *referential excess*, an excess on the basis of which the real leaves its trace on meaning. (79–80)

The "referential excess" is the precipitate of the dialogic situation of the speech act. What is left over after the referentiality of language is accounted for is the illocutionary force of the utterance. Although I usually frown on the use of pseudomathematical formulas in literary analysis, I believe that the following shorthand may help to clarify (without being reductive) the thrust of Felman's thinking and its relationship to the problematics of the occasion.

> For Benveniste: language = referent
> (and, by analogy, its relevance for my thinking):
> text = occasion
>
> For Austin: language = referent + x (illocutionary force)
> text = occasion + x (?)

The "residue" I mentioned with regard to the Pound and Apollinaire texts could therefore be explained as a poetic excess that we might understand in terms of Jakobson's formula for communication, also a dialogic situation in which the Addresser and the Addressee, two of the six different functions of language, communicate through one or more of the other four functions, Context, Message, Contact, and/or Code. According to Jakobson, the nature of any message (be it emotive, conative, referential, poetic, phatic, or metalinguistic) will be determined by the hierarchical order in which the different functions are emphasized in that message (353–57).[12] The "poetic" message, not necessarily restricted to literature, focuses "on the message for its own sake. . . . This function, by promoting the palpability of signs, deepens the fundamental dichotomy of signs and objects" (356). The excess left after the referential aspect of the occasional poem has been identified might well be this poetic focusing of language on the message itself. This is precisely what we have already discerned in "Toast funèbre": above and beyond Mallarmé's references to Gautier the text registers an excess that I described above as Mallarmé's turning toward the occasion of his own writing—a cogent illustration of the message focusing on itself as message.

It ought now to be clear that this description of the functioning of the occasional text will not fit into the historical framework adumbrated above. While it is tempting to read the "history" of occasional poetry as moving from a constative to a performative view of language, this is clearly not the case. To the degree that Felman shows the performative in some sense as already including the referential function of language as well as its illocutionary force, occasional poetry always both refers to its occasion and exceeds it. This is, of course, tantamount to saying that occasional literature is neither a genre, a subgenre, or even a specific mode of writing, but that all texts are, to a greater or lesser extent, occasional, whether the occasion be pre-textual or read as a product of the text itself.

Let us now consider the problem of the referent from yet another angle. As I mentioned earlier, the verse "J'offre ma coupe vide où souffre un monstre d'or!" is one of the most glossed lines in all of Mallarmé's poetry. Any number of interpretations (from the ingenious to the unlikely) have been offered to explain the unexpected appearance of the monster, and certainly my own suspicion that the golden monstrosity is in some sense metalinguistic, a comment on the very problematic of interpreting the line, is no more or no less defensible than the other readings proposed. In any case it seems fair to say that the problem of reading the line has itself been deformed into a kind of suffering monster and that this fact stands in need of comment.

Aside from the question of how the monster could possibly be either on or in the empty cup, the debate has been fueled by the famous anecdote passed down concerning Mallarmé's own questioning of the verse. Most commentators (myself included) feel obligated to reprint it, even if, like Davies, they cannot assure its veracity ("Whether this anecdote is true or not, it is difficult to find another explanation for this monster who writhes at the bottom of the cup" [*"Tombeaux"* 18]). The anecdote is attributed to Heredia:

The other day, just after dawn, I saw our enigmatic Mallarmé rush up to me, waking me with a start. Without preface he said to me: "I've just created a superb piece, but I don't quite understand its meaning and I've come to you so that you can explain it to me. And he read me his poem. Among other mysterious alexandrine verses, there was this one: "J'offre ma coupe vide où souffre un monstre d'or." It rhymed with "un sombre corridor." In order to repay his confidence in my faculties as seer I gave him this explanation: "It's quite clear. It's about an ancient cup on which an artist, a goldsmith, Benvenuto Cellini, if you will, engraved in the massive gold a monster who writhes with an expression of suffering." Upon hearing me Stéphane leaped up and cried out: "How beautiful! How rich! How moving!" And he left me beaming and grateful, happy to have understood himself, saying: "I've risen in my own esteem, and you, my dear man, as well!" (quoted in Davies, *"Tombeaux"* 18)

The anecdote seems to me to engage two problematics: the ontological status of the occasion and the praxis of exegesis. If we speculate with Lawler that Mallarmé may have been "trying out on a fel-

low poet a new system of expression; [and] that, having an ulterior
aim in view such as might concern the structural integration of his
language, he rejoiced to see that his image retained also for a sensitive
reader an immediate and satisfying impact" (6), we reinstitute the
very conception that Lawler subsequently tries to do away with, that
"Mallarmé's image is basically a plastic one; that, as an ornamental
poet, he is describing with intricate art an ideal glass, an elegant dec-
orative design, which might be compared to the fans and bracelets,
the mirrors and diadems of his other poems" (7). That is, as plastic
image, the "monstre d'or" must in some way "preexist" the text,
either as a "real" cup engraved with a monster or as a mental image,
which Mallarmé then sought to represent in the poem. In either case,
the situation is emblematic of the question of the ontological status
of the occasion; that is, whether the occasion is necessarily prior to
writing.

As Lawler points out, the majority of critics have "adopted by and
large Heredia's reading, even though his tone as reproduced in these
lines appears to be far from serious" (6). Among the half-dozen critics
that Lawler cites there would appear to be variants on two basic inter-
pretations: that there was a cup with a real engraving, or that the
monster is but a moving reflection of light or sunlight on the concave
surface of the cup. This second possibility is somewhat analogous to
the question of the change in status of the referent discussed above.
The monster as reflection suggests that it is imaginatively created, not
real, and that it is the poetic text that creates a monster, which then,
retroactively, is taken as the basis for reproduction in the text.

The second problematic mentioned above, that of the praxis of ex-
egesis, must also be brought into play. Through the anecdote the hy-
pothesized plastic image of the suffering monster engraved on the cup
is converted into a "reality," which then, paradoxically, is used to
explain the enigma in the poetry. The problem is how critical exe-
gesis appropriates such "explanations," naturalizes them, and turns
them into fodder for use as explications. Criticism's repeated "per-
formances" of such material as "events" endow them with what ap-
pears to be an extratextual status that is then hard to disassociate from
the text.[13]

Thus, we must perhaps modify our conclusions about the status of
the occasion reached above. The question of whether the occasion
produces the text or the text produces the occasion cannot be simply

resolved by choosing either the former (seemingly more traditional) interpretation or the latter. In fact, we reach the same aporia that Freud himself was ultimately forced to acknowledge as a consequence of his study of the Wolf-man case, that in a sense it matters little whether the "primal scene" or occasion really is primary or secondary, real or imagined. The productions of the texts, as well as the historical, critical, or legendary apparatus that comes to surround it, in fact become part of its frame.

In the following chapter I will pose once again the problem of representation and the occasional poem that has concerned us in Chapters 1 and 2, this time in terms of two Mallarméan texts from the 1880's. The texts provide two models for conceiving the relationship between text and world. In the first, "Prose pour des Esseintes," I reconsider the question of occasion and the poetic remainder discussed above, reading poetry itself as the excess that precipitates out of the text. The "too tall gladiolus" is the hyperbole whose exclamation opens the poem, the very figure of the poetic. In the second, the prose poem "La Déclaration foraine," I explore the question of the occasional text as subverting the alternatives of the text as either reproductive of a prior occasion or of producing the occasion itself.

Chapter Three

Allegories of the Poetics of the Occasion: "Prose pour des Esseintes" and "La Déclaration foraine"

> The analysis of the relation between the artist and his occasion, a relation always regarded as indispensable, does not seem to have been very productive . . . the reason being perhaps that it lost its way in disquisitions on the nature of occasion. It is obvious that for the artist obsessed with his expressive vocation, anything and everything is doomed to become occasion, including . . . the pursuit of occasion.
> —Beckett, "Three Dialogues"

In my Introduction I noted that occasional poetry appeared to belong to a class of texts that Paul de Man has termed "hybrid" in that they are considered to be "partly literary and partly referential" (*Allegories* 3). Although de Man created this category merely to point to it as a current literary fashion, and not to take up the problem per se of the hybrid text, this he does, to a greater extent, in a later piece entitled "Autobiography as De-facement." In describing previous attempts at circumscribing autobiographical writing by contrasting it with fiction, he states that "autobiography seems to depend on actual and potentially verifiable events in a less ambivalent way than fiction does. It seems to belong to a simpler mode of referentiality, of representation, and of diegesis" (920). What interests me here is the "fiction" of a "simpler mode of referentiality" that de Man delineates, for it will allow us to retrace certain steps made in the previous two chapters and to lay the groundwork for a new poetics of writing. Although he discredits it only a few paragraphs later, de Man elaborates on what form this "simpler mode" might take by challenging the very comparison he sets forth: "But are we so certain that autobiography depends on reference, as a photograph depends on its subject or a (realistic) picture on its model?" (920). The simpler (are we to understand more direct? more exact? less rhetorical?) mode of referentiality would seem to be patterned after the representative visual arts, and one senses with a certain unease the return of the centuries-old *ut pictura poesis* controversy, aesthetic speculation describing or prescribing the similarity between the literary and the visual arts. De Man's question posits the total objectivity of the camera lens and supposes that by focusing on the object exclusively and not letting one's eye (or mind) wander, a model of perfect referentiality could be produced, and this then imitated by literature.

But clearly one must refute de Man's example of a simpler mode of referentiality even as he proceeds to invalidate the term as applied to autobiography. It is simply not the case that the photographer or the realist painter focuses his subject in any more direct or simple mode than the autobiographer. Photographs are as constructed and mediated as any other type of representation. Roland Barthes had already pointed to the "new space-time category" of the photograph, that is, the essential spatial and temporal difference that intervenes between the photograph and its subject. The photograph, and by extension, the realistic picture painted from a model, shows not the presence of the subject but its absent presence, its "having been there" ("Rhetoric of the Image" 44). And in addition to the spatio-temporal distancing of the subject, the photograph's capacity for being wholly objective is marred irremediably by another form of spatial and temporal limitation, the frame. No snapshot can give the "total" picture at once because the limitations of film make not only selection but disposition essential; that is, not only what is included or excluded from the frame but also the disposition of the subject(s) within the frame as regards centrality, peripherality, juxtaposition with or distancing from other objects, and so on: rhetoric always returns to visual representation.

In "Autobiography as De-facement" de Man goes on to examine autobiography in terms of the nonreferentiality of language. In the final analysis, then, not only does autobiography not function according to a simpler mode of referentiality, but it does not work within a system of referentiality at all.[1] Language is rather a series of tropes that refer endlessly to one another but cannot afford access to extralinguistic reality (de Man remarks that for Wordsworth's deaf "gentle Dalesman" the outside world has "always been a book, a succession of voiceless tropes" [930]). His conclusion is: "To the extent that language is figure (or metaphor, or prosopopeia) it is indeed not the thing itself but the representation, the picture of the thing and, as such, it is silent, mute as pictures are mute" (930). De Man's statement would appear to be a deliberate echoing, for the purpose of refutation, of the pre-Horatian comparison of painting and poetry, "Poema pictura loquens, pictura poema silens" (poetry is a speaking picture, painting a silent [mute] poetry). De Man's assertion that language is not the thing itself but the picture of the thing would seem to bring us full circle, in a contradictory sort of way. Whereas at the beginning of the article he sought to differentiate the complex referentiality of autobiography from the simpler referentiality of the photograph or realistic painting, at the end he states their identity in a mode of nonreferentiality.

That de Man's comments on the similarity or dissimilarity of language and painting quite literally frame his text, stressing first their incompatibility and then their identity, may be read either as an oversight and internal contradiction or, in a more de Manian sense, as a case of the insight of critical blindness. The crossover pays tribute to the internal logic of the piece: de Man's purpose is to show that prosopopoeia is the true figure of autobiography and that it is read specifically in terms of the chiasmus, the "mutual reflexive substitution" that defines the autobiographical moment in an alignment between the two subjects involved in the process of reading, the author and himself, the subject of his own understanding. In any case this excursion into autobiography and photography will have helped, I hope, to refocus some of the problems of occasional literature. As we have to some extent already shown, occasional poetry, like autobiography, would seem to belong to a simpler mode of referentiality and representation. That is, the very definition of "occasional" seems to point to specific circumstances or events in the real world that could be then transported, intact, into the framework of the poem. But the temporal logic suggested here is not an essential one, and often, what is taken as cause or origin can be reversed with effect or product.[2] De Man finds this to be the complicating factor in the question of the referentiality of autobiography:

We assume that life *produces* the autobiography as an act produces its consequences, but can we not suggest, with equal justice, that the autobiographical project may itself produce and determine the life and that whatever the writer *does* is in fact governed by the technical demands of self-portraiture and thus determined, in all its aspects, by the resources of his medium? And since the mimesis here assumed to be operative is one mode of figuration among others, does the referent determine the figure, or is it the other way round: is the illusion of reference not a correlation of the structure of the figure, that is to say no longer clearly and simply a referent at all but something more akin to a fiction which then, however, in its own turn, acquires a degree of referential productivity? (920)

I hope in this chapter to show, in parallel fashion, the interchangeability between occasion and text. The occasional poem is not only *produced by* but *productive of* its occasion. Two texts, "Prose pour des Esseintes" and "La Déclaration foraine," function, I claim, to problematize the notion of a simpler mode of referentiality and representation in their attempts to formulate an allegory of the problematics of the occasion. That both texts take on the concept of the frame in confrontational terms, as well as posit fundamental oppositions between language and silence and between speech and the silent gaze, and the breakdown of these same oppositions (precisely those broached above in connection with the de Man article) is indicative of the way in which the problem of representation unfolds in texts that underscore the conflicting claims of referentiality and self-reflexivity.

"Prose pour des Esseintes" is considered one of Mallarmé's most difficult pieces. The ambiguity of the problematics of occasional poetry is perhaps pointed up by the equivocal "occasional" status of the poem itself. Is it an occasional piece? The title, with its reference to des Esseintes, the decadent hero of Huysmans's *A rebours*, would appear to indicate that this is so. But biographical evidence shows that the text (with the possible exception of the last two stanzas) may have been written before the appearance of the novel and thus may have received its dedication as an afterthought (Olds 16–17). The question is hardly moot when one considers the impressive array of ingenious scholarly back flips that have been performed in attempting to discern a relation between the poem and Huysmans's protagonist (see, for example, Kristeva 259–62). The dedication, whether by pointing to extratextual circumstances in terms of a "simple referentiality" or by obscuring the relationship between the occasion of the writing and the writing itself, has nevertheless conditioned the poem's reception and oriented its critical exegesis. The occasion, no matter how sketchily hinted at or how incongruously inconsistent with the text itself, cannot be ignored. Especially in the most difficult of Mallarmé's texts, the occasion often proves itself an obstacle that must be overcome in order to put forward a coherent exegesis of the text.

Similar contortions have also been performed in an attempt to explain or explain away the assignation of the term "prose" to what is undoubtedly one of Mallarmé's richest texts with regard to the conventional poetic categories of rhyme and rhythm. Some have seen the title as referring to the "proses chrétiennes," Latin hymns of the Byzantine period that Mallarmé mentioned in the prose poem "Plainte d'automne" (Cohn, *Toward* 241; Olds 18). Others read the title as ironic (given the poem's extravagant rhyming patterns) or apologetic and self-deprecatory (indicating Mallarmé's professed inability to write the "Grand Œuvre") (Noulet 113; Cohn, *Toward* 241). All these interpretations have claim to legitimacy. It is clear, however, that "Prose" points as well to the problematics of the "récit," the central portion of the poem, as a potential object of representation. I propose to read the text as an allegory of representation by focusing on the contrapositioning of the poem's inner narrative stanzas with the problem of the poetic reinscription of experience depicted in the framing outer stanzas.[3] In this way the production of "prose," or of a narrative rendering of experience, will be seen as the ultimate but elusory goal of poetry.

The poem can be divided into three zones of activity that successively encase one another like Chinese boxes. At the core are stanzas 3 and 6–9, which narrate the poet's account of his trip with his mysterious "sister" to the uncharted isle where, as the couple watches in silence, flowers uncannily propagate themselves. Framing this anterior episode is a present time (stanzas 1, 2, and 11–14) that is singularly preoccupied with the narrated past experience. In the earliest version of "Prose" the first two stanzas were set off from the rest, and in the poem's final form they seem to retain their introductory function. But the very first word has a dislocating effect: the speaking voice calls on and calls out "Hyperbole!" At once vocative and exclamatory, hyperbole/a sets in motion a network of resonances from the rhetorical to the mathematical, and from exaggeration to tumescence to ascension. The thrust of the opening stanzas is to invoke the muse of memory from whose depths will rise the island experience to be submitted to a poetic and scientific "installation" wrought through patience. This tranquil assurance and uncynical view of the poetic process, however, reigns only briefly. The fourth and fifth stanzas interject the troubling "ère [air] d'autorité," opening a Pandora's box through the intervention of words (ellipsis used to clarify syntax):

> L'ère d'autorité se trouble
> Lorsque, sans nul motif, on dit
> De ce midi . . .
>
> Que . . . son site
> . . .
> Ne porte pas de nom que cite
> L'or de la trompette d'Eté
>
> The era of authority becomes troubled
> When, with no reason, they say
> About this south land . . .
>
> That . . . its site
> . . .
> Bears no name that cites
> The gold of the trumpet of Summer

This negativity returns again in stanza 10, threatening the *locus amoenus* of the island experience with an unmotivated, unprovoked atmosphere of intimidation.

The antithesis of innermost to outermost stanzas is built up and reinforced through a proliferation of oppositions. The narrated idyllic experience is recounted entirely in the past tense, emphasizing the island's temporal as well as spatial remoteness and the futility of attempting to locate it. The preponderance of present tense verbs in the framing stanzas suggests that the problem of dealing with such past experiences is a recurring one, a routine task of the poetic vocation: "Car j'installe, par la science, / . . . / En l'œuvre de ma patience" ("For I install, by means of science, / . . . / In the work of my patience"). The insistence on the duality of the subject at the beginning of the narrative portion ["(Nous fûmes deux, je le maintiens)" "(We were two, I so maintain)"], and the already defensive gesture of its parenthetical insertion, betray an uneasiness about the accuracy of the visual perception that is later echoed in the very suggestive but ultimately indeterminate line that describes the island as charged

"De vue et non de visions" ("With insight and not visions"). The possibility of erroneous vision and its corollary sense of anxiety seems to have its figurative echoing in the hyperbolic blossoming of the island flowers that reaches threatening proportions: "Que de lis multiples la tige / Grandissait trop pour nos raisons" ("That with multiple lilies the stem / Grew too much for our reason"). Nevertheless, dual vision guarantees neither accuracy of perception nor the kind of mastery inherent in verbal representation. Overwhelmed by the profuse island growth, the two are reduced to silence ("Toute fleur s'étalait plus large / Sans que nous en devisions" ["Every flower displayed itself more grand / Without us talking about it"]), and it is precisely their inability to speak that in turn promotes the spectacular display of burgeoning irises. If in the inner text the subject is double and silent, in the outer stanzas it is always single and verbal, from the male "je" ("I") who opens the discourse to the "elle" ("she") whose final pronouncements close it. The preoccupation with the exercise of language (written or spoken) of the outer stanzas is almost too sharply contrasted with the couple's status as silent witnesses. If, as has often been the case, the poem is read as an *art poétique* with the profusion of flora as the metaphor for poetic production, then a grave contradiction rends the statement even as it is being made. The inner narration prescribes silence as the vehicle of poetic production, while in the outer stanzas there is a singular progression toward verbalization and naming as a kind of ultimate act.

The profusion of natural growth that characterizes the island experience sets up yet another opposition, a recurring one in Mallarmé's poetry. The inner stanzas present a world of nature in a totally undomesticated state, differing vastly from the sphere of consciousness and poetic activity of the outer frame that seeks to master it through poetic representation. The inherently repetitious nature of representation is flaunted on several levels as the poem then ostentatiously indulges in a number of self-reflexive moves. The opposition of unbridled nature with the harnessing effect of the poetic task ("Car j'installe, par la science, / . . . / En l'œuvre de ma patience," and "L'enfant . . . docte déjà par chemins" ["For I install, by means of science, / . . . / In the work of my patience," and "The child . . . already learned in ways"]) is embellished by a not very subtle underscoring of sexual symbolism. In each sphere a hyperbolic rise and fall plays off against the ever-rising phallic flowers. The island experience is, in effect, a figurative rendering of the typical activity of narrative with its rise to climax and ensuing denouement. The couple, partaking of the charms of the landscape, silently observes the blooming flowers in the "charged" air. The immensity of the flowers at once stimulates and matches the growth of desire: "Gloire du long désir, Idées / Tout en moi s'exaltait de voir" ("Glory of long desire, Ideas / Everything in me exalted to see"). The opening of stanza 9, however, with the simple but devastating "Mais" ("But"), signals the end of the heightening passion. Unwilling to continue in her role as spectator/voyeur, the sister withdraws her glance and forces a denouement and the end to narrative, not through consummation, but by denial. In parallel fashion, the rising movement of the first stanza seems to reach the height of climax in the eleventh ("A vouloir que l'ampleur arrive / Parmi mon jeune étonnement" ["In wishing that abundance arrives / Among my young surprise"]) only to have the tide turn ("Par le flot même qui s'écarte" ["By the very wave that ebbs away"]) and the child (again?) "abdicate" her ecstasy. The curve of narration, like the curve of inflated and deflated (or satisfied) desire, is self-parodically none other than the hyperbola whose invocation opens the poem. And the juxtaposed hyperbolas would seem to sketch out the silhouettes of two tombstones standing like a pair of matched bookends boxing in the poem, the hyperbola of the first stanza mirroring the sepulcher of the last.

Rather than working as a mediating force between the opposition of inner and outer stanzas, the vaguely threatening "ère d'autorité" ("era of authority") and the "Esprit de litige" ("Spirit of litigation"), the third sphere of activity I have distinguished, serve only to aggravate their irreconcilability. The key term is "authority," and the problem is knowing from whence it derives its power. The anxiety introduced by the middle stanzas seems to center on the question of contesting the existence and/or name of the paradisiacal island. The past tense of the inner narrative and the clarity of its recounting as memory suggest that it both precedes and exceeds the text; that is, that the island experience is both prior to and separable from the attempt to re-present it depicted in the outer stanzas. The middle stanzas, however, refuse to acknowledge the extratextual status of the island. The litigious spirit of the poem, in fact, points to an epistemological problem, as is clear from the strategic positioning and repetition of the verbs *savoir* ("to know") and *porter* ("to carry or bear") each repeated three times, whereas no other verb appears more than once. In the fifth stanza *savoir* and *porter* come together: It is said

> Que, sol des cent iris, son site,
> Ils savent s'il a bien été,
> Ne porte pas de nom que cite
> L'or de la trompette d'Eté.
>
> That, land of a hundred irises, its site,
> They know if it really existed,
> Bears no name that cites
> The gold of the trumpet of Summer.

Here the "ère d'autorité" and the "Esprit de litige" (stanza 10: "Oh! sache l'Esprit de litige" ["Oh! let the Spirit of litigation know"]) derive their power explicitly from the assertion of knowledge about the site's lack of a name, *ils savent que le site ne porte pas de nom que cite* ("they know that the site does not bear a name that cites"). But the affirmative and negative valences of the verbs can be reversed to paraphrase the fundamental epistemological problem of the poem that states the speaker's lack of knowledge of the name of the island: *il ne sait pas le nom que porte l'île* ("he does not know the name the island bears"). The major textual problematic can be seen to revolve around a typically Mallarméan play on words. The speaker's inability to *citer le site* (cite the site), that is, to find the name or location of the enchanted isle on the map (*savoir le nom qu'il porte*) is precisely identical to his powerlessness to *situer la citation* (site the cite) or to assign a place of origin to or identify a recognizable vocable uttered by the "trompette d'Eté." The problem adumbrated here is no less than the calling into question of the very possibility of literary representation. Does the island exist outside the poem as a verifiable, tangible, extraliterary site (citable and sightable, "De vue et non de visions"), that is then re-presented in the poem? Or is it only a fiction created by the poem itself that pretends to re-present the island? Can poetic objects and events ever be extrapoetic, or does the poem only refer to itself and the products of its fabrication? Is there a world of nature at the center of the poem that would oppose itself to the sphere of poetic activity, as indicated above, or is it merely textual allegory? The "je," as speaker of a poem, traditionally draws his power from his position of knowledge; it is, in fact, knowledge of his subject that allows him to constitute himself as speaker.[4] But here, as we have shown, the "authoritative" and "litigious" middle stanzas exert their power without ever assuming the first person stance that would direct poetic discourse. They split the poem asunder even as they are confined to third person status, and finally undermine the speaker's authority. The male poet at the opening of the poem later appears to be annihilated in the flood that contests ("Par le flot même qui s'écarte" ["By the very wave that ebbs away"]) the existence of the idyllic country. His inability to *citer le site* signals his fall from the position of knowledge and power he had falsely assumed with the inauguration of his discourse. This image of failure is then illusorily supplanted by the birth or annexation of a new poetic figure, "l'enfant" ("the child"), who would appear to be identifiable with the "sœur" ("sister") of the inner stanzas. Described as "docte déjà par chemins" ("already learned in ways"), her knowledge is not such as to permit her to speak in first person, although her cry, "Anastase!"—the one spoken word in the text—clearly represents an attempt at naming that the male speaker was unable to muster.

A problem with previous readings of "Prose" has derived from critics' inability to situate the "ère d'autorité / Esprit de litige": like the island itself, it has no site ("Sous aucun climat" ["In no climate"]), and the origins of its voice of authority are uncitable. Typically, where commentators have not entirely suppressed this aspect of the poem (as in Richard, Noulet, or Gans), they have pointed to the pervading "atmosphere of contention" that allows us to see the poem as "a kind of debate or trial" (Olds 27) in which the "know-it-all attitude of the debunking, dull-spirited, rationalistic carpers" (Cohn, *Toward* 246) "lament that the island does not exist, and deny that the sense of elevation and amplitude reported by the poet had any proper basis" (Bowie 36). In every case the larger structural force of the poem is conceived of as a binary opposition (from Boulay's Platonic dualism between the absolute Idea and its linguistic representation [54] to Kristeva's reading of the title, "Prose," as an "inversion" of *vers* and consequently of *versus* and *à rebours*, forming a complexity of identifications and differentiations between Mallarmé's and Huysmans's texts [260–61]).[5] A binary conception of the poem quite literally allows no place for the "ère d'autorité / Esprit de litige" complex, excluding it by repeating the despotic gesture thematized in the poem whereby the location and hence existence of the idyllic island are denied by an unjustified assumption of absolute power by the era of authority itself.

It is not, however, merely in arguing for a triadic conception of the poem that the principal interest of my reading may lie. Triads are, after all, implied by every dualism to the extent that binarism presupposes a boundary, limit, or other liminal configuration to demarcate the division between opposing structures. The recognition of a lack of difference between double and tripartite structures may indeed be a significant though nonexplicit by-product of Derrida's discussion of the parergon (although it is essential to note that the boundary itself can never constitute a third term [Derrida, *Positions* 43]). Derrida notes that "the parergonal frame is distinguished from two grounds [ergon and milieu], but in relation to each of these, it disappears into the other" ("Parergon" 24). This accounts for both the irrefutable "existence" of the boundary or frame and the fact that such a "middle articulation" declares itself as "a place deprived of place" ("Parergon" 5). The era of authority/spirit of litigation complex is at once outer frame to the recounting of the island experience and inner frame to the sphere of poetic consciousness depicted in the opening and closing stanzas, and yet is as unchartable as the island whose existence it refutes. It is elicited both by its inner and outer limits: without the gap between the island memory and the attempt to re-present it, the poem fails to cohere. The thrust of the hyperbola/e, etymologically a "throwing beyond" that would seek to bridge the gap, functions as a symbol of the poem at work. Thus the parergonal structure (I refer here to the middle frame, though each of the "frames" might well be considered parergonal with respect to the others) simultaneously "warps as it works" ("Parergon" 34), and is a "form which had traditionally been determined not by distinguishing itself, but by disappearing, sinking in, obliterating itself, dissolving just as it expends its greatest energy" (26). At once self-constituting and self-destructive, the era of authority joins the disparate elements of "Prose" precisely by threatening their very disjunction.

What I hope my analysis will call attention to, then, is not the simple demarcation of the era of authority as border, but what Derrida has called the "thickness" of the frame (24). The "ils" whose authority lies vested in their knowledge ("Ils savent s'il a bien été") of the paradisiacal island's *lack* of site and *lack* of name are the protagonists of the dramatization of the frame as frame, a kind of performance of the activity of the frame. "Parerga," Derrida goes on to say, "exert pressure at the boundary" (20). The orchestration of the frame is necessarily a repressive, even violent one, framing in even as the canvas framed exerts pressure from the other side. The images of organic and nonorganic hypertrophy threatening to burst its limits in the poem are legion: the "book of spells / Clad in a book of iron"; the air charged "With insight and not visions"; the overgrown flowers ("Every flower displayed itself more grand") that ornament themselves "With a lucid contour, lacuna, / That separated it from the gardens"; the desire that builds in the speaker ("Everything in me exalted to see"); the multiple lilies that overburden the stem that "Grew too much for our reason"; and the river that threatens to overrun its banks—to mention only the most explicit.

These images of borders simultaneously besieged and oppressing curiously recall the singular second line of the prologue to Huysmans's *A rebours*: des Esseintes's ancestors, as portrayed in the few surviving family portraits are "Imprisoned in old picture frames which were scarcely wide enough for their broad shoulders" (17). The frame *is* authority, *is* the giver and recipient for the (negative) spirit of litigation at the same time it unceasingly bestows and receives the (affirmative) action of attesting: "Sans fin attestés sur mes pas" ("Unendingly attested in my wake"). This middle frame of "Prose" is then, both thematically and formally—to borrow a pun from Cynthia Chase—a kind of paragon of parergons.

The voice of authority belongs to neither the inside nor the outside, but brings the two together, not by harmoniously joining them, but by casting doubt on the very possibility of their juncture. Thus the opposition of inner and outer frames *is* finally addressed, but without providing any satisfying resolution. The cumulative effort of the outer stanzas to circumvent the doubting era of authority/spirit of litigation results finally in the production of a word. Yet the name pronounced by the child does not appear to refer to the inner stanza experience. "Anastase!" a resurrection or rising up, necessarily leads us back to the introductory stanzas of the poem, to the invocation of hyperbole: "Triomphalement ne sais-tu / Te lever" ("Triumphantly do you not know / How to rise up"). The word pronounced is not a representation of experience, but a representation of the process of representation itself. The child's mode of attending to the occasion is thus not to attend to it at all. This may explain why the poem is considered so impenetrably obscure: our difficulty in reading it is doubtless a result of the fact that the attempt to represent the island experience in speech produces not mimesis but a swerving from it. The centrality of narrative is here displaced at the same time as occasion is demoted to the rank of mere pretext for a writing about writing.

Like the mute and silent language de Man designates at the close of "Autobiography as De-facement," this language, proffered as the pronouncing of names, seems unable to break through to the extra-textual "reality" posited by the poem, the island paradise. The linguistic effort made to get at the experience of the burgeoning flowers is no more successful than that attempted in the inner narrative, where the speaker and his sisterly companion watched the flowers silently. Their clear, silent gaze thus becomes in some way the equivalent, and not the opposite, of the child's enunciation of "Anastase!" or of the tombstone's written inscription, "Pulchérie!" Both speech and the silent gaze fail to posit an equivalence between the text and its occasion.

In its historical context the poem itself bespeaks this same lesson of the skewing of text and occasion. We have already mentioned the likelihood that the poem was written before Mallarmé read *A rebours*. When the verse was dedicated to des Esseintes, it became linked to a specific occasion. As occasional poem, it finally found itself in that its subject became the possibility of its own existence; that is, the possibility of writing a poem about an occasion. As we have seen, the only comment on the island experience voiced in the poem is the word "Anastase!" ("Né pour d'éternels parchemins" ["Born for eternal parchments"]), which refers not to its occasion but to its own production. Just as "Prose pour des Esseintes" has little to do with des Esseintes, the frame can only vaguely interact with the story it contains, except to question that very interaction.

The possibility of writing about an event as a way of domesticating it, freezing it, or monumentalizing it through inscription on the "éternels parchemins" seems therefore to be very much in question. Yet another pun seems to mock the enterprise: the equivalent positioning of "sépulcre ne rie" ("sepulcher laughs") with "Pulchérie!" is intimately linked to "Anastase!" and consequently with the opening invocation to the rising hyperbole: "ne sais-tu / Te lever" ("do you not know / How to rise up"). Anagrammatically, "sépulcre" is hidden in "Pulchérie," just as the secrets of the "grimoire" ("book of spells") are locked in the ironclad book. If the ultimate sign of death, the sepulcher or tombstone, is hidden in the poetic pronouncement of beauty, then writing about occasions (and here the only "writing" produced is the "Anastase/Pulchérie" inscription) seems to contain a secret and destructive message, which is the blotting out of the occasion itself.

The final irony, however, is yet to be played out. The seemingly authoritative pronunciation/inscription of "Anastase!" and "Pulchérie!"—summational last words (signatures, we might argue) in this allegory of representation—have hardly been proffered when they are mocked in all of their vainglorious pretensions. Supposedly destined for eternal parchments such as the inscription (as epitaph) on the sepulcher of the last stanza, they in turn are hidden by an insuppressible remainder from the island experience they did not deign to represent. The destiny of the parchment/tombstone is to be overshadowed, that is, erased by the island flower: "Caché par le trop grand glaïeul" ("Hidden by the too tall gladiolus"). The inner stanzas ultimately break out and end up boxing in the frame itself, obscuring the writing. If the gap opened by the link between "Anastase!" and "Hyperbole!" signaled the auto-referentiality of the process of representation and the elision of occasion, the poem's final line shows that this is by no means the last word on representation. The too tall gladiolus shows how occasion, in turn, eliminates the very writing that displaced occasion. Rather than the occasion being boxed-in or contained by the poem's two principal images of immobile, circumscribed writing (the ironclad book of the first stanza and the tombstone inscription of the last), the occasion quite literally "flowers" beyond control. The framing process, rather than providing a hierarchy of controlled juxtaposition, breaks down into a kind of relational frenzy.[6] If the poem can indeed be read, as I am suggesting, as an allegory of the problematics of the occasion, then the final lesson to be garnered would be not the elision of occasion but its inevitable reassertion, the occasion as an indestructible remainder, a precipitate of what Beckett has called in our epigraph the "pursuit of occasion."

To claim that the "too tall gladiolus" "reasserts" the occasion at the end of "Prose" is, of course, something of an exaggeration, my own hyperbolic way of making a point. First, it might be argued, the occasion is never actually elided, for it remains squarely at the center of the poem (stanzas 3 and 6–9) from one reading to the next. One might even say that reading "Anastase!" as referring exclusively to the poem's opening and to the initial representation of the poetic process is premature, in that the combination of "Anastase!" and "Pulchérie!" re-presents the proliferation of flowers, the hyperbolic rising up of Beauty, the contemplation of which is the thematic focus of the inner stanzas. Nevertheless, I would counter, "Anastase!" does bring us back, inevitably, to the initial invocation of poetic hyperbole. Both "Anastase!" and "Pulchérie!" are nominal forms that accrue a certain verbal force (an exhortation to rise up) that is accentuated when followed, as they are, by the exclamation point.

A second argument might point out that the evocation of the gladiolus at the poem's conclusion does not bring the "occasion" back in its entirety but merely represents it. Such a line of reasoning, however, is largely dismissible in that it is precisely the flower's final position of detachment that is of interest. Expelled, rejected from the inner stanzas, it hovers over the outer stanzas like a remainder, a leftover impossible to get rid of because of the hopelessness of disguising it. Occasion keeps coming back or turning up, we might say, like the proverbial bad penny.

This is precisely the main point of one of the few contemporary "theoretical" discourses on the role of occasion in art, Samuel Beckett's "Three Dialogues." Beckett's discussion takes the form of brief conversations between B (presumably Beckett himself) and D (the French abstract painter Georges Duthuit) each centering on a different contemporary artist. B argues for an art that would turn its back on occasion, rid itself of the delusion Western painting has labored under since its conception, namely, that art is expressive of preexisting concepts, feelings, objects, or vistas. He advocates an art of "the expression that there is nothing to express, nothing with which to express, nothing from which to express, no power to express, no desire to express, together with the obligation to express" (139). Art should concern itself not with reproducing objects or occasions but rather with the "anxiety of the relation" between "the aliment, from fruits on plates to low mathematics and self-commiseration, and its manner of dispatch" (144–45). The proper subject of art, then, lies in the spaces between subject and object, between occasion and its representation. The artist seeks not to illuminate, bemoan, or celebrate this void but to "submit wholly to the incoercible absence of relations" in the recognition that "to be an artist is to fail, as no other dare fail, that failure is his world" (145).

Beckett fully recognizes the untenability of his claim that an art devoid of occasion is possible. In a deliberately melodramatic moment of mock tension D questions him about the validity of his exalted claims for the artist van Velde:

D: One moment. Are you suggesting that the painting of van Velde is inexpressive?
B: (A fortnight later) Yes.
D: You realise the absurdity of what you advance?
B: I hope I do. (143)

Beckett is acutely aware of the impossibility of the contention that an inexpressive art can remain so. The "inexpressivity" of art immediately opens itself to recuperation, just as the void of failure immediately dissolves into the failure of void: "I know that all that is required now, in order to bring even this horrible matter to an acceptable conclusion, is to make of this submission, this fidelity to failure, a new occasion, a new term of relation, and of the act which, unable to act, obliged to act, he makes, an expressive act, even if only of itself, of its impossibility, of its obligation" (145). To repeat once again my epigraph: "Anything and everything is doomed to become occasion, including . . . the pursuit of occasion" (144).

The pretension to a lack of occasion is necessarily recuperated as the occasion of a lack; this we have seen dramatized if not explicitly thematized in "Prose." The void created by the elision of the island experience and the absence that the sepulcher marks are both in turn voided: the tomblike mark of absence, "sous aucun climat," was only a self-mocking phantom, an absent sign marking a cenotaph. The seeming elision of occasion was immediately filled by the shadow of the too tall gladiolus. Is, indeed, an art of expression and representation inescapable? Is a truly abstract art, one incapable of recuperation as art whose subject is its own inability to represent, possible?

Beckett winds up the third dialogue with a glimpse at his "unenviable situation, familiar to psychiatrists," a "coloured plane, that was not there before" (145), terms that suggest that he sees, even if his art does not yet fully enact, an alternative. But this moment of insight is short-lived. The final exchange of the dialogue is a total non sequitur to D's admonition that B has only completed the first of his promised "two parts," the first to say what he thought and the second. . . . The response? "B: (Remembering warmly) Yes, yes, I am mistaken, I am mistaken" (145). The mirrorlike repetition of first the affirmative and then the acknowledgment of error suggests more than a gentle and innocuous lunacy. Beckett's "mistakenness" may well work to undermine the possibility of alternative forms of art, if not his entire discussion. But if an art of expression is inevitable, must we continue along the line already established in which "the numerous attempts made to make painting independent of its occasion have only succeeded in enlarging its repertory" (143)? What other relationships between occasion and its representation might be explored?

"Three Dialogues" enacts rather than discloses a response. This "theoretical" discussion, it must be remembered, takes place under the guise of theater. The text is a critical fiction dramatizing Beckett's ideas in which D plays straight man to B much as Didi and Gogo or Hamm and Clov play off each other. The longest single exchange, which occurs at the end of the final dialogue and contains the most sustained critical discourse, is itself presented as B's fiction, what he is "pleased to fancy he [van Velde] is, fancy he does" (144). There is something vaguely reminiscent of Lucky's long-winded speech and the proportional space it occupies in *Waiting for Godot* in B's major statement ("There are many ways in which the thing I am trying to say may be tried in vain to be said" [144]). Here, a novel role for occasion is staged: theoretical discourse becomes the occasion for art, rather than vice versa. When, in turn, we read the "Three Dialogues" as art, the text occasions critical discourse. This notion of a reciprocity between art and occasion, which echoes the undecidability between life and autobiography considered above, will be crucial for the discussion of "La Déclaration foraine" that follows.

Given the many thematic, structural, formal, and theoretical concerns shared by "La Déclaration foraine" (1887) and "Prose pour des Esseintes" (1884), it is surprising that the two texts have not yet been the focus of a comparative study. The prose poem, although not occasional in the strictest sense of the term, is, like "Prose," exclusively preoccupied with the question of the relation of occasion to text and can also be read as an allegory of the problem of representation. The exposition of the problematics of the occasion can be discussed within two fields of discourse, each identifying a major set of oppositional forces in the text: first, the question of the prose/poetry controversy inherent in the prose poem form itself, and second, a consideration of the oppositional pairing of silence/declaration and speech/silent gaze set up in the text's opening paragraphs.

"La Déclaration foraine" is, like "Prose," the tale of a couple on excursion, this time not to an exotic island setting but out for a more mundane drive in the country. On impulse, the woman suggests that they stop at a country fair. In one of its remote corners a deserted booth is found in which the woman promptly mounts a table. Her companion assumes the role of barker as a drummer summons a crowd for their performance. In spite of his conviction that her beauty is in itself a sufficient show for the entrance fee they charge, the man, with a last-minute glance at her hair, recites a sonnet. The two, quite pleased with themselves and the outcome of their unpremeditated production, banter lightly about their improvisation as they wend their way back to the carriage.

Also like "Prose," in which the "poeticity" of a traditional form of fourteen octosyllabic stanzas of extremely rich rhyme is challenged by its contrary title, "La Déclaration foraine" flaunts a certain capriciousness with regard to the question of its classification as prose or poetry. As if to maximize the conflicting claims of prose and poetry that characterize the prose poem genre, the text contains, within the confines of its poetic prose, a poem in verse. The verse, in sonnet form, is set off from its context by a frame of blank space. Because one of Webster's definitions for *margin* is "the blank space around the printed or written area on a page or sheet," it would seem appropriate to take that wording quite literally in order to frame a discussion of the margins/borders/limits between prose and poetry in "La Déclaration foraine."

That opposition already existed more or less explicitly in "Prose." There we were able to distinguish between the outer stanzas (the sphere of poetic activity, of the hyperbolic rise of inspiration and its accompanying science and patience that occasioned "Anastase!," the "poetic production" at the poem's closing) and the inner stanzas, the anecdotal rendition of the couple's visit to the flowering island. The two spheres were mediated by a third, the era of authority/spirit of litigation complex, which defined them less by bringing them together than by pointing to their absolute incompatibility. "La Décla-ration foraine" carries the frame format of "Prose" to a visual ex-treme. Its three "spheres" are distinguished formally as well as the-matically in that the sonnet is quite visibly framed by the white space of the page that in turn is framed by the prose.

But here a chiasmic reversal occurs as the prose narrative portion moves to the outside frame, with the poetry now enclosed within. The transposition is potentially significant, especially in the light of Mallarmé's celebrated statement, "tout, au monde, existe pour abou-tir à un livre" (*O.c.* 378) ("everything in the world exists to end up in a book"). Is it the task of poetry to comprehend anecdote, or, al-ternatively, as suggested by "La Déclaration foraine," does the an-ecdotal encompass poetry? We will return to a discussion of the pos-sible ramifications of these conditions further on.

Whereas the frame format is more prominent because of the clarity of its disposition on the page, in "La Déclaration foraine" the func-tional thematic oppositions (many of which are remarkably similar to those of "Prose") are no longer coincident with the inner and outer portions of the text. Instead, they inhabit each of the frames. The result is a skewing rather than reinforcing of the prose/poetry polar-ity. The prose section does not present itself as a uniform entity; it is instead broken quite literally in two by the sonnet. Its integrity is further shaken by the pairs of oppositions generated almost too con-spicuously as the narrative portion progresses: the possibility and goal of declaration, set forth in the title, is pitted against the poem's first words: "Le Silence!" The male poet-persona plainly functions in a different sphere and with motives different from those of his female companion. His contentment with the isolation of the mobile car-riage, enveloped in silence, is quite clearly broken and contrasted with her "command" to stop the car and to participate in the "ca-cophony" of the crowded fairground. The move from the protected interior of the carriage to the exposed exterior of the fair thus incites the shift from silence to declaration, from the private to the public sphere, from the rocking mobility of the carriage to the curious im-mobility of Madame poised on the stage.

In parallel fashion the sonnet features the opposition of the "nudi-ty" of the tender hero to the simple but glorious adornment of the woman by her loosened hair and the omnipresent oscillation between the mobile and the immobile suggested by the pervasive symbol of the flickering torch. The fact that the prose poem's visually obvious antithesis of prose to poetry is tempered and complicated by a series of internal conflicts should make us suspect that again, as with "Prose," a simple binary model will not be sufficient to account for the poem's complexities. Here we will have to consider instead a more dynamic model that will encompass a certain instability of categories and a propensity toward a vacillation between the mobile and the immobile.

Interposed between the prose and sonnet is an ambiguous blank space, a frame that, having no "materiality" of its own, would appear to be no frame at all. But here again I would like to call attention to the "thickness" of the frame. Certainly the attribution of an intrinsic value to blank space can be well documented in Mallarmé. In the draft of a letter to Charles Morice, Mallarmé had written:

L'armature intellectuelle du poème, se dissimule et—a lieu—tient dans l'espace qui isole les strophes et parmi le blanc du papier; significatif silence qu'il n'est past moins beau de composer que les vers. (*Propos* 164; included in *Le Livre* as fragment 2)

The intellectual armature of the poem conceals itself and—takes place—holds together in the space that isolates the stanzas and amidst the white of the paper; significant silence that is no less beautiful to compose than poetry.

Such statements allow us to infer a certain tangibility to the border itself that engages what Derrida has called "the entire problematic of inscription in a milieu, of distinguishing the work from a ground" ("Parergon" 24). Where, in fact, is the ergon, the art object, and where is its natural ground or parergon (artificial ground)? What ought to be the real object of our study in "La Déclaration foraine," the prose, the sonnet, or (if we push Mallarmé's notion of "significant silence" to its logical limit) the blank space that separates them?

The question of blank space becomes even more acute in what has often been called Mallarmé's most radical poem, "Un Coup de dés." The preface (shall we read it as parergon or part of the ergon itself?) contains his famous formulation of "l'espacement de la lecture": "Les 'blancs,' en effet, assument l'importance, frappent d'abord; la versification en exigea, comme silence alentour" (*O.c.* 455) ("The blank spaces, in effect, assume importance, strike first; versification demanded them, like surrounding silence"). There the work itself is inseparable from its generous disposition on the page; the paper "intervenes" as images cease or return. Like the silence of a musical composition, the "advantage" of blank space is to accelerate or slow down movement, punctuating it with the proper stresses, imitating that movement according to a simultaneous vision of the page taken as a "natural" unity (*O.c.* 455).

How ought the critic deal with this white space and the relationship of poem to prose? Certainly one sort of legitimate investigation would fall within the domain of historical scholarship: were the prose poem and sonnet conceived together? If not, which is prior and what motivated their combination? The consensus of Mallarmé scholarship is that the two were written independently and that the sonnet predates the prose poem, but definitive answers and exact composition dates have yet to be provided. A minor critical rift exists between those, led by Richard, who read the sonnet in terms of the prose poem, and those, principally Cohn, who have tried to resist the introduction of the circumstances of the prose into their interpretation of the sonnet. Cohn argues that

the sonnet was, without doubt, written separately and was combined with the prose as an afterthought; its imagery is occasionally inconsistent with the unlikely situation. This view is supported by the fact that Mallarmé published it separately in his *Poésies* and therefore its imagery must be independent of any notion [such as Richard's] of a crowd-public. (*Toward* 147)

At stake, of course, is whether the sonnet *can* or *must* be read independently or together with the prose. Can a poem be divorced from its context and still be read properly? Is the poem that Mallarmé published separately in his *Poésies* in some way a different poem from that which appears in the text of "La Déclaration foraine"?

Furthermore, the actual relationship between prose and sonnet is significant to the extent it becomes revelatory of our notions of "simple" referentiality. I noted at the opening of this chapter that de Man "invented" this hypothetical category to oppose it, implicitly, to more nuanced or complex modes of reference and representation. But Cohn's claim that the "imagery [of the poem] is occasionally inconsistent with the unlikely situation" (147) should make us question the likelihood or even possibility of a complete "consistency" between the imagery of any poem and its context, and even the desirability of such.

The purpose of these queries will undoubtedly become less opaque now as I try to elucidate the relationship between the particular concerns of "La Déclaration foraine" and the larger problematics of the occasional poem. As Barbara Johnson has noted in her remarkable essay on Mallarmé's prose poem, it is "the story of the recitation of an occasional poem" that "concludes with a discussion of what constitutes a poem's occasion" (*Critical Difference* 54). Yet this perspective, however intriguing it may sound, raises as many questions as it solves. It compels us to pose once again the question that informs this entire study, namely, what is an occasional poem and how does it relate to its occasion? If, as Barbara Johnson contends, "La Chevelure vol d'une flamme" is an occasional poem, it can be so considered only in the context of the prose poem frame; independently it makes no gesture to specific extratextual circumstances. It is also rather unorthodox, as occasional poems go, in that the "event" that it ostensibly celebrates (even within the context of the prose poem) does not precede the writing but rather is simultaneous with the poem's improvised composition. Finally, the poem itself would seem not to treat the circumstances from which it arises but rather to obscure them as much as possible.

Thus we have an uneasy and equivocal relationship between the poem and its occasion, which will readily be seen as a variant of that outlined above concerning the correspondence of the prose to the sonnet. What exactly is at stake at the margins of the verse, in the blank space that both separates and joins poetry and prose, the poem and its occasion? Does the prose poem provide the occasion for the sonnet, as Barbara Johnson's reading seems to suggest, or conversely, does it make more sense to speak of the sonnet as providing the "occasion" for the prose?

Let us explore the first possibility. If the prose poem "occasions" the verse, as, for instance, the death of a public figure may occasion an elegy or epitaph, we should expect to find a logic of cause and effect at work: the circumstances recounted leading up to the recitation of the verse ought to be represented (to a greater or lesser extent) in the verse itself. But the sonnet "La Chevelure" does not reproduce mimetically any event that precedes it (that is, in the first part of the prose poem), nor does it slavishly describe the woman who has so boldly placed herself on a makeshift pedestal. Like the words "Anastase!" and "Pulchérie!" produced at the end of "Prose," which refer to the framed anecdote but in no way reiterate it, the sonnet of "La Déclaration foraine" seems to point to aspects of the surrounding prose without re-presenting (in any accepted sense of the term) the events narrated therein. Rather than clarifying its relationship to its circumstances, the sonnet foregrounds its own inability or refusal to represent them.

What, then, is the sonnet about? Cohn has noted, and Barbara Johnson has quoted him as stating, that it is "a celebration of a woman whose looks, featuring magnificent hair, need no outer adornment" (Cohn, *Toward* 147; Johnson, *Critical Difference* 53). Johnson carries this to its logical conclusion: "In its simultaneous act of naming and exhibiting, the poem can thus be said to relate to the lady as a sign to its referent" (53). She goes on, of course, to deconstruct this notion of a simple mode of referentiality and finally concludes that in the sonnet

reference is not denied: it is problematized beyond reconciliation. The lady remains the referent of the poem, but only insofar as the poem says absolutely nothing about her. . . . What is revolutionary in Mallarmé's poetics is less the elimination of the "object" than this very type of construction of a systematic set of self-emptying, nonintuitive meanings. Mallarmé's famous obscurity lies not in his devious befogging of the obvious but in his radical transformation of intelligibility itself through the ceaseless production of seemingly mutually exclusive readings of the same piece of language. *This* is what constitutes Mallarmé's break with referentiality, and not the simple abolition of the object, which would still be an entirely referential gesture. Reference is here not denied but suspended. The sonnet simultaneously takes on and discards meaning only to the extent that its contact with the lady's presence is contradictorily deferred. (64–65)

I reached much the same conclusion in Chapter 1. In the poems there considered, especially "Ses purs ongles" and the "Ouverture ancienne d'Hérodiade," reference was thematically as well as structurally deferred, and this at the level of the image as well as in the larger units to which Johnson alludes. She declares that in "La Déclaration foraine" the "sonnet is talking less directly about the lady than about its relation to the lady. It is less about *something* than about *being about*. Simultaneously asserting both the necessity and the undesirability of its own existence, the poem refers to its own referring and not directly to its referent" (63). Granted. But one wonders if this would not be an accurate description of *every* late Mallarmé poem (and every obscure Modernist poem?) to the extent that these texts by their very difficulty foreground their own problematization of referentiality. Michel Foucault summed up current understanding of the radical break in literature from the nineteenth century onward as follows: "Literature was reconstituting itself . . . in an independent form, difficult of access, folded back upon the enigma of its own origin and existing wholly in reference to the pure act of writing" (300). The auto-referentiality of late-nineteenth- and twentieth-century literature has become a cliché of contemporary criticism.

What then specifically accounts for the difficulty of "La Chevelure"? The poem is one of five categorized as sonnets to Méry Laurent, all written, presumably, between 1885 and 1887. The sonnets evidence a remarkably stable repertoire of images: the golden *chevelure*, associated with the cloud, the flag, and the silk; sunset, associated with other fire images and the torch; jewels, especially rubies and diamonds; flowers, most often the rose; and the motifs of royalty and chivalry. On a purely anecdotal level we find in each poem an intimate scene between the lover and his beloved set in an implicitly or explicitly theatrical space (as in Mallarmé's intimate theater of the mime, "un milieu, pur, de fiction" ["a pure fictional space"]), allowing for "une notation de sentiments par phrases point proférées" (*O. c.* 310) ("a notation of feelings by phrases not uttered"). Upon this stage Mallarmé does not describe the woman physically, nor does he enumerate her spiritual qualities; rather, he pays tribute to her by representing the play of emotions, of passions, the "fils de ces rapports qui forment les vers et les orchestres" ("threads of these relations that form verses and orchestras") that fill the atmosphere of their presence together. Each of the love sonnets is syntactically difficult in that it is often impossible to determine the subject of any particular verb. This dissociated movement of affectivity entirely displaces the traditional narrative patterns of passion; all that is apparent is movement or lack of it. Each poem is a ballet of contours traced in the air. "La chevelure" ("Hair") harshly juxtaposed with "vol d'une flamme" ("flight [or theft] of a flame") is quite incomprehensible until the metaphor is translated by the last verse: "Ainsi qu'une joyeuse et tutélaire torche" ("Like a joyous and tutelary torch"). The flickering motion of the hair-torch is depicted in the poem by the movement traced by verbs or verbal nouns: "vol . . . déployer . . . se pose . . . mourir . . . soupirer . . . ignition . . . continue . . . diffame . . . ne mouvant

. . . simplifier . . . accomplit . . . fulgurante . . . semer . . . écorche" ("flight/theft . . . unfurl . . . perches . . . to die . . . to sigh . . . ignition . . . continues . . . slanders . . . not moving . . . to simplify . . . accomplishes . . . lightning . . . to sow . . . flays"). Passion hovers between explosion and extinction, staging the very contours of eroticism.

The extreme capriciousness of the sonnet, a kind of *va-et-vient* between the wildly mobile and the completely immobile is itself a commentary on the process of reading Mallarmé: we forge ahead only to slow down, to stop, to continually reread, to continually reformulate. As the text performs for us, it forces us to perform in predictable ways. We might speculate as to whether the text and this process are infinitely repeatable. And the performance itself? The fickle movement suggests the strange mobility of the couple in the prose poem, in the carriage moving, now stopping, and preparing to set off again. One begins to suspect that this might not have been their only stop that day, and that the same show, complete with elevated pedestal and sonnet, might have been "improvised" down the road a bit before yet another audience demanding a spectacle for their money. The very "mobility" of the title word, "foraine," which can mean anything from foreign or alien, to outdoors, to pertaining to fairs, to strolling or itinerant, would seem to sanction such a hypothesis.

If then the sonnet can clearly be shown *not* to function after the fashion of the prototypical occasional poem and, indeed, if in its flurry of mobility it denies rather than points to the specificity of its occasion, perhaps another brand of relationship between text and occasion, between prose and poetry can be discovered. This leads us directly to the second possibility adumbrated above and to a much broader-based problematization of the notion of the occasion in "La Déclaration foraine." But first let us reconsider some ground already covered. The "readerliness" of my synopsis of the prose poem belies the actual experience of the text, which any reader of Mallarmé will acknowledge to be a slow, difficult process given his hermeticism and tortuous syntax. Any attempt, therefore, to delimit the relationship between the prose and the poetry is at best an approximation. The notion of a poem that occasions its circumstances, as the sonnet perhaps does, can then be seen as a parable of the reading situation itself. That is, our first step in reading poetry is to naturalize the text by creating an occasion for it: we tell a story about it much as

Mallarmé's prose poem provides a story that, however tangentially, "explains" his obscure sonnet (the poet was out driving with his beloved when . . .). Our impromptu "performance" of reading the sonnet can only repeat Mallarmé's production of the prose poem that narrates the young man's extemporaneous composition of the sonnet. The sonnet therefore engenders the prose that in turn engenders the sonnet. Can the vicious circle be arrested? Can the sonnet or the prose finally be labeled as "occasion" and "re-presentation" and their relationship specified?

The question is likely to remain unresolved and is, perhaps, ultimately undecidable. Here, as with "Prose," the piece's obscurity may lie not only in Mallarmé's syntax but in his eschewing the conventional techniques of representation. When, as in these texts, the problem of representation becomes the principal thematic concern and demands itself to be represented, the temporal scheme implicit in the "re" of representation is nullified. Occasion is no longer necessarily prior to its representation in writing and may be, as the prose poem has evidenced, more product than origin. The lesson of "La Déclaration foraine" is then finally a demonstration of the ultimate commutability of occasion and its textual representation.

If we then return to our initial question about the margins of prose and poetry in the prose poem, we may read the blank space that separates them as the visible manifestation of a lack. Derrida notes that without the parerga (in Kant's examples, the frames of pictures, the draperies on statues, or the colonnades of palaces) "the lack within the work would appear or, what amounts to the same, would not appear. It is not simply their exteriority that constitutes them as parerga, but the internal structural link by which they are inseparable from a lack within the ergon. And this lack makes for the very unity of the ergon. Without it, the ergon would have no need of a parergon" ("Parergon" 24). The work cannot be conceived as such, as a coherent, identifiable, integral structure without its frame to distinguish inside from outside, the internal from that which is exterior. But conversely, the lack that creates the frame is created by the frame; it is the very act of framing that makes the internal lack apparent.

In "La Déclaration foraine," just as poetry and prose function both as text and as occasion, both can be read as ergon or parergon. And, as stated above, the blank space that intervenes may itself make claims to such a dual status. Does the embedding of the sonnet rend a gap in the prose, forcing white space? Or does the gap already in some sense elicit the intervention of the poetry? Clearly, blank space at its margins is a conventional sign of verse, but in the prose poem, or any short narrative piece, a certain margin is also elicited and works to unify the text.[7] In either case, however, blank space sets the text on a pedestal of sorts and attracts a specific audience.

The recognition of the structural equivalency of blank space, pedestal, and audience, in fact, seems essential to a proper reading of "La Déclaration foraine." At different levels, each makes possible the interpolation of the sonnet, each provides the space in which the relationship between the poem and its occasion is at once discernible and the point of a total absence of readability. Like the blank space, the woman's placing herself on the table/pedestal seems to initiate a lack that must be filled, just as the couple's happening on the empty booth *demands* a presentation therein. Thus the frame frames its own lack, calling attention to the missing show ("l'hallucination d'une merveille à montrer" [*O.c.* 280] ["the hallucination of a marvel to be shown"]), the absence of a presence. Madame's silent and statuesque performance is seemingly absolute, complete in itself, filling the lack of the empty stage. And yet it is coexistent with the very lack it disclaims, creating the need for the word. Indeed, the problematics of the poem seem to revolve around a dynamic opposition engendered in the space between the title and the very first words of the text: declaration/silence.

Each time there is a void, a silence hinted at or created in the text, words rush in to stop the gap. The prose poem would seem to open on a scene of "tacite félicité": the couple moving along pleasurably, rocking gently to the motion of the carriage. The insistence on silence is reiterated: "Le Silence! . . . toute femme . . . m'exempte de l'effort à proférer un vocable" ("Silence! . . . any woman . . . exempts me from the effort of uttering a word"). This tranquillity, we know, however, is destined to be broken: the words "vocifération," "rire strident ordinaire des choses et de leur cuivrerie triomphale" ("usual strident laughter of things and their triumphal brassiness"), and "la cacophonie" soon overpower the text (*O.c.* 279). But on closer examination one begins to suspect that silence is a very rare commodity in "La Déclaration foraine," for even the opening exclamation or apostrophe that calls on silence nevertheless calls it out, breaking the very soundlessness it would seek to describe. And while the poem's speaker seemingly rejoices in his exemption from speech, his extreme volubility in describing his quietude belies his very claims. He inundates us with his own cacophony, that peculiarly replete Mallarméan prose style that leaves one absolutely breathless as words pile up on words. The entire first paragraph, in fact, is composed of only two sentences. It would be difficult to find another passage in literature where the described lack of speech is so verbosely overstated, and one wonders, finally, if the stated preference for silence is not entirely dismissible.

Again, when the woman emerges on the empty stage, perched on the makeshift pedestal, silent and motionless, it is her companion, not she, who feels overwhelmingly obliged to compensate for the sensed void with words. Indeed, there is a telltale gap between his ability to "see" the situation properly and his inability simply to let it stand as is. A marvelous Mallarméan pun translates this incompatibility between speech and the gaze: in the first paragraph of the text it is the man who self-interestedly reads the woman's ability to see clearly, "voit clair" ("j'en sais une qui voit clair ici" ["I know one who sees clearly here"]), and then, in the second paragraph, it is her clear voice, "voix claire" (" nomma l'enfant . . . la voix claire d'aucun ennui" ["said the child . . . her voice clear of any annoyance"]), that names the provincial fair they have happened on. Although the male persona, taking one last glance at her hair, clearly sees that the woman's "performance" needs no accompaniment, he nevertheless understands his "devoir en le péril de la subtile exhibition" ("duty in the peril of the subtle exhibition") and feels compelled to speak, to "dégoiser jusqu'à l'éclaircissement" (*O.c.* 281) ("spout off until seeing the elucidation").

Speech, again, would seem to overpower the silent gaze in that only language, not silence, is capable of providing "elucidation." Does silence punctuate language as conventional understanding would have it, or is the reverse true? (This can be read as yet another version of the question of whether blank space intervenes between words, or whether words punctuate blank space.) What, in fact, constitutes the real performance (prose, poem, or blank space?) set on that improvised stage? Is the woman's placing herself on display the real show? If so, and if, as the speaker states, it is clear that she, without supplement of dance or song, *amply* repays the entrance fee charged, why is this consummate performance nevertheless supple-

mented by the recitation of the sonnet? Is this a textual manifestation
of the lack in the ergon producing the parergon? This "ornamenta-
tion" then elicits its own supplement, for the male, as if to counter
the as yet unexpressed dissatisfaction of the crowd, provides a "plain
folks" paraphrase ("maintenant de plain-pied avec l'entendement des
visiteurs" [O.c. 282] ["now on the level of the understanding of our
visitors"]) of the hermetic sonnet he has just recited. In doing so, he
reiterates the fact that Madame needs no "costume ou aucun acces-
soire usuel de théâtre" ("costume or any customary theater props"),
denying the very necessity of his having spoken at all. Why is the
crowd in fact given three performances when anticipating only one?
(And, by extension, why is the reader provided with prose, sonnet,
and blank space?)

Before we are able to answer these questions we must return to the
problematic of silence versus declaration, reading it this time in terms
of the dichotomy between speaker and hearer, writer and reader as
thematized in the text. If, indeed, a declaration is to be made, it nec-
essarily presupposes both speech and silence, both speaker and
hearer(s) and their coming together on a common ground. I have
shown how both the blank space on the page and the pedestal the
woman mounts function similarly to provide a common ground or
enabling space for the recitation of the sonnet. In the light banter
following the couple's presentation, the sonnet itself is referred to as
the "lieu commun d'une esthétique" (O.c. 283) ("commonplace of
an aesthetic"), seemingly demoting its potentially exalted place as
serious artistic endeavor to a mere cliché of a response to the given
situation. But the locution functions on several different levels.
Taken literally, it is the "common place" where speaker and hearer
come together, placing emphasis on the improvised stage that allows
for the enunciation of the sonnet. The interpolation of the sonnet
thus takes place (*a lieu*) both because of and in the space of this *lieu
commun*. Furthermore, the male's offhand dismissal of his compan-
ion's arcane appreciation of the sonnet ([She:] "J'ai dans l'esprit le
souvenir de choses qui ne s'oublient" ["I have in mind the memory
of things that are not forgotten"]; [He:] "Oh! rien que lieu commun
d'une esthétique" ["Oh! it was nothing but the commonplace of an
aesthetic"]) functions to exempt him from admitting that he has in-
deed proffered a formal "declaration" to the lady. In the conversation

that follows, she suggests that in the "conjoint isolement" of their carriage he might never have gotten around to formulating even this "lieu commun," except for the considerable stimulus provided by an impatient audience: "le coup de poing brutal à l'estomac, que cause une impatience de gens auxquels coûte que coûte et soudain il faut proclamer quelque chose fût-ce la rêverie" (*O.c.* 283) ("the brutal punch to the stomach that the impatience of people to whom one must suddenly proclaim something at any cost, even if it is only reverie").

The audience then provides yet another plane of signification for the "lieu commun" in that it is the middle ground that enables the bringing together of the male speaker and his female companion in terms of the sonnet declaration. As we have seen, the woman credits the audience for the jolt that made possible his spoken declaration, while the man, recognizing the initiating role the public may play in such situations, wonders if Madame might not have heard his words so "irrefutably" if they had not been pronounced in front of an audience:

Qui s'ignore et se lance nue de peur, en travers du public; c'est vrai. Comme vous, Madame, ne l'auriez entendu si irréfutablement, malgré sa réduplication sur une rime du trait final, mon boniment d'après un mode primitif du sonnet, je le gage, si chaque terme ne s'en était répercuté jusqu'à vous par de variés tympans, pour charmer un esprit ouvert à la compréhension multiple. (*O.c.* 283)

She who forgets herself and dashes, naked with fear, among the public, it's true. Just as for you, Madame, who would not have heard it so irrefutably, in spite of its reduplication on a rhyme of the final part, my charlatanry in the form of the primitive mode of a sonnet, I bet, if each term did not reverberate back to you off various eardrums, to charm a mind open to multiple understandings.

Like the virtual blank space on the written page, like the table waiting to be read as stage and pedestal, the audience functions to mediate (and, indeed, to prompt) the recitation of the sonnet. Neither quite passive nor active, it works as a catalyst to enable the production of language. Ursula Franklin aptly terms this facilitating role the "midwifery of the public" (133). The frustrated silence that reigned at the opening of the text finally falls into language; the recitation of the

sonnet is followed by the lovers' repartee, a reproduction of the un-
spoken communication at the beginning of the poem. But where are
the lovers at the end, having gone through silence to speech?

There would seem to be a dichotomy drawn between the limits and
borders of the private sphere as opposed to the public. What exactly
is involved in the transfer from the privacy of the carriage to the pub-
lic stage? The conditions of privacy, silence, and chastity would seem
to be linked to and specifically set off against the speech and (admit-
tedly restrained) passion of the public demonstration, whereas con-
ventional etiquette (especially that of the nineteenth century) would
lead us to expect passion to be confined to the private sphere. We
may well raise the question of what the public is actually paying to
see, the woman on the pedestal, the poetic recitation, or a public
display of affection? Certainly, the importance of the role of the third-
party audience shades our understanding of the declaration, and we
may wonder why the kind of language meant for private ears is served
up for public consumption.

In fact, a double seduction is being attempted on the provincial
stage. The woman is seduced by the poetry of her companion (the
"declaration" of the title), and at the same time, the crowd is seduced
by the couple's performance. But the seductions are not merely si-
multaneous; they are, as we have seen, highly dependent on each
other. Clearly, an element of exhibitionism is a contributing factor
in the seduction of the woman, making the crowd the secondary ad-
dressee of that seduction as well as the medium through which the
seduction takes place. And the seduction of the public is concomi-
tantly a formalization and legitimation of voyeurism, the crowd's very
seduction excited and promoted by witnessing the declaration. The
appearance of the sonnet in this unlikely setting is linked to what
contemporary parlance would term a "flashing," a "streaking," a re-
vealing of oneself before the public. Both the prose and the poetry
make references to this self-display: "Qui s'ignore et se lance nue de
peur, en travers du public" (*O.c.* 283) ("She who forgets herself and
dashes, naked with fear, among the public") and "Une nudité de
héros tendre diffame / Celle qui ne mouvant astre ni feux au doigt"
(*O.c.* 282) ("A nakedness of tender hero slanders / Her who neither
moving star nor fires on her finger"). The nakedness appears to be a
transposition between man and woman: she, needing no adornment,
"denudes" herself as she places herself on the pedestal; he conse-

quently feels denuded by her exhibitionism. This public display shares with all of Mallarmé's love poetry its affectlessness; it is a kind of sublimated sex act more suggested than realized. (Note, for example, the play of "semer" and "écorche" in the first line of the sonnet's rhymed couplet: "De semer de rubis le doute qu'elle écorche" ["To sow with rubies the doubt that she flays"].) But, does the seduction actually take place? That is, if the couple's sudden leave-taking is explained by a pretense of returning to the "authenticité du spectacle," what one translator has rendered as the "real show" (Bosley 233), and if the woman's remark, "j'ai dans l'esprit le souvenir de choses qui ne s'oublient" ("I have in mind the memory of things that are not forgotten"), can be read as pointing to the "upcoming" scene that will transpire once they return to the carriage, are we to understand that the spectacle we have just witnessed in the fairground booth is not the "real" show and that it is only a prolegomenon to another, more private spectacle?

If this is the case, it is unclear who is seducer and who is seducee: who controls the events of the day? Most critics have read the text in terms of nineteenth-century male domination, with the woman playing the role of silent adjunct. But in fact, is it not the woman (with the already formulated project of forcing the declaration?) who manipulates her companion out of the silence of their carriage into the tumult of the fair, who summons the crowd by commanding that the drum be beaten, and who places herself on the stage? When the male speaker resigns himself to entering the fairground, "ce déchaînement exprès et haïssable" ("this willed and odious outburst"), he finds his companion more than acquiescent: she is "prête et ne témoignant de surprise à la modification dans notre programme" (*O.c.* 280) ("ready and showing no surprise at the change in our plans"). She initiates the "show" as she unhesitatingly mounts the makeshift stage (it is her "secret": "ce qu'avait su faire avec ce lieu sans rêve l'initiative d'une contemporaine de nos soirs" [*O.c.* 281] ["that which the initiative of a fashionable lady contemporary of our evenings had known how to do with this dreamless place"]), whereas the man is quite at a loss as to what his role ought to be. If the conventional model for seduction is one in which the woman is seduced into silence, here we have an important reversal. It is rather the woman who, through her silent exhibition, appears to be seducing her male companion into words.

That seduction *into* words may in fact repeatedly only tell the se-
duction *of* words is perhaps the principal lesson of the prose poem.
The "lieu commun" discussed above can be read at at least one more
level, one that largely challenges the various interpretations already
advanced. If it is true that the sonnet is the "common place" that
brings the male and female interlocutors together in the presence of
the audience (that is, the speaker and his multiple hearers) and that
the sonnet is only produced because this common ground is created,
it is nevertheless highly questionable whether the sonnet provides
any common ground on which speaker and audience actually meet.
The syntactical difficulties and ambiguities of the sonnet have been
well documented (see especially Johnson, *Critical Difference* 61–66;
Goodkin 135–55): there is no reason to believe that the provincial
audience is any less puzzled by the hermetic recitation than are we as
readers of the sonnet. The confrontation of speaker and audience in
the prose poem, in fact, sets itself up as a fable of a certain relationship
of writer to reader. In the text the immediate presence of the speaker
to his audience seems to provide none of the advantages Western
metaphysics has traditionally accorded to speech over writing. There
appears to be, instead, an enormous gulf between the two: even as
the woman initiates the performance, and before the crowd has had
time to register its satisfaction or dissatisfaction with the spectacle,
the speaker has already in somewhat paranoid fashion assumed the
incomprehension and potentially violent response of the assembled
provincials:

du même trait je comprends mon devoir en le péril de la subtile exhibition,
ou qu'il n'y avait au monde pour conjurer la défection dans les curiosités que
de recourir à quelque puissance absolue, comme d'une Métaphore. Vite, dé-
goiser jusqu'à l'éclaircissement, sur maintes physionomies, de leur sécurité
qui, ne saississant tout du coup, se rend à l'évidence, même ardue, impli-
quée en la parole et consent à échanger son billon contre des présomptions
exactes et supérieures, bref, la certitude pour chacun de n'être pas refait.
(*O.c.* 281)

in the same flash I understand my duty in the peril of the subtle exhibition,
that there was no way in the world to conjure away defection from these
curiosities than to resort to some absolute power, like a Metaphor. Fast,
spout off until seeing, upon many a face, the elucidation of their security
that, not grasping everything all at once, renders itself to the evidence, even
though with difficulty, implied in their speech, and consents to exchange his

base coin for exact and superior presumptions, in brief, the certitude for each one not to get taken in.

The sonnet itself, supposedly an "absolute power, like a Metaphor," is permitted to function no more as an absolute performance than was Madame's silent self-exhibition. Words rush in to explain the unexplainable; there is, as we have already noted, an obsessive impulse repeatedly portrayed in the poem to "spout off until seeing the elucidation." The compulsion to see clearly, "voir clair," is expressed by repeated attempts to produce a clear voice, "voix claire."

We are now perhaps in a better position to answer the question posed some pages back concerning the treating of the crowd to three performances when it anticipated only one. The speaker offers the sonnet to supplement Madame's statuelike "performance," which is followed by his unnecessary supplementation of that supplement, the paraphrasing of his sonnet in which he states that the woman needs no adornment, this last functioning both as a restatement of the poem and a repudiation of it. The problem the poem seems to be posing is the communicability of poetry: What, if anything, is communicated between speaker and audience in this privileged "lieu commun"? What place does a hermetic art have in the "lieu commun"? Surely, little semantic content passes between the interlocutors. And the illocutionary or perlocutionary force of the poem would appear to be a very vague concept of "art" itself, as well as a kind of verbosity for verbosity's sake. The crowd is overcome by verbiage, and the speaker somewhat intoxicated with his own compulsion to proffer words. He refers to his fear that he has not spoken enough, "peut-être faute chez moi de faconde ultérieure" (*O.c.* 282) ("perhaps because of my lack of further loquacity"), and later to his "boniment" (*O.c.* 283) ("charlatanry").

But the speaker's verbal acrobatics are only the textual echo of Mallarmé's own performance as writer. We, as readers, are in the position of the crowd, and we, like the spectators at the fairground, are treated to a barrage of elucidations that both repeat and repudiate what has gone on before. Like the compulsive and vaguely paranoid persona in his poem, Mallarmé offers us a series of explanations of his text that finally comprise the text itself. Our final question then, to return to Barbara Johnson, may be phrased as follows: What is the occasion for the occasion of a writing about occasional poetry? If the first half of the prose provides the occasion for the production of the sonnet, and the second half of the prose asks, as Johnson states, what constitutes a poem's occasion, what then is the occasion for calling the occasion into question?

My preliminary reading of "Prose" suggested that occasion had been elided, displaced by a representation of the problem of the representation of occasion. But the "remainder" at the end of the text, the "too tall gladiolus," forces me to alter that conclusion. Instead, I read the too tall gladiolus as reinstating the occasion, as representing the island experience (the occasion) as outside the outermost frame, that is, in a symbolic sense, as outside the framing of representation itself. Occasion, it seemed, could not be dismissed with, and the attempts to obviate it succeeded only in reasserting it. This same conclusion was reached, cast in the tragic dimension, in Beckett's "Three Dialogues."

In "La Déclaration foraine" Mallarmé has not exactly succeeded in abolishing occasion, but the distinction between text and occasion has been considerably flattened in that the two terms become interchangeable: as "occasion," the prose produces the sonnet, which then furnishes the "occasion" for the composition of the prose, which produces the sonnet, and so on. Occasion is abolished to the extent that all textuality becomes occasion and all occasion, text. The text is shown here to perpetuate itself by a continual supplementation, and if we can subscribe to the possibility suggested above that this "déclaration foraine" is but one in a potentially infinite series, the mobility of succeeding occasions begins to approximate the final version of the poetics of the occasion that we shall be examining in the last chapter in the discussion of Mallarmé's *Vers de circonstance*.

Chapter Four

Displacing the Monumental:
The "Tombeaux" Poems

Not marble nor the gilded monuments
Of princes shall outlive this pow'rful rime
—Shakespeare, Sonnet 55

There are but two strong conquerors of the forgetfulness of men,
Poetry and Architecture; and the latter in some sort includes the
former, and is mightier in its reality; it is well to have, not only what
men have thought and felt, but what their hands have handled, and
their strength wrought, and their eyes beheld, all the days of their
life.   —Ruskin, *The Lamp of Memory*

Occasional poetry, as we have seen, encompasses a broad
spectrum of poetic endeavor ranging from the funeral elegy and se-
rious pieces composed for historic occasions to a more domestic va-
riety of verse penned by whim or fancy as invitation, gift, or mere
playful banter. In the interest of expediency I have employed a crit-
ical shorthand and allowed these poles of the occasional to be la-
beled, respectively, the monumental and the trivial, without rigor-
ously defining the terms. In this chapter and the next I will attempt
to put these polarities into focus in terms of the Mallarméan text.

Any attempt to stake out the site of the monumental necessarily
invokes a series of framing strategies. The monumental is not a lo-
calizable absolute but rather a relative point that can be specified only
in terms of its diacritical difference from an equally unspecific notion
of the trivial. That is, a text or work of art is monumental only with
respect to another; and at any moment the metaphorical concept of
the monumental may shift to redefine their relationship. Jonathan
Culler offers a rather succinct account of the process in the distinct

but parallel context of convention and the naturalization of the poetic text:

Once a purpose is postulated (praise of a mistress, meditation on death, etc.) one has a focal point which governs the interpretation of metaphor, the organization of oppositions and the identification of relevant formal features. . . . It is perfectly possible to write a poem in order to invite a friend to dinner, but if we admit the poem to the institution of literature we thereby contract to read it as a statement which coheres on another level. Thus, Ben Jonson's "Inviting a Friend to Supper" becomes the evocation of a particular style of life and is read as enacting through the tone and posture of the verse the values that support and recommend this mode of life. The invitation becomes a formal device rather than thematic centre, and what might have been explained as elements of an invitation are given another function. (*Structuralist Poetics* 147)

Culler's choice of an occasional poem as his example is, for my purposes, a particularly fortunate one. In the circumstances of its writing, delivery, and acceptance, Jonson's poem would be categorized as a trivial piece. Its rather detailed evocation of the proposed dinner fare with its comical rhyme "palate/salad" and reference to the "short-legged hen" works to support this classification:

> Yet shall you have, to rectify your palate,
>   An olive, capers, or some better salad
> Ushering the mutton; with a short-legged hen,
>   If we can get her, full of eggs, and then
> Lemons and wine for sauce; (In Abrams 1223)

And yet, through the centuries, the nearly unanimous inclusion of this poem in anthologies inevitably distinguishes it, endowing it with monumental stature and securing it a place in the canon. The poem is removed from its original private, functional context, framed and, so to speak, hung on the museum wall like a Duchamp readymade to be revered publicly as an object of artistic contemplation. The frame of the anthology (the literary equivalent of the museum?) provides the text with a kind of monumentalization.

Given this definition, any poem, properly framed, becomes a potential candidate for the monumental. Thus Mallarmé's decision to include the three "Eventail" poems in the 1899 Deman edition of his *Poésies* gives them a special status he never accorded to the "Eventails" now collected in the *Vers de circonstance*. Similarly, the sonnet

"Toast," pronounced at Saint-Charlemagne at the Collège Rollin in February 1895 (*O.c.* 178), in spite of its lexical and thematic parallels with "Salut" and "Toast funèbre," is considered a minor piece. I believe, nevertheless, that Mallarmé's most interesting comments on the nature of monumentality and, by extension, on the question of occasion can best be seen by an analysis of the monuments he erects in the "Tombeaux" poems where the monument is an explicit thematic concern. This strategy has the further advantage of allowing me to consider the phenomenon of monument building from the mutually illuminating perspectives pointed up in my epigraphs: poetry and architecture.

Monuments, whether they be literary or architectural, conjure up a constellation of associated concepts: memorialization, durability, solidity, dignity, serenity, largeness of scale, a certain didacticism, and a fundamental emotional impact.[1] To visit a monument is to enter into contact with a "historical sacred" (Barthes, *Eiffel Tower* 8). As Lewis Mumford has noted, for the ancients it was the dead that were the first to have a permanent dwelling. Their ceremonious burial in graves marked by a cairn, a tree, or a tall rock were landmarks to which the living probably returned at intervals to commune with ancestral spirits (*City in History* 7 and Graphic Section I, Plate 1). As the quest for continuity in place was concomitant with a desire for permanence through time, the monument came to symbolize immortality. Since well before Horace's boast that his poetic monuments would outlast those of bronze ("Exegi monumentum aere perennius" [*Odes* 3.30]) a polemic has raged as to which of the arts, literary or visual, best achieves the ends of monumentality.

Throughout the centuries of debate, however, an even more basic question has remained unresolved: what exactly is the purpose poetry and architecture each claim to serve better? Lawrence Lipking's observation that the word "tomb" designates either the burial place or the monument erected over it (138) points to the fundamental paradox of monumental art, and perhaps of all art: even as it works toward preservation and memorialization, it operates through destruction. We bury to remember, we write funeral elegies to resurrect. The "tombeau," in writing or in stone, serves the dead as it serves the living. It is simultaneously the sign of absence and presence, of the presence of one's absence. The occasion of death calls for a memorialization, the transformation of the ephemeral into the eternal through its inscription in text or rock. Like the casting of one's likeness in bronze, the setting down of an event into writing gives it a monumental quality ("writing is a hardened language which is self-contained") that removes it from the "flow of empty signs, the movement of which alone is significant" that characterizes speech (Barthes, *Writing Degree Zero* 19). Yet this supreme act of perpetuating the occasion is the circumstance by which the occasion is violently erased, annihilated by the text or rock that rewrites or replaces it. The attempt to register the occasion becomes the occasion for its own destruction.

That this is not an accident that befalls monumental art but rather part of its inherent nature of representation is a topic much discussed in current literary theory. Derrida writes, "[t]he book is often described as a tomb" ("Mallarmé" 370), a statement that approaches litotes when made in reference to Mallarmé. The implied juxtapositions in his works of book or poem to tomb or casket are ubiquitous and form, of course, the thematic core of the "Tombeaux" series. In the earlier, more traditional "Tombeaux" the text self-consciously exhibits (as does the camera, morbidly described as a "portable tomb" [Smithson, quoted in Hobbs 155]) its own propensity to efface the real in order to immobilize its idealized fictionalization (cf. "Toast funèbre": "Le rite est pour les mains d'éteindre le flambeau / Contre le fer épais des portes du tombeau:" ["The rite is for hands to put out the torch / Against the thick iron of the gates of the tomb:"] and "Quelqu'un de ces passants . . . / . . . se transmuait / En le vierge héros de l'attente posthume" ["One of those passing . . . / . . . was transformed / Into the virgin hero of posthumous expectation"]). It will be my purpose, however, to show how in the later "Tombeaux," the poem/monument has metamorphosed from the "livre de fer" ("book of iron") into an increasingly supple and accommodating structure.

In like manner the framing discussed above is never an innocent act: it too perpetrates a certain violence by wrenching the text from its circuit of communication and by placing it in an alien context. The text is preserved, monumentalized, but transfigured in the process. The immobilization involved in building or writing a monument necessarily contorts the object of one's attention. The mere fact that such a deformation occurs, however, does not imbue it with the qualities we associate with the monumental. What are the particular strategies conducive to monumentalization? What makes one rendition of an event monumental, and another not?

Such queries raise the question of the possibility of developing a typology of monuments in terms of their mode of representation. My initial work on Mallarmé's "Tombeaux" poems, in fact, was moving in this direction. Having noted the vastly different portrayals of the monument in "Le Tombeau d'Edgar Poe" and the "Tombeau" for Verlaine, the one a massive, stationary block of granite, the other a restless, raging black rock, I wondered if such variances existed among architectural conceptions of the monument and whether a corresponding rhetoric could be discerned. My interest was in exploring the relationship of the finished monument to the object, event, or personage memorialized: by what tropes does the monument come to represent that which occasions it?

Three of the best-known monuments in Washington, D.C., seemed to offer a promising analogy with linguistic representation. The Lincoln Memorial, with its imposing statue of the president sheltered in a templelike structure, draws its force from a mimetic reproduction of the man seated in his symbolic home (the thirty-six Doric columns represent the states of the Union at the time of his death). The statue is Lincoln's metaphor; it is the magnification of the man. Similarly, Jefferson's monument, by recalling the American classic revival style of Monticello, his Virginia mansion, stands in metonymical relationship to him; it depicts the man by representing his home and the style of house he used to design as a practicing architect. The Washington Monument, by contrast, bears no mimetic relation to the first president. The obelisk would seem to represent nothing but itself, an abstract symbol of power whose force is derived from the repetition of the form throughout history beginning with the shafts representing the rays of the sun used by the ancient Egyptians to record the conquests of the pharaohs.

Attractive as such classification schemes appeared, they were ultimately less than useful in dealing with Mallarmé's "Tombeaux" poems.[2] Certainly the sonnet form does not allow for the kind of discursiveness necessary for a descriptive portrait of the dead poet, and other metaphorical representations (such as the angel in the Poe "Tombeau") do not seem capable of dominating the poem as Lincoln's statue dominates the memorial structure. Metonymic means of representation abound in the "Tombeaux," primarily through references to the dead poets' verse, but this type of trope might be more fruitfully explored in terms of the level of citation in the poem. The question of the nonrepresentational has been examined in relation to the Verlaine poem,[3] but on quite a different level. The problem with this attempt at classification was that ultimately it was too reductive to be useful. Like Lewis Mumford's implication that there are finally only two forms of architectural monuments, those symbolizing the phallus and the womb (obelisks, columns, towers, and domed enclosures) (*City in History* 12–13), the categories are too all-encompassing and do not provide the tools necessary for nuancing the subtle differences in monumental representation.

In architectural criticism the problem of distinguishing among expressive systems has taken the form of a polemic between those believing in formal types leading to the possibility of a universal architectural theory (similar to the kind of classification suggested above) and those who contend that architectural styles are historical (flourishing and decaying within a specific historical context, i.e., Classical, Gothic, Renaissance, etc.). But given the relative stability of the formal funeral elegy since the ancients, the historical view seems equally unproductive for literature, and especially for pinpointing the specificity of the Mallarméan "tombeau." What appears to be developing, as we move through the sonnets, is a deformation of the monument and the concept of monumentalization. With the Verlaine poem, the last of the "Tombeaux," the monument has been so radically revised as to be nearly unrecognizable.

It has been said that architects tend to criticize the work of their colleagues (but not their own) as being a succession of monuments—monuments to the architects themselves and to their virtuosity rather than to abstract concepts (Creighton 13). The same is true for poets: they write elegies to fellow poets not only to honor them but to place themselves among them, to carve their own niches in literary history. Certainly Mallarmé's "predilection for necrological poems," as one critic noted (Nicolas 50), has contributed to the establishment of his own personal graveyard, much as Henry James's character, Stransom, built up his own altar to the dead. Mallarmé's graveyard, like the monuments of a city, can be read systemically or atomistically; the systemic resulting from the place of the individual "tombeau" in the system, the atomistic conceived of as residing in the poem itself. A problem with critiques of the "Tombeaux" up until now is that they have read the poems as individual monuments instead of as a "city." The following is an attempt to consider the sonnets as an architectural whole, that is, to discern how they function as an ensemble, each in its dialectical position within the "Tombeaux" series.

Perhaps the most striking point that can be made about the criticism of Mallarmé's "Tombeaux" poems is its uncommon consistency. Apart from the goal of general exegesis of the texts, which has been the dominant effort of Mallarmé studies during the past forty years, critics have been motivated, by and large, by two additional factors: (1) a uniform treatment of the sonnets, leading repeatedly to what I hope to expose as aberrant readings of the later "Tombeaux," and (2) a peculiar insistence on reading them as conventional tributes (with the possible exception of the Baudelaire poem)[4] in spite of the rather questionable qualities attributed to the dead and the depiction of their monumental "resting places." Certainly the poems are among Mallarmé's most difficult, and we can only be grateful to those who have wrestled with the texts' uncompromisingly idiosyncratic syntax. But the project of exegesis and the piecemeal manner in which it has been executed (resulting in collected anthologies of *explications de texte* of individual poems rather than in a coordinated effort at general interpretation) have tended to impose on each poem the same diagnostic grillwork, obscuring subtle gradations among points of thematic similarity.

I suggest that a new perspective be taken on Mallarmé's "Tombeaux," focusing on them as occasional poems. The shift of poetic emphasis mapped out in Chapter 2 on "Toast funèbre" (from the occasion of the poet's death to the occasion of Mallarmé's writing) would seem to be confirmed by the sonnets. Tracing a chronological path from "Le Tombeau d'Edgar Poe" through the sonnet "Sur les bois oubliés" and the Baudelaire and Verlaine poems, I believe we can detect Mallarmé's increasing discontent with a poetry that monumentalizes occasions and show how his changing concept of monumentality ushers in a radical revision of the nature of the poetic. This struggle with the question of the monument, it seems, is the real crisis underlying the *crise de vers* of the 1880's and 1890's. The poet's masterstroke of irony, of course, is to have staged the undoing of monumentality in the monument poems themselves.[5]

Mallarmé's literary impotence between 1866 and 1873 is often invoked in discussions of the "Crisis of Tournon" as a turning point in his career. Equally important is the fact that between 1873 (the publication date of "Toast funèbre") and 1884 ("Prose pour des Esseintes"), although busily occupied with journalistic and quasi-linguistic pieces and the inauguration of the weekly gatherings that were to establish him as *chef d'école* of the young symbolists, Mallarmé

seems to have written extraordinarily little poetry. In this period he
worked on only three new poems, "Le Tombeau d'Edgar Poe," "Sur
les bois oubliés," and the never-completed "Tombeau" for his son,
Anatole, who died in the fall of 1879. Thus, during nearly twenty
years (1866–84) death would seem to be the only circumstance oc-
casioning poetry. Given the enormous difference between the early
and late works, it is tempting to read this poetic silence, broken only
by elegies, as a period of contemplation on the nature of death and
its relation to poetic composition.

These early elegies suggest that literature in some sense is able to
erase the finitude of mortality and to fill the void that is death. In
fact, a current runs throughout Mallarmé's oeuvre suggesting that po-
etry exists to supplement a lack, the most succinct statement being
that in "Crise de vers" where Mallarmé laments that the words *jour*
and *nuit* so contradictorily reflect each other's timbres: "obscur ici, là
clair" ("dark here, light there"). Although we might wish that lan-
guage would more accurately reflect the world, as such it would elim-
inate the need for poetry: "*Seulement, sachons n'existerait pas le vers*:
lui, philosophiquement rémunère le défaut des langues, complément
supérieur" (*O.c.* 364) ("*Only*, know that *poetry would not exist*: a su-
perior complement, it philosophically remunerates the defects of lan-
guages"). Lawrence Lipking's observation that each of the three most
famous "Tombeaux" poems recounts a particular disgrace (the
twenty-six years that Americans failed to honor Poe's grave, the
twenty-five years that had already passed without a monument to
Baudelaire, and the insignificant burial spot where Verlaine had been
laid to rest [138]) could be invoked to support this view. Disgrace,
here the result of a lack of recognition and monumentalization, be-
comes the immediate occasion for poetry. A textual monument is
erected to supplement the lack of reverence that would be symbolized
by a stone monument.

In parallel fashion, in Mallarmé's notes for the "Tombeau" for
Anatole, the poem as monument is destined to replace his son's bi-
ological absence with the peculiar ubiquitous "presence" of the lit-
erary text, procuring for Anatole the longevity denied him by his
sickness. But, as I sketched out in more general terms above, a certain
perversity necessarily inhabits the erection of the monument. Tex-
tual immortality can only be achieved by sacrifice: the real Anatole
must die so that his ideal projection can live. The occasion of the

poem (Anatole's death) must take place so that the poem itself can exist; real death is the prelude to literary life. In contrast to the view of literature as supplementing the lack of reality that I have just been discussing, here literature must murder reality to assure its own survival. The terrible space between the occasion of the writing and the scene of writing itself is perceived as a macabre struggle between poet father and living son: "lutte des deux père et fils l'un pour conserver fils en pensée—idéal—l'autre pour vivre" (f. 195) ("struggle of the two, father and son, the one to preserve son in thought—ideal—the other to live").[6] The violence of the act of writing is rendered by the harshness of fragments 32–34:

moment où il faut rompre avec le souvenir vivant, pour l'ensevelir—le mettre en bière, le cacher—avec les *brutalités* de la mise en bière contact rude, etc. / pour ne plus le voir qu'idéalisé—après, non plus lui vivant là— mais germe de son être repris en soi—germe permettant de penser pour lui— de le voir [et de] / vision (idéalité de l'état) et de parler pour lui

moment when one must break with the living memory, in order to bury it— put it in a coffin, hide it—with the *brutalities* of putting it into a coffin, rough contact, etc. / in order to no longer see him except idealized—after, no longer him living there, but seed of his being taken back into itself—a seed permitting one to think for him—to see him [and to] / vision (ideality of the state) and to speak for him

Even in this most solemn of moments and earnest efforts at literary tribute, the "tombeau" or literary monument suffers from the ambivalence inherent in the act of literary representation itself. As Leo Bersani has written in a review of the manuscript translation, it is as if Mallarmé had

backed away from a work that would have implicitly reduced Anatole's illness to the status of a metaphor for the inferiority of life to art. The principal interest of "A Tomb For Anatole" lies in this tension between the annihilating idealizations of literature and the intractable realities of physical life and death. Mallarmé's failure to complete the Anatole epic is perhaps the sign of a reluctance to reduce life to the trivializing nobility of a redemption through art. ("Mallarmé in Mourning" 10)

My reading of the principal "Tombeaux" sonnets not only confirms this but demonstrates, moreover, a progressive breakdown of the monumentalizing function of literature itself: from the "Tombeau" for Poe to that of Verlaine, the clear distinction between the monumental and the trivial is gradually obscured, producing a trivialization of the monumental that is tempting to read as a monumentalization of the trivial (see the following chapter).

Le Tombeau d'Edgar Poe

Tel qu'en Lui-même enfin l'éternité le change,
Le Poëte suscite avec un glaive nu
Son siècle épouvanté de n'avoir pas connu
Que la mort triomphait dans cette voix étrange!

Eux, comme un vil sursaut d'hydre oyant jadis l'ange   5
Donner un sens plus pur aux mots de la tribu
Proclamèrent très haut le sortilège bu
Dans le flot sans honneur de quelque noir mélange.

Du sol et de la nue hostiles, ô grief!
Si notre idée avec ne sculpte un bas-relief   10
Dont la tombe de Poe éblouissante s'orne,

Calme bloc ici-bas chu d'un désastre obscur,
Que ce granit du moins montre à jamais sa borne
Aux noirs vols du Blasphème épars dans le futur.

The Tomb of Edgar Poe

Such as into Himself eternity at last changes him,
The Poet rouses with a naked sword
His century, terror-stricken not to have known
That death triumphed in that strange voice!

They, like a vile recoil of a hydra long ago hearing the angel   5
To give a purer meaning to the words of the tribe
[They] Proclaimed very loudly the magic potion drunk
In the honorless wave of some black mixture.

Of the land and the cloud hostile, O grievance!
If our idea does not sculpt a bas-relief with this   10
Which the dazzling tomb of Poe decorates itself

Calm block fallen down here from an obscure disaster
Let this granite at least display forever its barrier
To the black flights of Blasphemy scattered in the future.[7]

The most celebrated of the "Tombeaux," Mallarmé's poem to Poe, would seem to have all the earmarks of the unshakeable literary trib-

ute of the apprentice poet to his self-proclaimed master, "le cas lit-
téraire absolu" (*O.c.* 531) ("the absolute literary case"). Composed
in the stately alexandrine, its somber, eloquent tone appears to place
it squarely in line with the earlier funerary tribute, "Toast funèbre."
Emilie Noulet has remarked, in fact, that the two poems share "[the]
same thought: the only immortality is that of works of art. In fact,
the admirable first verse, 'Such as into Himself eternity at last
changes him,' could serve as epigraph or epilogue to 'Toast funèbre' "
(53). Like "The solid sepulcher in which lies all that blights" and
"the beautiful monument [that] encloses him altogether" of the Gau-
tier poem, Poe's "Calme bloc ici-bas chu d'un désastre obscur"
("Calm block fallen down here from an obscure disaster") gives the
impression of absolute solidity and insuperable limits: "Que ce granit
du moins montre à jamais sa borne" ("Let this granite at least display
forever its barrier"). Assured in the specificity of their solid materials,
porphyry and granite, respectively, the two texts work to convey an
equal sense of security about the immaterial monument, the poems
themselves. The inscription on Poe's monument, itself monumental
("Si notre idée avec ne sculpte un bas-relief / Dont la tombe de Poe
éblouissante s'orne" ["If our idea does not sculpt a bas-relief with this /
Which the dazzling tomb of Poe decorates itself"]), provides a kind
of eternal double protection against the "noirs vols du Blasphème
épars dans le futur" ("black flights of Blasphemy scattered in the fu-
ture"). Similarly, in the Gautier poem, the "agitation solennelle par
l'air / De paroles" ("solemn agitation through the air / Of words"),
plainly metacommentary on Mallarmé's poem itself, miraculously
coats the poetic "fleurs dont nulle ne se fane" ("flowers of which none
wilt"), granting them perfection and immortality.

Clearly, a good case can be made for explicating the Poe "Tom-
beau" straightforwardly in this manner. I support this kind of reading
in general, especially the characterization of the monument as im-
mobile and solid. I am, however, troubled by what might be termed
Mallarmé's inability to fix the occasion of the poem. He wrote no less
than three significantly different versions recounting the occasion of
the erection of the Poe monument. This problematization of the oc-
casion is triggered by the note in the "Bibliographie" affixed to the
Deman edition of the *Poésies*. Here, Mallarmé painstakingly (in his
own words, with "so much attention to detail") recorded the occa-
sion of "Le Tombeau d'Edgar Poe": "Mêlé au cérémonial, il y fut ré-

cité, en l'érection d'un monument de Poe, à Baltimore, un bloc de basalte que l'Amérique appuya sur l'ombre légère du Poëte, pour sa sécurité qu'elle ne ressortît jamais" (*O.c.* 78) ("Integrated into the ceremonial, it was recited there, in Baltimore, during the erection of a monument to Poe, a block of basalt that America propped against the light shade of the Poet, for his security, so that it would never again spring forth"). But, as the notes to the Pléiade edition indicate, the monument was erected in mid-November 1875, and Mallarmé did not even accept the offer to contribute "quelques vers écrits ... commémoratifs de la grande cérémonie de l'automne dernier" (*O.c.* 1492) ("some written verse ... commemorative of the great ceremony of last autumn") until the following April.

In itself, the lack of historical accuracy about the circumstances of the poem's composition and recital is hardly worth noting. Nor, I suppose, is that fact that the monument described in the "Bibliographie" is made of basalt and that in the poem, of granite.[8] Somewhat more curious, however, is the discrepancy between versions concerning the monument's "function." In the sonnet a clear opposition is constructed in the first and second quatrains between "Le Poëte" and Them, "Eux." The poet, now apparently silent, "speaking" only with his "glaive nu," is distinguished from "them" precisely in that he is guardian of a knowledge about speaking: "That death triumphed in that strange voice!" "They," on the other hand, defined by their lack of knowledge ("His century, terror-stricken not to have known"), are those who speak, and speak loudly: "[They] Proclaimed very loudly the magic potion drunk." In the sonnet the monument functions as a massive obstacle or limiting force, a sort of container set up to protect the poet from the black flights of blasphemy certain to be hurled in the future by the uncomprehending "Eux." In the bibliography note, however, it is "they," "l'Amérique," who employ the monument in order to protect Poe from himself: like an immense lid on a jack-in-the-box, the monument leans on Poe's shade to assure "that it would never again spring forth." The monument shifts from an arbiter between knowledge and speech, between poet and "they," to be aligned with the enemy (his compatriots) in an effort to suppress all knowledge and speech.

It is precisely this shifting that I see as the "problem" with the Poe sonnet. In the *Scolies* appended to his translation of Poe's verse, Mallarmé included a rather extensive note on his own sonnet, which served as frontispiece to the translation. There he characterized Poe's plight as follows: "Son tort fut simplement de n'être placé dans le milieu exact, là où l'on exige du poëte qu'il impose sa puissance" (O.c. 226) ("His mistake was simply to not be placed in the exact spot, there where one demands from the poet that he impose his strength"). Apart from the conviction that "la fleur éclatante et nette de sa pensée" ("the clear and dazzling flower of his thought") was "dépaysée" ("out of its element") in America and certain to find its "sol authentique" ("authentic ground") in France (O.c. 224), Mallarmé evidently attributes Poe's problem to a general displacement, or lack of place. The occasion of Poe's death ought to provide the opportunity to find the "place" he never had; but in fact, rather than being a site from which he can "impose" his force, it is a place that imposes on him, suppressing his poetic voice. In the "Bibliographie" his volatile "light shade" is corked like a genie in a bottle: death is an entrapment rather than a source of dazzling splendor ("Poe éblouissant"). The sonnet's famous first line has been traditionally interpreted as a kind of prototype of the finding of one's place: "Tel qu'en Lui-même enfin l'éternité le change" ("Such as into Himself eternity at last changes him"). But seldom is it observed the degree to which the verse builds to what should only be read as an anticlimactic end: all emphasis finally "reposes" on the final word: *change*. Rather than finding a final resting place, Poe seems to be set adrift in a never-ending series of displacements.

The *Scolies* offer another version of the poetic occasion with a further twist to the circumstances represented:

Aussi je ne cesserai d'admirer le pratique moyen dont ces gens, incommodés par tant de mystère insoluble, à jamais émanant du coin de terre où gisait depuis un quart de siècle la dépouille abandonnée de Poe, ont, sous le couvert d'un inutile et retardataire tombeau, roulé là une pierre, immense, informe, lourde, déprécatoire, comme pour bien boucher l'endroit d'où s'exhalerait vers le ciel, ainsi qu'une pestilence, la juste revendication d'une existence de Poëte par tous interdite. (O.c. 226)

Thus I shall never cease to admire the practical means by which these people, put out by so much insoluble mystery forever emanating from the corner of earth where the abandoned remains of Poe have lain for a quarter of a century, have, under the cover of a useless and belated tombstone, rolled there a boulder, immense, misshapen, heavy, deprecatory, as if to fully stop up the place from which might give forth toward the sky, like a pestilence, the just demands of a Poet's existence censored by all.

In both the sonnet and the bibliography note, in spite of other discrepancies, the monument clearly functions in a useful and protective fashion in the interest of guarding the security of the dead poet. But here, in the most satiric account yet, the "monument" becomes the instrument by which a hostile public, deceptively pretending to honor Poe but achieving quite the opposite, plugs up his abandoned remains much as one puts a lid on a garbage can or quarantines a leper. The "calm block" is demoted to a simple and unadorned rock, useless, belated, immense, misshapen, heavy, and deprecatory, a poor masquerade for a tombstone. The insoluble mystery that Poe represents is the ultimate evidence of a lack of knowledge on the part of the American people. Placing the rock/tombstone over Poe's remains irrevocably assures that speech will never again issue forth from that point, and that Poe will never find a place from which to "impose his strength." From the sonnet to the *Scolies* the emphasis shifts from stifling blasphemies about the poet to stifling the poet himself.

A reconsideration of the sonnet in the light of this last version of the poetic occasion changes the cosmic and spiritual aspects of the poem into rather ironic commentary. Eternity, the subject of the first verse and agent of the final transformation of Poe, can be seen no longer as a godlike force but rather as the hardly disguised vengefulness of the American public. Similarly, the obscure disaster that, in meteorlike fashion, had caused the calm block to fall mysteriously to the ground can only be seen as the all too human force that has "roulé là une pierre . . . pour bien boucher l'endroit" ("rolled there a boulder . . . to fully stop up the place"). The resounding cosmic overtones of the sonnet (Cohn speaks of the hostile *sol* and *nue* as a "lightning-like opposition [or struggle] and union—a drama—of the two supreme poles of nature, earth and sky, in this baroque flash of grief and beauty . . . [that] express for Mallarmé the cosmic, or metaphysical, depth of Poe's art" [*Toward* 156]) are considerably deflated when they are read as controlled by the American public. Even the seemingly indisputable tribute paid to Poe in the *Médaillons et Portraits* can be called into question. There it is Poe himself who is compared to an imposing rocklike substance: "comme un aérolithe; stellaire, de foudre, projeté des desseins finis humains, très loin de nous contemporainement à qui il éclata en pierreries d'une couronne pour personne, dans maint siècle d'ici" (*O.c.* 531) ("like an aerolite; stellar, lightninglike, projected from finite human designs, very far from us contemporaneously to whom he burst into jewels of a crown for no one, many centuries from now"). By substituting the Poe aerolite into the *Scolies* version, we see Poe allowing his blasphemers to make him the very agent of his own disgrace and gagging.

One might object that the discrepancies among these different versions are unfortunate or strangely contradictory but ultimately inconclusive, at least in terms of the monument conceived as tombstone and physical marker. It will be remembered, however, that the "tombeau" is always text as well as rock, always Mallarmé's poem itself as well as the stone it describes. In this case, then, it matters considerably whether the "tombeau" functions as protector or suppressor of Poe, as the nature of the tribute (or lack thereof) is a crucial element not only for literary history but for understanding the place this particular sonnet holds in relation to the other "Tombeaux" and to Mallarmé's oeuvre. Does the poem function to resurrect Poe, to render him homage and secure his immortality as most critics have asserted? Or rather, as Leo Bersani has claimed, does it work toward carrying out a kind of masterplot of burying the poets so that Mallarmé can begin writing (*Death* 33–35)? Was the occasion for the writing a move to support or suppress knowledge? What does this say about the relationship between writing and knowledge?

The purpose of this problematization has not been to propose a new interpretation of the Poe sonnet. I would much prefer to keep in play the more traditional reading with the possible qualifications suggested by these findings. The problematization of the monumental will become increasingly clear in the succeeding poems, allowing me to establish an interdisciplinary working rhetoric of the monument focusing on the intersections and divergences of the monumental in Mallarmé and in nineteenth- and twentieth-century architectural conceptions of the monument.

Sonnet
(*Pour votre chère morte, son ami.*)
   2 novembre 1877.

"Sur les bois oubliés quand passe l'hiver sombre
Tu te plains, ô captif solitaire du seuil,

Que ce sépulcre à deux qui fera notre orgueil
Hélas! du manque seul des lourds bouquets s'encombre.

Sans écouter Minuit qui jeta son vain nombre,   5
Une veille t'exalte à ne pas fermer l'œil
Avant que dans les bras de l'ancien fauteuil
Le suprême tison n'ait éclairé mon Ombre.

Qui veut souvent avoir la Visite ne doit
Par trop de fleurs charger la pierre que mon doigt   10
Soulève avec l'ennui d'une force défunte.

Ame au si clair foyer tremblante de m'asseoir,
Pour revivre il suffit qu'à tes lèvres j'emprunte
Le souffle de mon nom murmuré tout un soir."

Sonnet
(For your dear deceased one, her friend.)
    November 2, 1877.

"Over the forgotten woods when the somber winter passes
You complain, O solitary captive of the threshold,
That this sepulcher for two that will make us proud,
Alas! is encumbered only by the lack of heavy bouquets.

Without hearing Midnight that threw off its vain number,   5
A vigil exalts you not to sleep a wink
Until in the arms of the old armchair
The supreme fire-brand illuminates my Shade.

He who often wants to have the Visit should not
With too many flowers overburden the stone that my finger   10
Lifts with the boredom of a defunct force.

Soul at the so bright hearth trembling to be seated,
To live again it suffices that from your lips I borrow
The whispering of my name murmured all evening long."

If the Poe poem is one of Mallarmé's most renowned, most often
analyzed, and curiously, the only poem that Mallarmé commented
on so extensively himself (consider the *Scolies* and his own translation
complete with explanatory notes), "Sur les bois oubliés" is one of the
least known and most neglected of the major pieces. The sonnet of-
fers an excellent example of the functioning of the problematic of the
occasion in terms of the biographical and historical information sur-
rounding a text that is available to critics. In 1945, at the time of the

Sonnet

—

2 Novembre 1877

Sur les bois oubliés quand passe l'hiver sombre,
Tu te plains, ô captif solitaire du seuil,
Que ce sépulcre à deux qui fera notre orgueil
Hélas! du manque seul des lourds bouquets s'encombre.

Sans écouter Minuit qui jeta son vain nombre,
Une veille t'exalte à ne pas fermer l'œil
Avant que dans les bras de l'ancien fauteuil
Le suprême tison n'ait éclairé mon Ombre.

Qui veut souvent avoir la Visite ne doit
Par trop de fleurs charger la pierre que mon doigt
Soulève avec l'ennui d'une force défunte.

Âme au si clair foyer tremblante de m'asseoir,
Pour revivre il suffit qu'à tes lèvres j'emprunte
Le souffle de mon nom murmuré tout un soir.

(Pour votre chère morte,
son ami)
Stéphane Mallarmé

Manuscript of "Sur les bois oubliés . . ." (Bibliothèque Littéraire Jacques Doucet).

publication of the Pléiade version of the complete works, the editors lamented the fact that neither Mallarmé's daughter nor his son-in-law, who first published the poem, was willing or able to reveal the identity of the dead woman whose homage it sings: "We would wish for more light on one of the poet's purest achievements" (*O.c.* 1491). And yet the poem repeatedly insists on its occasional status in that it contains a plethora of deictics pointing to extraliterary circumstances. The dedication, extremely rare in Mallarmé (only three other of the *Poésies* are so addressed), is placed within parentheses, which conventionally function to interject qualifying information or explanation. Although a dedication normally orients the reading of a poem by pointing to a specific *hors-texte*, here the parenthetical material ironically seems to obscure more than it clarifies in that the excess of nonassignable deictics renders it essentially unreadable. "Pour votre chère morte, son ami" ("For your dear deceased one, her friend") is followed by the date, "2 novembre 1877," which marks the "fête des morts," and is presumably the date of the writing of the sonnet, but possibly the date of decease or the date of the sonnet's presentation. At least three persons, in addition to and in an unspecifiable relation to the poet, are implicated, the "chère morte," the person addressed as "votre," and yet another figure designated by the "son ami." By pointing everywhere at once, the proliferation of possessive pronouns (complicated by the sonnet itself, in which we find "tes," "notre," and "mon" ["your," "our," and "my"] as well) seems to invite a search for referents without allowing any one to establish itself as dominant.

The case is a curious one: it is an occasional poem without a specifically identifiable occasion. We might speculate to what degree this single factor is responsible for the lack of critical attention the poem has received. With the publication of the Flammarion edition of the complete works in 1983, however, the missing "center" of the poem has been restored and what appeared in the dedication to be deviant syntax on Mallarmé's part is now made clear. The sonnet was composed in memory of Ettie Maspero (née Yapp), the former fiancée of Mallarmé's good friend and correspondent, Henri Cazalis. Addressed to the widower, Maspero, and signed by Mallarmé, the dedication's difficulties are dissipated: "Pour votre [Maspero] chère morte [Ettie], [de] son ami, Stéphane Mallarmé" ("For your [Maspero's] dear defunct one [Ettie], [from] her friend, Stéphane Mallarmé"). Even the curious circumstances of the poem (the dead woman addressing her living lover from beyond the grave) become demystified when we learn that Mallarmé knew that Maspero had become interested in the theosophy of Mme Blavatsky and was trying to use spiritist exercises to put himself into contact with his dead wife (*Œuvres complètes* [Flammarion] 1:280–81).

The decor of the poem has much in common with the poems of the 1860's and with "Toast funèbre" and "Le Tombeau d'Edgar Poe." The midnight setting is lugubrious and wintry; again there is a wakefulness combined with a certain sterility. The peculiar brand of oxymoronic locution we have already seen in "Ouverture ancienne d'Hérodiade" and "Ses purs ongles" in which noun and adjective seem to cancel each other out is also apparent in this poem in its "bois oubliés," "vain nombre," "force défunte," and the "manque seul des lourds bouquets" ("forgotten woods," "vain number," "defunct force," and the "lack of heavy bouquets"). But there are a number of significantly distinct features that compel attention in other directions. In the Poe sonnet the monument, no matter how questionable its commemorative qualities, is weighty and imposing, especially when compared to the "light shade" (*O.c.* 78) of the poet it houses. But in "Sur les bois oubliés" the tombstone is curiously characterized by an inexplicable lightness. Instead of being itself imposing, it is weighed on by the merest and most conventional of adornments, flowers. The point is not to be ignored, considering that the tomb itself is twice invoked, each time in connection to the flowers that encumber it: "ce sépulcre . . . qui . . . du manque seul des lourds bouquets s'encombre" and "ne doit / Par trop de fleurs charger la pierre que mon doigt / Soulève avec l'ennui d'une force défunte" ("this sepulcher . . . that . . . is encumbered only by the lack of heavy bouquets" and "should not / With too many flowers overburden the stone that my finger / Lifts with the boredom of a defunct force"). This lightness, which in no way is accompanied by a levity in tone, recalls the magnificent moment that concludes "Toast," where the solid sepulcher seems to rise up from its site. In "Toast," however, the vertical motion, though apparently autonomous, is only hypothetical, appearing in the subjunctive ("Afin que . . . Surgisse . . . Le sépulcre solide où gît tout ce qui nuit" [note the wordplay on *gît/surgisse*] ["In order that . . . Rise up . . . The solid sepulcher in which lies all that blights"]). In "Sur les bois oubliés" the stone appears to be actually lifted: "la pierre que mon doigt / Soulève" ("the stone that my finger / Lifts").

What kind of "tombeau" is it that is spoken by the deceased herself from beyond the grave? The poem stages the dead woman's gentle chastising of her bereaved lover for sitting in his armchair futilely awaiting her apparition, mourning her in traditional fashion, with flowers, insomnia, and laments. He who wishes to have the dead return from the grave, she admonishes, need only murmur her name repeatedly: "Pour revivre il suffit qu'à tes lèvres j'emprunte / Le souffle de mon nom murmuré tout un soir" ("To live again it suffices that from your lips I borrow / The breath of my name murmured all evening long"). Jean-Pierre Richard has linked the sentiment to Mallarmé's wish that "the word *create*, and even materially, the reality that it names" (Richard 530). Mallarmé's best-known formulation of this is of course the celebrated passage beginning with "Je dis une fleur" ("I say a flower") upon which the absent of all bouquets magically arises. The same mechanism seems to be at work in this poem: we are given to understand that speaking her name will, ideally, bring her back. But this represents a curious shift from the situation in "Toast" (lines 3–6):

> Ne crois pas qu'au magique espoir du corridor
> J'offre ma coupe vide où souffre un monstre d'or!
> Ton apparition ne va pas me suffire:
> Car je t'ai mis, moi-même, en un lieu de porphyre. (*O.c.* 54)

> Do not believe that to the magic hope of the corridor
> I offer my empty cup where suffers a golden monster!
> Your apparition will not suffice me:
> For I put you, myself, in a place of porphyry.

There the problem of raising the lost one from the dead is immensely complicated in that the act seems neither possible nor even desirable. (Cf. the *Médaillons et Portraits*, where Mallarmé clearly states that Verlaine's presence would only serve to "obscure . . . his glory" [*O.c.* 510].) But the act of resurrection itself is never treated lightly; a great solemnity surrounds the possibility and the implications of its performance. In "Sur les bois oubliés," however, a contrast is set up between the apparent grief of the addressee and the casualness, even ennui of the speaker. In its very effortlessness the image of the finger raising the tombstone with the boredom of a dead force is strangely powerful. Why has the monument become so light? Why is so little invested in the question of the dead returning from their graves? There is something in the "il suffit" of the penultimate verse ("Pour revivre il suffit qu'à tes lèvres j'emprunte" ["To live again it suffices that from your lips I borrow"]) that suggests a radical departure from poetic and metaphysical norms. The very possibility of taking a nonchalant, even bored attitude toward life's greatest crisis, its termination, is inconsistent not only with what we have seen previously in Mallarmé but with the entire tradition of Western civilization.

The answer may lie not in the poem's psychology or metaphysics but in its rhetorical structure. As Paul de Man has shown, prosopopoeia, "the fiction of an apostrophe to an absent, deceased or voiceless entity, which posits the possibility of the latter's reply and confers upon it the power of speech" ("Autobiography as De-facement" 926), is the "dominant figure of the epitaphic or autobiographical discourse" (927). In his analysis of Wordsworth's discussion of Milton's elegy "On Shakespeare," de Man quotes the following lines, which Wordsworth curiously omits: "Then thou our fancy of itself bereaving / Dost make us marble with too much conceiving" as well as Isabel McCaffrey's paraphrase of them: "Our imaginations are rapt 'out of ourselves' leaving behind our soulless bodies like statues." De Man reads this as evoking "the latent threat that inhabits prosopopeia, namely, that by making the death [sic] speak, the symmetrical structure of the trope implies, by the same token, that the living are struck dumb, frozen in their own death" (928). As Michael Riffaterre has pointed out in his discussion of the de Man article, "Prosopopeia thus stakes out a figural space for the chiasmic interpretation: either the subject will take over the object, or it will be penetrated by the object" ("Prosopopeia" 112).

"Sur les bois oubliés" offers a number of curious complications of the conventional form of the figure. Within the anecdotal core of the poem itself it is instead the dead who apostrophize the living: with "ô captif solitaire du seuil" ("O solitary captive of the threshold") the "dear defunct one" seeks to make her bereaved husband speak to her. As Riffaterre writes, "the address calls for a reply of the addressee, the gaze that perceives animation invites gazing back from the animated object to the subject daydreaming a Narcissistic reflection of itself in things" ("Prosopopeia" 112). She beseeches him to murmur her name, which amounts to her apostrophizing him to respond in kind with an apostrophe. But the possibility of the living speaking in this sonnet appears to be less likely than the "presence" of her supernatural voice. The symmetrical structure of the trope—that the living and the dead may exchange places—here seems to be actualized by the text. The woman's voice and her self-characterization as the "Ame au si clair foyer tremblante de m'asseoir" ("Soul at the so bright hearth trembling to be seated") make her seem remarkably more alive than her lover who, captive, deaf to his surroundings, and unblinking ("solitary captive of the threshold," "without hearing Midnight," and "not sleep[ing] a wink"), is more statuelike than human. The text explicitly states, in fact, that her force and vitality are capable, literally, of taking his breath away: "Pour revivre il suffit qu'à tes lèvres j'emprunte / Le souffle de mon nom murmuré tout un soir" ("To live again it suffices that from your lips I borrow / The whispering of my name murmured all evening long"). Through the chiasmus of prosopopeia, she, inanimate but animated, converts him into the living dead.

In his discussion of the poem, Davies (*"Tombeaux"* 127) points out a similar use of the verb "revivre" in one of the *Vers de circonstance* written on glazed fruits (*O.c.* 128):

> Le Temps
>   nous y succombons
> Sans l'amitié pour revivre
> Ne glace que ces bonbons
> A son plumage de givre.

> Time
>   to it we succumb
> Without friendship to relive
> It glazes only these bonbons
> With its plumage of frost.

The quatrain, however, offers parallels with the sonnet beyond that one word. The disjunctive disposition of the first verse is in fact iconic: "nous y succombons" (from the Latin, "to lie under") literally is placed under "Le Temps," which itself weightless nevertheless oppresses, much as in the sonnet the flowers (or lack thereof) encumber the tombstone. Death, the freezing action of Time's hoary wing to

which we all eventually succumb, is cleverly equated with yet an-
other figure of weightless superimposition, the overlaying of the can-
dies with glaze. The verb "succombons," in spite of its comical rhyme
with "bonbons," suggests in rather macabre fashion the visit of a suc-
cubus or incubus, the latter again repeating the dominant figure of
the sonnet, the illogical encumbrance of the immaterial. This lends
a rather pointedly erotic (even indecorous, given the poem's occa-
sion) sense to the notion of the "visit" of the departed one ("Qui veut
souvent avoir la Visite" ["He who often wants to have the Visit"])
that is not, however, uncharacteristic of Mallarmé.[9]

But the problematic of the sonnet extends beyond its anecdotal
core. As Jonathan Culler has remarked in his study of the apostrophe,
"the simple oppositional structure of the *I-Thou* model leaves out of
account the fact that a poem is a verbal composition which will be
read by an audience. What is the effect of introducing this third
term?" (*Pursuit* 141). We, as readers, are all the addressees of the
"chère morte," and we are equally "captif[s] solitaire[s] du seuil" in
the prototypical stance of the reader ensconced in "les bras de l'an-
cien fauteuil" and liable to be rendered statuelike as is the sonnet's
bereaved lover. The dead speaker moves from the personal "tu" ("Tu
te plains") in the quatrains to the gnomic "Qui" ("Qui veut souvent
avoir la Visite") in the first tercet, and then back to the familiar ad-
dress in the last tercet. This shifting rather neatly engages another
level of chiasmus between the grieving lover and us as readers. But
"Sur les bois oubliés" incorporates a fourth term as well, that of the
poet. The "chère morte" speaks through the poet who in turn speaks
through her. Moreover, as poet, Mallarmé necessarily addresses the
reader and, in the dedication ("Pour *votre* chère morte"), he directly
addresses the lover himself. We might diagram the intricate web of
textual chiasmus as follows:

We are now in a position to suggest an answer to the question of
why death seems to be treated so lightly in this sonnet. Here the line
between the dead and the living is apparently not seen as an insu-

perable barrier. Through the chiasmus of prosopopoeia an eerie trans-
formation occurs whereby the living are also dead and the dead also
living: all four terms of the chiasmus hover between death and life.
One interpretation of the Milton lines quoted above suggests that
"the monuments of Shakespeare's tomb are all the enchanted and
motionless readers of his book" (Abrams 1304). Thus, if we as living
readers are also lifeless monuments, the great apotheosis of poet into
the essentialized version of himself ("Tel qu'en Lui-même enfin l'é-
ternité le change") is itself dethroned. If we are all monuments, then
it follows that we are as well nonmonuments. The same is true for
poetic production: if all poetry is monumental, it is equally all trivial,
and consequently the usual hierarchies dominating the institution of
poetry are erased.

Therefore, the characterization of the monument in the sonnet as
light rather than massive is both sign and symptom of a fundamental
shift in Mallarmé's thinking. The poem ends, evocatively, with the
remedy for the lover's melancholia: all he need do is murmur the dead
woman's name. But in terms of the conventional function of the
monument the purported panacea is unworkable and caustically
ironic. The name itself, on or in the monument (be it text or stone),
is perhaps the most recognizable sign of death: once the name is en-
graved on the stone, the fact of death is ostensibly irrevocable. Here
the engraved monument is somehow superseded: the name itself,
rather than portending and pronouncing death, is said to bring the
dead back to life. Thus the finality associated with death and its com-
memorative monument is seriously challenged.

Yet a further irony inhabits the situation to the extent that the son-
net offers a critique of its own premises. If all that is needed to end
the man's grieving is to murmur the beloved's name, why isn't the
name murmured? Why, instead, is this poem written? The sonnet
perversely suggests that the appropriate response to the occasion
would not at all be poetry, but rather it would be the repeated enun-
ciation of the woman's name. And in this sonnet it is particularly
derisory that the woman's name is not pronounced (note that in the
Gautier, Poe, and Baudelaire poems the name of the deceased ap-
pears once; in the Verlaine poem, twice) and that it is precisely the
lack of her name that for so long presented the chief mystification
surrounding the poem and prevented us from pinpointing the poem's
occasion.

Le Tombeau de Charles Baudelaire

Le temple enseveli divulgue par la bouche
Sépulcrale d'égout bavant boue et rubis
Abominablement quelque idole Anubis
Tout le museau flambé comme un aboi farouche

Ou que le gaz récent torde la mèche louche   5
Essuyeuse on le sait des opprobres subis
Il allume hagard un immortel pubis
Dont le vol selon le réverbère découche

Quel feuillage séché dans les cités sans soir
Votif pourra bénir comme elle se rasseoir   10
Contre le marbre vainement de Baudelaire

Au voile qui la ceint absente avec frissons
Celle son Ombre même un poison tutélaire
Toujours à respirer si nous en périssons.

The Tomb of Charles Baudelaire

The buried temple divulges by its sepulchral
Sewer mouth slobbering mud and rubies
Abominably some idol Anubis
Its whole muzzle flaming like a ferocious bark

Or rather the recent gaslight contorts the suspicious wick   5
Wiper it is known of disgraces undergone
Haggard it lights up an immortal pubis
Whose flight according to the lamppost, sleeps out

What dried up leaves in the cities
Without votive evenings could bless, just as it sits down again   10
In vain against the marble of Baudelaire

To the veil that girdles it, absent with shivers
Its Shade even a tutelary poison
Always to be breathed in [even] if we die of it.

With each "tombeau" he wrote, Mallarmé seems to have become increasingly disenchanted with the form and suspicious of its tradition. This debilitation of the monument continues with the 1893 "Le Tombeau de Charles Baudelaire." The monument, as such, is hardly recognizable in the Baudelaire poem. It is templelike but buried, no longer working as a visible reminder of death, as if to do away with

Hommage

Le temple enseveli divulgue par la bouche
Sépulcrale d'égout bavant boue et rubis
Abominablement quelque idole Anubis
Tout le museau flambé comme un aboi farouche

Ou que le gaz récent torde la mèche louche
Essuyeuse on le sait des opprobres subis
Elle allume hagard un immortel pubis
Dont le vol selon le réverbère découche

Quel feuillage séché dans les cités sans soir
Triste pourra bénir comme elle se rasseoir
Contre le marbre simplement de Baudelaire

Au voile qui la ceint absente avec frissons
Celle son Ombre même un poison tutélaire
Toujours à respirer si nous en périssons

— Stéphane Mallarmé

Manuscript of "Le Tombeau de Charles Baudelaire" (Bibliothèque Littéraire Jacques Doucet).

the monumentality of the monument itself. It knows no repose. Sewerlike, it is actively producing an abominable babbling spittle of mud and rubies (most critics have noted the poem's insistent alliteration of Baudelaire's initial: it is repeated eighteen times throughout the poem) through its sepulchral sewer mouth, "bouche sépulcrale d'égout" (Cohn has cleverly pointed out the pun *d'égout/dégout* [*Toward* 160]). The Baudelaire poem proceeds repulsively through an evocation of the flaming muzzle of a dog, the prostitute's pubis, and the tutelary poison that saturates the poetic atmosphere. The verbs map out the poem's itinerary: "torde . . . découche . . . périssons" ("writhes . . . sleeps out . . . we perish"). The "tombeau," throughout, writhes in agony, as if in its own death throes.

The editors of the Pléiade edition, echoing the dismay of early critics, reluctantly acknowledged the unconventionality of the Baudelaire poem: "Strangely enough, it is to the poet of *Fleurs du mal* for whom he had the greatest admiration and who was the major influence of his youth that Mallarmé rendered, in verse, his most obscure and least convincing homage" (*O.c.* 1495). Considering Mallarmé's participation in projects to erect monuments in Paris to Baudelaire and to Banville and later, his presidency of a committee destined to finance a monument to Verlaine, it is hardly surprising that critics have largely exhibited a certain blindness to the textual evidence and have continued to contort their readings of the poem to produce a semblance of the conventional funerary tribute.

That the sonnet evokes more a rank garbage dump, a rotting compost pile than a monument is evident when we compare the depiction of the tombstone in the first tercet ("Quel feuillage séché dans les cités sans soir / Votif pourra bénir comme elle se rasseoir / Contre le marbre vainement de Baudelaire") with the "beautiful monument" and the "thick iron of the gates of the tomb" of "Toast" or with the "calm block" adorned with a sculpted bas-relief of the Poe poem. The blasphemy against which the Poe monument claimed to serve as guarantee has, in the Baudelaire poem, now invaded the "tombeau" itself. Rather than warding off refuse and putrefaction, the tombstone is now the site of the collection of debris: the image is that of a city resembling the dissipation of the Joycean Nighttown; here leaves and trash are blown about, their flight absorbed by the monument itself. Mallarmé's "tribute" to Baudelaire tellingly echoes the "Tableaux parisiens" and "Le Spleen de Paris" itself and in turn becomes the negative model for the Modernists' evocation of the city. (A poem that immediately comes to mind is Eliot's "Preludes," in which a "gusty shower wraps / The grimy scraps / Of withered leaves about your feet / And newspapers from vacant lots;" and where "[you] watched the night revealing / The thousand sordid images / of which your soul was constituted;" [13–14].) The monument no longer functions as barrier or veil to keep good and evil separate: absent or torn, or simply so flimsy as to fly about in the wind, it encloses only absence. Baudelaire's "tutelary poison" passes back and forth through it, gaslike, and we, no longer having any monumental protection from it, must breathe it even if we perish.

The "Tombeau" for Baudelaire is, in fact, so unrelentingly abstruse a poem that except for the title and the mention of the dead poet's name in the first tercet, it would be difficult to even hazard guesses about what the occasion of the writing could possibly have to do with the actual writing of the occasion. Critics have had to struggle to find some thread that would connect pre-text to text, to find some "key" that would link them. (An exegesis of this poem is conspicuously absent in the chapter on the series of "Tombeaux" and homages in Chassé, who based one of his critical texts on Mallarmé on the concept of lexical "keys" discovered in *Littré*.) It occurs to me, however, that the problem is less interesting in terms of finding "keys" or "links" than in the symptomatic need to do so itself. The presumption that the particulars of a literary effort are all motivated by the circumstances that occasion them is indeed a powerful one, borne out, as we have seen, by centuries of literary tradition. But Mallarmé's evolving notion of the occasional poem challenges the simple assumptions of one-to-one correspondences we have operated on in the past. The incongruity of the Baudelaire monument and the difficulty we have in reading it need not be seen as a deficiency in the text that must be filled up with meaningful connections. It should not be necessary to recuperate the text in order to read it. Instead, we can read the surfaces of its dissonances, and try to understand them in and of themselves.

Once we exclude the possibility of the conventional tribute, the Baudelaire poem need not be viewed as irreverent or as some black farce perpetrated by Mallarmé to denigrate his predecessor. Nor need it, I believe, be seen as the by-product of a Mallarméan anxiety of influence. The image of the monument speaks forcefully for itself. It is the monument's dirge that is being sung here, and we see the poetic funerary tribute captured in the final paroxysms of its demise. Just as the Gautier poem can be read as the occasion for the celebration of the inauguration of the poetics of the occasion, "Le Tombeau de Charles Baudelaire" can be seen to herald the end of the monumentality of the poetic occasion. Mallarmé still wrestles with the urge to preserve intact the appropriate conventions of commemoration: this accounts for the presence of the temple, the marble, and the *réverbère* (lamppost) (see Baudelaire's "Les Phares") in the poem. But the images are tainted: the temple is buried, divulging rather than silently providing testimonial; the marble is depicted as vulnerable: it is cluttered with dried leaves that it tries in vain to ward off; and the lamplight, haggard, only sheds light on the "immortel pubis" in restless flight. The monument is besieged by a clutter of ugly detail that totally obscures its glory. The attempt to write a tribute to Baudelaire became for Mallarmé the crisis point (not psychological, but rather rhetorical) after which the monumental vein as such had to be abandoned.

Tombeau

Anniversaire—Janvier 1897

Le noir roc courroucé que la bise le roule
Ne s'arrêtera ni sous de pieuses mains
Tâtant sa ressemblance avec les maux humains
Comme pour en bénir quelque funeste moule.

Ici presque toujours si le ramier roucoule   5
Cet immatériel deuil opprime de maints
Nubiles plis l'astre mûri des lendemains
Dont un scintillement argentera la foule.

Qui cherche, parcourant le solitaire bond
Tantôt extérieur de notre vagabond—   10
Verlaine? Il est caché parmi l'herbe, Verlaine

A ne surprendre que naïvement d'accord
La lèvre sans y boire ou tarir son haleine
Un peu profond ruisseau calomnié la mort.

Tombeau

Anniversaire – Janvier 1897

Le noir roc courroucé que la bise le roule
Ne s'arrêtera ni sous de pieuses mains
Tâtant sa ressemblance avec les maux humains
Comme pour en bénir quelque funeste moule.

Ici presque toujours si le ramier roucoule
Cet immatériel deuil opprime de maints
Nubiles plis l'astre mûri des lendemains
Dont un scintillement argentera la foule.

Qui cherche, parcourant le solitaire bond
Tantôt extérieur de notre vagabond –
Verlaine ? Il est caché parmi l'herbe, Verlaine

à ne surprendre que naïvement d'accord
La lèvre sans y boire ou tarir son haleine
Un peu profond ruisseau calomnié la mort.

Stéphane Mallarmé

Manuscript of the "Tombeau" for Verlaine (Bibliothèque Littéraire Jacques Doucet).

Tomb

Anniversary—January 1897

The black rock enraged that the north wind rolls it
Will not stop even under pious hands
Probing its resemblance with human troubles
As if to bless thereof some tragic mold.

Here almost always if the ringdove coos   5
This immaterial mourning oppresses with many a
Nubile fold the ripened star of tomorrows
Whose scintillation will besilver the crowd.

Who seeks, surveying the solitary bound
Now and then exterior of our vagabond—   10
Verlaine? He is hidden among the grass, Verlaine

To surprise only naively in accord
The lip without drinking from it or drying up his breath
A shallow little river calumniated death.

If the Baudelaire poem shows us the monument in full crisis, the
"Tombeau" for Verlaine, written at least four years later and only one
year before Mallarmé's death, can be seen as a step toward resolution.
The monument, as we know it, has been phased out. The tombstone
is here a "noir roc courroucé" ("raging black rock") rolled by the
wind, unable to stop even under the most pious of hands, even by
those who most zealously desire to preserve some semblance of tra-
ditional monumentality. The poem is rent by motion. Riffaterre has
pointed out the relevancy of two hypograms of the poem's first line,
the proverb "Pierre qui roule n'amasse pas mousse" ("A rolling stone
gathers no moss") as well as the "quintessential" Verlainian verses
from "Chanson d'automne": "Et je m'en vais / Au vent mauvais / Qui
m'emporte / Deçà delà" ("And I go away / Conveyed by the bad wind /
That carries me / Here and there") ("Prosopopeia" 115). The cooing
of the dove, the "nubile" folds (suggesting both a full potentiality for
sexual activity and a sky of drifting clouds), the scintillation of the
"ripe" sun through those clouds, the indecorous displacement of the
vagabond Verlaine, and the final image of the shallow river slandered
as death, more fittingly attest to the fluctuations of life than to the
immutability of death.

But the most extraordinary aspect of the poem can be found in the first tercet. Here an entirely unsuspected tone creeps into the "Tombeau." If the monument has been increasingly challenged in the Poe and Baudelaire poems, this has been accomplished with a kind of massive counterforce, as if Mallarmé were convinced that only a monumental assault could eradicate the claims of monumentality. But this remarkable tercet represents what I would like to read as the realization that the monumental would be felled not by a knockout but rather by the very lightest of touches. This is the kind of force already glimpsed at in "Sur les bois oubliés," the disarming power of the single finger flicking in boredom. The monumental (and here I hope to invoke as well something like the "power of the poetic" and the concept of mastery) no longer resides in massiveness, profundity, and solidity. In fact, it doesn't "reside" at all; it is rather a kinetic surface effect, a playing along a veneered edge that points to no inner depths, much as the "shallow little river" runs along interminably in the poem providing no source from which to drink ("The lip without drinking from it").

And yet the monument is not entirely effaced. We must still acknowledge its presence in the Verlaine piece, its transmutation from the immobile to the mobile, and from the integral to the fragmentary. The monument is broken down into pieces, "bribes," that scintillate like the immaterial "nubile folds" that oppress the star (note the repetition of the weightless oppression already seen in "Sur les bois oubliés"). The first tercet is one such "bribe":

> Qui cherche, parcourant le solitaire bond
> Tantôt extérieur de notre vagabond—
> Verlaine? Il est caché parmi l'herbe, Verlaine

> Who seeks, surveying the solitary bound
> Now and then exterior of our vagabond—
> Verlaine? He is hidden among the grass, Verlaine

Composed of a question and a response that is more of a non sequitur than an answer, the tercet becomes emblematic of a new Mallarméan ontology. The "proper" response to a query is no longer necessarily its logical answer, but rather a slight movement to the side of the question. Who looks for Verlaine? is answered not by *who* but by *where*. The trajectory traced out by the linguistic exchange is already inscribed in the question itself: it takes the form of the "solitaire bond / Tantôt extérieur." Instead of cause and effect, we get a horizontal move along the surface, a nomadic vagabonding rather than the possibility of settling in any one predetermined place.

The third verse of the tercet provides a miniallegory of the problem of the occasional poem in that Verlaine's relationship to the grass (which can be read as pre-text to text) is unstable. Grammar and semantics tell us that Verlaine is hidden in the grass ("Il est caché parmi l'herbe"), but the syntax performs quite a different operation. Because the line both begins and ends with "Verlaine," the grass is also hidden by Verlaine, couched between the repetitions of his name. Mallarméan wordplay takes the problem one step further. With a minor pronunciation adjustment to allow for the difference in gender, "Verlaine" is also quite clearly "verte laine," which is simply a poetic rendition of grass, a green wool. If Verlaine is hidden in the grass, then the green woolly grass is equally hidden in "Verlaine." This is perhaps how we might interpret being "caché *parmi* l'herbe" (among) rather than "*dans* l'herbe" (in), which would have been the more orthodox lexical choice. To be hidden *in* supposes a real possibility of concealment, whereas to be hidden *among* is ostensibly more of a scattering, a dissemination. Verlaine is hidden only by his very visibility, much as the large letters across a map are more difficult to read than the single locatable site of a small city or village.

He who looks for Verlaine, therefore, is destined not to find him, because Verlaine is everywhere at once. The monument is his mobility itself; the homage is to his mutability. The "beautiful monument" to Gautier and the "calm block" to Poe, which attested to a kind of assurance that a poet (if not his poetry) could eventually be essentialized, that he would be changed "Tel qu'en Lui-même" by eternity, or more radically, that he could finally be buried and silenced so that another discourse could be opened, is now metamorphosed into the "raging black rock" that knows no repose. The restless Verlainian monument becomes the emblem of a mobile, non-totalizable poetry. With the precision of a mathematical equation, especially as it delights in its extension across the blank space of a page (see the myriad fragments of *Le Livre* inscribed solely with numerical calculations), the last verse of the first tercet can be transformed by the merest of touches to reinscribe and reinforce a changing poetics:

<pre>
Verlaine?   Il . . . l'herbe,   Verlaine
            (He . . . grass,   Verlaine)

Verlaine = Il . . . l'herbe = Verlaine
           (He . . . grass = Verlaine)
</pre>

Thus the poem asks not only who looks for Verlaine, but also who is Verlaine? He is immediately identified by a response that answers without differentiation; he is simply "Il," the protean pronoun whose identity is constituted only by the specific instance of discourse. If Verlaine is "he" here, by the end of the verse he has already been transmuted and now appears in apposition to "l'herbe," the grass. The question mark separating "Verlaine" and "Il" is replaced by the comma of apposition, but both function as indices of equivalence. "Verlaine = Il" is, of course, a common and perfectly acceptable grammatical transposition, but "l'herbe = Verlaine" moves out of grammar into rhetorical wordplay. I submit that this represents, presented in the most concise of contours, a profile of the major shift in Mallarmé's poetics of the occasion that it is the purpose of this book to outline, a shift from a conventional immobilizing form of monumental representation to a mobile and trivializing performative that de-hierarchizes and collapses occasion and its writing. At the conclusion of this chapter, and throughout the following one, I provide evidence that develops this premise in a speculative mode.

This degree of playfulness is certainly not uncommon in Mallarmé. Gardner Davies has pointed out a number of other occurrences of palindrome-like effects in the *Poésies*: "*De qui* les longs regrets et les tiges *de qui*" ("Hérodiade"), "*La tienne* si toujours le délice! *la tienne*" ("Victorieusement fui"), as well as the "gigantic chiasmus" of "Un Coup de dés," "*Un Coup de dés . . . Comme si . . . comme si . . . Un Coup de dés*" (*Vers une explication* 79; emphasis added). But such wordplay, especially with the proper name, is most characteristic of the *Vers de circonstance*. Verlaine was the addressee of a number of the *Loisirs de la poste*, verse containing the names and addresses of Mallarmé's correspondents. Consider, for example, this quatrain in which "Verlaine" undergoes yet further metamorphosis (*O.c.* 82):

> Je te lance mon pied vers l'aine
> Facteur, si tu ne vas où c'est

Que rêve mon ami Verlaine
Ru' Didot, Hôpital Broussais.

I'll kick my foot towards your groin
Postman, if you don't go where it is
That my friend Verlaine dreams
Rue Didot, Broussais Hospital.

The "monument" to Verlaine is thus, as is the swift kick in the groin envisioned in the quatrain, threatened but never enacted. It would be unfair to say that no monument at all is erected, however, because undoubtedly Verlaine's "Tombeau" is written and has been read as a tribute. But the monument, never immobilized, lacks the grandeur and sweep of more traditional "tombeaux." As conventional expression it is somehow crippled by its first tercet; its repose disturbed by the too facetious verses. There is here a flirtatious courting of the trivial that smacks of irreverence, not a brand of irreverence that tends to reinforce the monument and the institutions it stands for, but a destructive one. One is left, ultimately, with a monumental "bribe," a fragment that gestures toward monumental expression just as that very gesture is undermined from within. The Verlaine monument has no site: it hovers in between the mobile and the immobile, between the integral and the fragmented, and between the monumental and the trivial. Neither monument nor quite antimonument, it represents an important transition point in Mallarmé's poetics.

The "peu profond ruisseau" carries, then, precisely as Mallarmé says, a calumny of conventional tributes to death. The monumental conception of poetry, of a poetry whose depths must be sounded to bring out its full resonance, is both represented by and eroded through a constant flow of shallow water. The elements of a new poetic conception flow in the stream, as they have for years on end. But they cannot be seen as such until the last remnants of monumentality have been forsaken, and until the shallow stream can be seen for itself instead of in terms of the monumental fragments it carries along.

The full implications of Mallarmé's tampering with the monumental can perhaps best be elucidated by the interdisciplinary approach suggested by the epigraphs at the head of this chapter. Throughout history in the various arts, conceptions of the monumental have remained relatively parallel, even up to the disjuncture outlined in the preceding discussion. In the following pages I would like to juxtapose a (necessarily brief, but I hope not misrepresented) account of the recent history of the monument in architecture with the kind of development and rupture I have traced in Mallarmé.

In the discussion of "Toast funèbre" (Chapter 2) I showed to what degree the nineteenth-century French elegy still clung to the patterns of classical rhetorical styles. Mallarmé, like the other contributors to the Gautier "Tombeau," drew from a stockpile of rhetorical conventions on which he superimposed his personal thematic, formal, stylistic, and lexical flourishes. Writing a "tombeau," in fact, was not unlike borrowing from a cemetery of tradition,[10] a graveyard of rhetoric, and ghoulishly reassembling certain standard parts according to one's particular needs. The situation was much the same for nineteenth-century architecture, which was largely characterized by its imitation of past period styles. The early nineteenth century developed no monumental style of its own, but instead relied on pastiches of the classic and gothic traditions. The architectural critic Sigfried Giedion has analyzed the problem of monumentality in nineteenth- and twentieth-century architecture in great detail. Contributing to a symposium entitled "In Search of a New Monumentality" in the British journal *Architectural Review*, Giedion speaks of architecture of the past century in terms of a "pseudomonumentality" that arose within the sphere of Napoleonic society, emulating the manner of the former ruling classes. He argues that it actually has little or nothing to do with the Roman, Greek, or other styles or traditions it imitated. To illustrate this point he describes a "recipe" for a monument as it was represented in the lectures of J. N. L. Durand (1760–1834), the "Précis de leçons d'architecture" (1801–5), which were frequently translated and followed by architects of every country in the early part of the century. There the lesson for achieving an expression of monumentality is always the same: take some curtains of columns and put them in front of any building, whatever its purpose, and to whatever consequences it might lead.[11] Giedion writes further that even the considerable advances in building techniques, especially at the end of the century, seemed to have brought with them only the practical problems involved in using new methods to produce old effects ("In Search" 126–27). In spite of the increasing output of monumental sculpture and architecture that characterized the first half of the century and the "statuomania" that swept France with the fervor of the revolution after 1848, it was evident that no genuine and distinctive tradition could emerge from the medley of inherited forms that overlaid the architecture of the period.

In contrast, the early-twentieth-century attitude toward the monument can be summed up by Lewis Mumford's oft-quoted statement: "The notion of a modern monument is veritably a contradiction in terms; if it is a monument it is not modern, and if it is modern, it cannot be a monument" (*Culture of Cities* 438). The wave of architectural thinking that accompanied the technical advances in building materials rejected the monument as antiquated, antidemocratic, unprogressive, and oppressive. Walter Gropius, the founder and director of the Bauhaus and one of the most influential practicing architects of the period, saw the problem in these terms: "The very idea of resuming monumental expression through static form symbols as in the past should be alien to the creative mind of our period. For modern man has made the important discovery that there is no such thing as finality nor eternal truth. The old monument was the symbol for a static conception of this world, now overruled" ("In Search" 127). Manifesto after manifesto denounced the monument, making it the chief scapegoat for the lamentable state of contemporary architecture.

For the nineteenth-century architect, monumentality had simply been a problem of expression; that is, determining what style best expressed the qualities of the particular figure or event to be commemorated. In the twentieth century, however, the problem of the monument has shifted considerably. The question is no longer simply *how* to express, but more radically, *what* and even *whether* to express. First, as Thomas Creighton has written, "Monumentality is fundamentally a problem in *expression*, not in function, technology, or economics. The expression of a monumental concept in classic, or in pompous imperialistic terms is not too difficult; it is simply boring" (9). In other cases the monument has been seen as thoroughly objectionable for social and political reasons: "Monumentality is not desirable. . . . The totalitarian society has always taken monumentality into its service to strengthen its power over people, the democratic society in conformity with its nature is anti-monumental" ("In Search" 123).

In fact, however, the antimonumental treatises of this century did not put an end to monument building. Monuments were still constructed along nineteenth-century lines and still accused of exhibiting pseudomonumentality. In spite of their revolutionary rhetoric, the modernists also engaged in monument building. Their constructs were no longer "useless" temples, but rather functional buildings: libraries, museums, and civic centers were given the names of civic leaders and other public figures and so came to memorialize them in the new architectural lexicon.

The antimonument furor began to settle considerably after the Second World War. The question of the monumental was posed again, this time in terms of finding a mode of expression that would be suitable for the twentieth century; no longer were the modern and the monumental seen as necessarily antagonistic. The problem, however, was to create a uniquely modern monument. The doubts that had been expressed as to whether the new materials, steel, concrete, glass, plastics, and the new building techniques actually excluded monumentality began to dissipate. Certain terms came to have more credence and a new rhetoric of the monument began to develop. Gropius, in a continuation of the passage quoted above, now would maintain that the monument, once the symbol of a static world, should come to symbolize a new world of relativity and changing energies. "I believe," he wrote, "that the equivalent for monumental expression is developing in the direction of a new physical pattern for a higher form of civic life, a pattern characterized by *flexibility for continuous growth and change*" ("In Search" 127). The critic Henry-Russell Hitchcock had expressed concern about whether contemporary methods of construction that emphasized demountability and presumed obsolescence did not tend to discourage monumental building ("In Search" 124). But it seems to me that "demountability" and "presumed obsolescence" may in fact be essential properties of the still emerging twentieth-century rhetoric of the monument. Sigfried Giedion has in fact suggested that the new monumentality may lie precisely in this direction. He has spoken of events such as the spectacle of waterplays, light, sound, and fireworks at the Paris exhibition of 1937 and the New York World's Fair two years later as a kind of "ephemeral architecture": "These spectacles form of [sic] the rare events where our modern possibilities are consciously applied by the architect-artists." He hoped that newly created civic centers might be the site for collective emotional events, in which the people play as important a role as the spectacle itself, and where a unity of the architectural background, the people, and the symbols conveyed by the spectacles would arise (Giedion 563 and 568). Such possibilities suggest a new notion of time projected for the monument, not of long duration and stability, but of an experienced and finite temporality. We shift from a conception of the monument as colossal object to one of its monumental performance.

If Giedion's idea expresses some kind of liminal moment for architectural and monumental expression, then a number of other architectural monuments, or plans for monuments, some of which were never constructed, may be seen as intervening steps in the process of developing a contemporary mode of expression. It is difficult, of course, to choose representative conceptions from the many avant-garde proposals for resolving the problem of modern architectural monumentality. I would like, however, to briefly present descriptions of selected proposed structures in some detail before returning to the problem of the monument in Mallarmé. The juxtaposition of twentieth-century architectural conceptions of the monument with Mallarmé's great monumental work of the later years, "Un Coup de dés jamais n'abolira le hasard" ("A Throw of Dice Will Never Abolish Chance"), provides a novel approach to the poem that I believe will prove mutually illuminating.

In 1919 V. E. Tatlin was commissioned to design a project for a monument to the Russian Revolution. His proposed *Monument to the Third International* was described by Nikolai Punin as an "entirely new" and "mathematically true form of monument." Note the emphasis on mobility and the preoccupation with current events rather than with commemorating past glories:

A succession of the simplest forms (cubes) is to contain halls for lectures and gymnastics, premises for agitation, and *other rooms which can be used for different purposes as required*; these premises, however, are not to be museums or libraries of any kind, their character should preferably be *shifting* the whole time. [A later account mentioned that the monument would consist of three great rooms moving at different speeds, one at one revolution per year, another at one revolution per month, and the uppermost, at one revolution per day (Punin 91).] The monument contains also an *agitation centre*, from which one can turn to the entire city with different types of appeals, proclamations and pamphlets. Special motorcycles and cars could constitute a highly *mobile*, continuously available tool of agitation for the government, and the monument therefore contains a garage. . . . In accordance with the latest invention, one part of the monument is to be equipped with a projector station that can write letters in light in the sky . . . with such letters it would be possible to compose different slogans in connection with current events. (Punin 86–87; emphasis mine)

Claes Oldenburg became immensely interested in the question of the monument in the 1960's and throughout that decade and the following drew up hundreds of proposals for gargantuan structures that ranged from the first drawings in which he placed a familiar object on a landscape making it appear "colossal" by equating it in size with the surrounding landscape (such as the *Giant Soft Shirt*) to a more studied relationship of object and site (*The Sculpture in the Form of a Trowel*, installed in the Sonsbeek Park, Arnhem, Holland, echoes the triangular shape of the park, is symbolic of the flatness of the country, and the word "trowel" has a Dutch sound to Oldenburg's ear). Barbara Haskell has described his thinking on the subject of the monument in these terms:

Whereas art has historically been concerned with permanence, with freezing things, with non-change, Oldenburg's work is very much involved with *change, movement and metamorphosis*. . . . Many of the hard works are composed of *several parts whose positions are constantly being altered and rearranged. The Giant Fagends*, for example, have no definite positions; they may be arbitrarily arranged to suit a particular space. . . . [His parodies of monuments] sometimes *literally depict movement*—as in the *Thrown Can of Paint* where the can and paint are frozen in various strobiscopic positions as they are hurled through the air. . . . *The Ice Bag* is the first of his colossal sculptures that not only moves, but does, in fact, convey a sense of life itself in its breathing movements. (9; emphasis mine)

Oldenburg's studies of the monument broadened to embrace ephemerality and entropy. "Some of his monuments literally depict the *process of decomposition* . . . the *Banana* shows stages of destruction or change through the eating process. The passage of time and the vicissitudes of life play upon the large outdoor monuments as well. The pieces are exposed to the vagaries of weather; they rust, fade, disintegrate" (Haskell 10; emphasis mine).

In the 1960's a competition was held to elicit suggestions for a proposed monument to Franklin Delano Roosevelt to be constructed in Washington, D.C. The event proved to be an international forum on theories of contemporary monumentality. Thomas Creighton, who analyzed the competition proposals, described the winning entry by architects Pederson and Tilney as consisting of "uprising shafts to

Vladimir Tatlin. *Model for Monument to the Third International*. 1919–20. Wood, iron, and glass. Russian State Museums, Leningrad. (Photograph courtesy of the Museum of Modern Art, New York.)

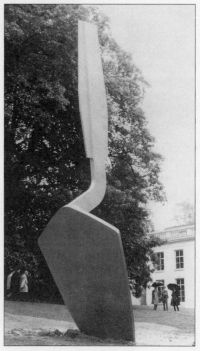

Claes Oldenburg. *Sculpture in the Form of a Trowel Stuck in the Ground*. 1971. 40′ high. Installed in the Sonsbeek Park, Arnhem, Holland. (From Barbara Haskell, *Claes Oldenburg: Object into Monument*, photograph by Hannah Wilke, courtesy of the Norton Simon Museum.)

create a three-dimensional effect without the medium of a building,
producing space, but *unenclosed space*, related to the rest of the site"
(44–45). The jury selecting the winner applauded its "vast concrete
tablets [that] *emphasize the intervening spaces as positive entities. . . . As
one moves onto the various levels of the platform the views change and new
spaces acquire significances.* As a monument it satisfies the visitor's de-
sire *to apprehend the whole from many approaches* and is visible, but
without massiveness, from the distance" (quoted in Creighton 38).
Wolf von Eckardt's assessment of the memorial poetically described
its concrete slabs as:

solemnly firm, silent and motionless as space itself, arrogantly indifferent
and yet benign as the cosmos. . . . The *visually overlapping slabs*, and the
variety of spaces they create, give the composition *animation* like that of a
body of deep, quiet water. There is *motion* too, in the infinite play of light
and shadow as the earth turns. The structure offers no shelter for womb-like
comfort, *nothing pretty to provide the security of familiar associations. . . .*
Whether you are in the center court or outside the arrangement, you, the
beholder, are a part of it. . . . *It is a dynamic composition variously experienced
and always relative.* (quoted in Creighton 41)

I have taken the liberty of highlighting numerous words and
phrases in the foregoing descriptions in order to outline the changing
conception of the architectural monument throughout this century.
We have arrived, it would seem, at the antipodes of the classical mon-
ument. Splendor, serenity, and immutability have been forsaken for
simplicity, an antiaristocratic openness, flexibility, mobility, a center
that no longer grounds the structure but generates its movement, the
integration of multiple elements rather than a single dominating per-
spective, the concepts of destruction and entropy, the intervention
of space as a positive entity, fragmentation, the dissolution of a nur-
turing sense of security, and the embracing of the trivial. But it
should be patently clear that the novelty or revolutionary quality of
these architectural components pales considerably when juxtaposed
with what might be considered a meditation on the question of mon-
umentality, one of Mallarmé's final poetic efforts, "Un Coup de dés."
Although by no means an occasional text, and certainly not a con-
ventional "tombeau," the poem can be read as offering a series of
speculations on the question of the monumental and its relationship
to literature.

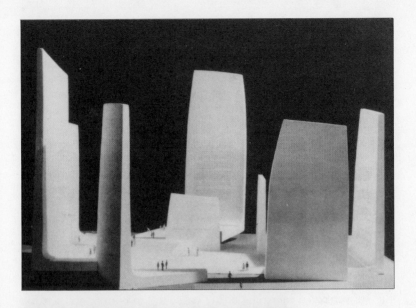

Pederson and Tilney and Associates. *Model for Franklin Delano Roosevelt Memorial.* 1961. (Photographs by, and copyright of, Louis Checkman.)

The very plasticity of the text is architectural in the most modern sense of the term in that it can be comprehended only in a series of experiences rather than all at once. Mallarmé has to a significant degree taken the simultaneity and the linearity of the usual poetic composition and elongated them to the point of unrecognizability. To this he appends a certain visual complexity of the plastic arts: the double pages are perhaps more interesting to the degree that they do not quite form ideograms but merely suggest writing's potential for doing so. In similar fashion the architectural conceptions described above (devoid of ornamentation imposed on simple geometric forms and the ubiquitous columns of the conventional monument) radically break with the forms prescribed by traditional architectural institutions. Because of the unorthodox distribution of words across the double pages and the multiplicity of typographical characters in Mallarmé's text, it becomes impossible to read the poem only in terms of the conventional hierarchy of the page, top to bottom and left to right. Rather, like Tatlin's *Monument*, with its "three great rooms which move at different speeds," the text is broken into a series of nonintegral but intertwined subtexts (i.e., "Un Coup de dés"; "Quand bien même lancé"; "(soit) que l'Abîme"; and the italics of pages 6 to 9). "Un Coup de dés" is highly flexible in that each new reading allows for previously unseen combinations of words and "verses." It therefore resembles the various levels of the platforms of the Pederson-Tilney group proposal for the FDR monument where "as one moves . . . the views change and new spaces acquire significances." The work addresses the "Lecteur habile," as in the epigraph to *Igitur*: "Ce Conte s'adresse à l'Intelligence du lecteur qui met les choses en scène, elle-même" (*O.c.* 433) ("This Tale addresses itself to the Intelligence of the reader that stages things itself"). It is the task of the viewer or reader to intervene in the work of art and to participate in the production of meaning.

New time and space categories are created by Mallarmé's composition. The oxymoronic "circonstances éternelles" of the dice throw lie somewhere between the immortal and the ephemeral, the permanent and the transient. Like Oldenburg's *Ice Bag*, neither fully animate nor inanimate, and like his colossal *Banana*, always decomposing but never decomposed, these textual and plastic artifacts redefine the transitional. It is no longer merely a passage between positive categories, but itself eternally in transition, canceling out the very possibility of the transitional by enacting a contradiction in terms. Mallarmé's famous revaluation of blank space as forming part of the text itself and not merely functioning as background ("Les 'blancs' en effet, assument l'importance, frappent d'abord; la versification en exigea, comme silence alentour" [*O.c.* 455] ["The blank spaces, in effect, assume importance, strike first; versification demanded them, like surrounding silence"]) predates the new architectural awareness of empty space (cf. "The vast concrete tablets emphasize the intervening spaces as positive entities" of the proposal for the monument to FDR). Space is not merely something to be enclosed by a structure, but it rather opens or encloses that structure in relation to surrounding areas. One of the conclusions of the *Architectural Review*'s symposium was that the new monument for the twentieth century may be conceived "scenically rather than structurally" ("In Search" 122); that is, that the frame of the monument may be extended from the concept of the structure to include the entire site. This parallels what Richard has written in connection with "Un Coup de dés": "Instead of the full being arranged around the empty, it is rather the empty that from now on will position itself amongst the full" (563).

The winning blueprints for the FDR monument called for the erection of a number of immense concrete slabs on which would have been inscribed quotations from the writings and speeches of FDR. These would form not a single monolithic edifice but, echoing a concept broached above, a series of monumental fragments or "bribes." In this way the monumentality of the structure is preserved even as its massive totality is fragmented. The concept is distinctly similar to that of "Un Coup de dés," which, in spite of its excessive fragmentation, still produces, perhaps because of the imposing nature of the project's scale, the "sacred shudder" that we associate with the traditional monument. The "bribes" of which the text is composed take on a quality of the monumental in themselves. In his excellent study of the poem, Malcolm Bowie has suggested that sound figuration of the kind found in phrases such as "l'ultérieur démon immémorial" and "tourbillon d'hilarité et d'horreur" ("the ulterior immemorial demon" and "whirlwind of hilarity and horror") "helps give these subunits of sentences an air of complete and often monumental statement" (135). The effect of the text as a whole, in fact, especially when compared to what might also be called the monumental "bribes" of *Le Livre*, suggests that of the "completed fragment." Because of its self-contradiction, the term itself is an uncomfortable one; but that discomfort is perhaps a definitive aspect of modern art. Just as the winning FDR proposal "offers no shelter for womb-like comfort, nothing pretty to provide the security of familiar associations," Mallarmé's "Un Coup de dés" is, again according to Bowie, the "least relaxing" of his works.[12] The ability of the artwork to shock the reader or spectator has in fact been identified as a major factor in modern art at least since the time of the Surrealists. That Mallarmé recognized and even savored the jarring effect his poem might have is evidenced by the remark he purportedly made to Valéry when showing him the manuscript: "Ne trouvez-vous pas que c'est un acte de démence?" ("Don't you think it's an act of madness?") (quoted in Davies, *Vers une explication* 12). What is perceived by the public as the outrageousness of the modern plastic arts often stems from a concept of art as obstacle. One commentator has written of Oldenburg's gargantuan sculptures: "These monuments are not just large sculptures. They behave quite differently on their site. Contemporary large-scale sculpture has a tendency to please the site, fitting into it and somehow echoing it in form and scale. But Oldenburg's monuments disrupt the site" (Fuchs 97). The concept of the monument as sheer obstacle, however, in spite of its utilization by many of the more radical members of the art community, may be read as just another reincarnation of the classic conception of the monument as symbol of absolute power. If the monument is to be conceived in a truly revolutionary fashion, its propensity to "behave" as barrier will have to be modified.

From what can be deduced from his frequent employment in his prose writings of the term "architecture" as substantive or modifier, Mallarmé's concept of the architectural was quite traditional. In the autobiographical letter to Verlaine, he described the "Grand Œuvre" in these terms. "Quoi? c'est difficile à dire: un livre, tout bonnement, en maints tomes, un livre qui soit un livre, architectural et prémédité, et non un recueil des inspirations de hasard fussent-elles merveilleuses" (*O.c.* 662–63) ("What? It's difficult to say: a book, all in all, in several volumes, a book that would be a book, architectural and premeditated, and not a collection of chance inspirations however marvelous they may be"). The opposition he constructs here between architecture and *hasard* then modulates in the succeeding paragraphs to one between the architectural and the fragment. The "livre" is architectural and premeditated whereas the "album" is a collection of chance inspirations, "mille bribes," "lambeaux," "fragment[s] [non-]exécuté[s]," and "portions [non] faites" ("a thousand odds and ends," "scraps," "unexecuted fragments," and "portions never done"). Related lexical choices abound,[13] and it would be futile to try to trace all of his uses of the term, but it is clear that Mallarmé's early sense of the architectural shares many of the qualities of the traditional monument as sketched out in the opening pages of this chapter. The conventionality of his use of the term is thoroughly belied, however, by the evidence of his own architectural "practice." The structures he designs, especially in the late poetry, are quite unlike those contained in the verse of other nineteenth-century poets, particularly the Parnassians (for example, Nerval's *chateaux* in "Fantaisie" and "Sylvie," the statues of Leconte de Lisle,[14] Banville, and Gautier, and especially the latter's evocation of an "art robuste": "Tout passe. L'art robuste / Seul a l'éternité; / Le buste / Survit à la cité" [131]) ("Everything passes. Only robust art / Possesses eternity; / The bust / Outlives the city"). We have already seen the extent to which Mallarmé's later "Tombeaux" are increasingly unconventional constructs. It is important to rule out the possibility of judging these antimonumental tombstones/poems merely as the fantasies of a psyche grappling with the anxiety caused by the death of his self-proclaimed poetic forefathers. Let us examine, then, two more examples of edifices constructed by Mallarmé to see if they corroborate our findings in the "Tombeaux" poems.

"Remémoration d'amis belges" is an occasional piece composed for a book destined to celebrate in 1893 the tenth anniversary of the Excelsior, a literary circle in Brussels where Mallarmé had three years earlier delivered his lecture on Villiers de l'Isle-Adam. A tribute to the poet friends he had made during his stay there, the poem in fact shifts the focus from a recounting of the circumstances of the visit to a poetic evocation of Brussels itself, its architecture, its canals, its swans. The text is controlled by a sense of slow leakage ("émeuve," "flotte," "épandre" ["stirring," "floating," "scattering"]) of fog, of "couleur encens" ("the color of incense"), of "baume antique" ("antique balm"), of the "multiplying" dawn punctuated by flights of suddenness (in the last verses of the quatrains and tercets, respectively: "la soudaineté de notre amitié neuve" and "A prompte irradier ainsi

qu'aile l'esprit") ("the suddenness of our new friendship" and "To ir-
radiate spirit like a prompt wing"). The image of the city as an ar-
chitectural whole is brilliantly communicated through the depiction
of the stone as floating and unanchored, gradually but insistently di-
vesting itself, fold by fold, of its very stoniness, much as a widow is
inevitably invaded by the absence of her departed husband (lines 1–
8):

> A des heures et sans que tel souffle l'émeuve
> Toute la vétusté presque couleur encens
> Comme furtive d'elle et visible je sens
> Que se dévêt pli selon pli la pierre veuve
>
> Flotte ou semble par soi n'apporter une preuve
> Sinon d'épandre pour baume antique le temps
> Nous immémoriaux quelques-uns si contents
> Sur la soudaineté de notre amitié neuve
>
> At odd hours and without such a breath stirring it
> All the antiquatedness almost the color of incense
> As if hiding from it and visible I feel
> That the widowed stone undresses fold after fold.
>
> Floating or seeming by itself to bring no proof
> Except to scatter time as an antique balm
> We immemorial few so content
> Over the suddenness of our new friendship

The vaguely erotic undressing of the stone comes to be a kind of
fog not only surrounding the actual event (i.e., the climatic condi-
tions of Brussels in February) but also clouding the event as it moves
into the poem: the "proof" that is never brought is the specificity of
the mimetic moment. The evaporating stone points to the erasure of
the monument even as it is being erected.

A strikingly similar image concludes page 8 of "Un Coup de dés"
where the "roc / faux manoir / . . . / qui imposa une borne à l'infini"
("rock / false manor / . . . / that imposed a limit on the infinite") is
doubly assaulted. Unceremoniously slapped by the tail of the sea-
maiden "en sa torsion de sirène" ("in her siren twisting"), it is then
swiftly devoured by the sea fog: "tout de suite / évaporé en brumes"
("suddenly / vanished in the fog"). The passage offers a series of mo-
ments that can be read as cynical metacommentary on a number of

the depictions of the monument we have analyzed above. The "roc" calls to mind the "noir roc courroucé" of the "Tombeau" for Verlaine, which, as the passé simple of "imposa" informs us, had in the past set a limit to the infinite. There would appear to be a conscious self-parody at work here in that the "borne à l'infini" tellingly recalls the "granit" of the Poe poem that was invoked to "montre à jamais sa borne / Aux noirs vols du Blasphème épars dans le futur" ("display forever its barrier / To the black flights of Blasphemy scattered in the future"). Considering the rather dubious circumstances we have uncovered in relation to the Poe tombstone as "borne," that is, its vacillation in Mallarmé's various writings on the subject between agent of security and of suppression, it is highly ironic that the rock is evoked in its function as insuperable obstacle even as it itself is being evaporated away in the fog. In its efforts to "impose" at the same time as it is gradually being worn away by the most insubstantial of elements, the image functions as an allegorical recounting of Mallarmé's differing conceptions of the monument. The "faux manoir" is also a locution particularly apt to recall the "Tombeaux" series in that the questioning of place, as Lipking has noted, pervades the texts: "Compulsively the poems reiterate a question: Where now is Gautier? Poe? Baudelaire? Verlaine?" (163). The "manoir" (from the Latin *manere*, to remain) is false in that the monument is no longer locatable: having lost its stability and permanence it is set adrift on a sea of letters, available to the shipwreck that forms the major thematic focus of the poem.

It might be argued that this evaporating monument is belied by the final image of the poem, "UNE CONSTELLATION / froide d'oubli et de désuétude" ("A CONSTELLATION / cold from forgetfulness and disuse"). The constellation has, in fact, been read as the harbinger of "total fixity, stopped by 'quelque point dernier qui le sacre'" (Michaud 161). But the final configuration is qualified by the visions of entropy that occur throughout the poem such as the rock discussed above and the falling pen/feather on page 9, buried in the "écumes originelles" ("originary foam"). Both images evoke a pristine past in which the object was viable, now superseded by its present state of degradation. Occupying approximately the same space on their respective pages, the lower right hand corner, traditionally the last position on the page, the two reiterate the contours of the defining throw of dice cast from the already defeated heights of the depths:

"LANCE DANS DES CIRCONSTANCES ETERNELLES / DU FOND D'UN
NAUFRAGE" ("THROWN INTO ETERNAL CIRCUMSTANCES / FROM THE
DEPTHS OF A SHIPWRECK"). The constellation ultimately achieves no
sense of finality. As Bonnie J. Isaac has shown, "the 'total number'
is in formation only, observed only at the moment *before* its supposed
consecration, the halting of its movement. The time of 'Un Coup de
dés' is the *futur antérieur*, of incomplete, deferred action . . . the con-
stellation does not 'take place' any more than does the 'place'" (835–
36). The endpoint of the transitional process is glimpsed at ("avant
de s'arrêter / à quelque point dernier qui le sacre" ["before stopping /
at some last point that consecrates it"]), but it can only be ap-
proached asymptotically. Ultimately the monument is condemned to
an eternal displacement ("le heurt successif . . . veillant doutant rou-
lant brillant et méditant" ["the successive shock . . . watching
doubting rolling shining and meditating"]) that is attested to by the
poem's final line, "Toute Pensée émet un Coup de Dés" ("All
Thought emits a Throw of Dice"). This, of course, repeats the text's
opening and relaunches the dice throw, enjoining us to read the poem
again.

Thus instead of a rejection of the monumental similar to that
staged by the architectural avant-garde of the early part of this cen-
tury, Mallarmé's texts document its gradual phasing out. His search
for a viable alternative to the monumental forms he no longer held
tenable is, I believe, more interesting in that it provides more radical
solutions than the architectural practice that has in the final analysis
never succeeded in doing away with conventional monumentality.
In the next chapter I examine the *Vers de circonstance* as constituting
this alternative in their intersections with and divergences from the
"portions faites" of the *Livre* itself, that is, the manuscript as pub-
lished and evaluated by Jacques Scherer. Mallarmé may have suc-
ceeded in envisioning an alternative not yet realized by the architec-
tural community (although, as I will show, it was an alternative that
has many parallels in the sculptural avant-garde). The *Vers de cir-
constance* can be read as enacting a new conception of poetry, a dem-
ocratic writing that evidences the other pole of the occasional, the
mobile/trivial rather than the immobile/monumental.

Chapter Five

Toward a New Poetics:
The *Vers de circonstance*

Mallarmé
Had too much to say:
He could never quite
Leave the paper white.
—W. H. Auden,
Academic Graffiti

Je donnerais les vêpres magnifiques du Rêve et leur or vierge, pour un quatrain, destiné à une tombe ou à un bonbon, qui fût *réussi*.
—Stéphane Mallarmé,
Letter to F. Coppée, April 20, 1868

In spite of Mallarmé's high visibility in continental and Anglo-American theory and criticism, the traditional image of him as ivory-tower poet, as the legendary insomniac isolated in provincial Tournon taunted by literary impotence and the merciless whiteness of the page, still prevails.[1] This version of the Mallarméan myth features a poet so obsessed with sterility and silence that even the prospect of dealing with the exigencies of his daily correspondence provokes a vengeful disgust: "J'ai horreur des lettres, et les crayonne le plus salement possible pour en dégoûter mes amis" (*Correspondance* 1:234) ("I abhor letters, and I scribble them as messily as I can in order to disgust my friends"). The predominant view of Mallarmé's attitude toward writing is summed up by Paul Bénichou's observation that "it is as if for Mallarmé the exercise of the mind and the use of language were marked with fundamental turmoil and pain" (72).

It would appear that notwithstanding the "revolution in poetic language" he produced and the frequent coincidences of his views with those of recent theorists like Barthes, Mallarmé was nevertheless denied the "pleasure of the text" and the "jouissance" we have come to associate with contemporary notions of textual practice.

There is one realm, however, in which we consistently encounter a certain species of Mallarméan "bonheur," where we glimpse an "other" Mallarmé, that suggested by the Auden epigraph, Mallarmé, the loquacious, author of numerous occasional pieces: translations, dedications, theater reviews, and of course, the *Vers de circonstance*. Although critics such as Jean-Pierre Richard periodically acknowledge this Mallarmé, they are by and large suspicious of him and how he might skew the "imaginary universe" so diligently constructed to exclude him. In speaking of the thematics of the going and coming, or *aller-retour*, in Mallarmé's works, Richard notes that from this perspective "one might more easily [and more comfortably] explain why Mallarmé took such pleasure in covering so many real fans with small dedicatory quatrains" (314).

As the subtly derogatory nuances of the Richard quote seem to indicate, even when recognized this Mallarmé is rarely accorded status or space. In recent publications of his selected works, the *Vers de circonstance* are either given token representation or, more frequently, omitted altogether; this despite the fact that in the still definitive Pléiade edition of the complete works the poems in the *Vers de circonstance* outnumber those in the *Poésies* (excluding the *Poèmes d'enfance et de jeunesse*) by two to one (approximately 104 pages to 50).

This suppression would have been easily understood even two decades ago when the institution of criticism still operated under the aegis of established conventions that obligated one to open a discussion of a minor work on an apologetic note; this to be followed with an authoritative claim to the forgotten work's intrinsic value, and a lament bordering on rebuke that critics have overlooked this text that now shall serve as focal point for a new perspective on the author. But today, when poststructuralist criticism has championed the marginal and when Jonathan Culler, the impresario of guidebooks to theory, acknowledges that a "common operation" of deconstruction is one that takes "a minor, unknown text and grafts it onto the main body of the tradition, or else takes an apparently marginal element of a text, such as a footnote, and transplants it to a vital spot" (*On Deconstruction* 139), it is surprising that the *Vers de circonstance* still remain virtually unknown.

It is with a reverse apology, then (not for focusing on a minor work,

but for what must seem merely the deployment of a typical decon-
structive strategy) that I propose to conclude my study of Mallarmé's
occasional poetry with the *Vers de circonstance*. In so doing I do not
wish to suggest that these quatrains and distichs ought to be included
in the canon, nor to simply reverse the hierarchy of the monumental
and the trivial, but to show that it is precisely with the example of
this writing that notions of canons and hierarchies tend to break
down. Certainly, as Jean Royère maintains, the poems are "petty
trinkets, at most decorative knick-knacks that exhibit an ingenious-
ness all the more rare where least playful," but it would be misguided
to conclude with him that "in complexity as in irony, this poetry
equals the major pieces" (146).

My goal is therefore not to set the *Vers de circonstance* up as suc-
cessors to the no longer viable monument discussed in the previous
chapter, nor is my goal to claim that what Mallarmé ostensibly con-
sidered an activity on the outermost peripheries of his literary en-
deavors was or ought to be regarded as central to the Mallarméan leg-
acy. Rather, I am interested in investigating the *Vers de circonstance*
as literary practice in order to understand what they represent in
terms of Mallarmé's poetic output and theory.

Whereas the "monumental" aspect of Mallarmé's work has a cer-
tain self-evident quality, the nature of its alternatives, both theoret-
ical and actual, is highly conjectural. Nevertheless, the death of the
monument would appear to be a prerequisite for the commencement
of a new mode of writing. In "Crise de vers" ("Crisis in Poetry"),
Mallarmé's essay that ostensibly describes an important juncture in
the history of literature ("La littérature ici subit une exquise crise,
fondamentale" [*O.c.* 360] ["Here literature undergoes an exquisite,
fundamental crisis"]), poetry quite respectfully defers its definitive
rupture until after the death of the "monument" Hugo: "Le vers, je
crois, avec respect attendit que le géant ['monument en ce désert']
qui l'identifiait à sa main tenace et plus ferme toujours de forgeron,
vînt à manquer; pour, lui, se rompre" (*O.c.* 361) ("The verse, I be-
lieve, waited with respect for the giant ['monument in this desert']
who identified it with his tenacious hand, firmer than that of a black-
smith, to be lacking; in order for it to break up"). But we must qualify
the attribution of the adjective "fundamental" to describe the nature
of the crisis in poetry in view of the fact that the death of the mon-
ument is not described as a full-scale demolition of a sacred architec-

ture (not upheavals, "des bouleversements"); it is rather depicted as an uneasy agitation with significant folds and perhaps a little tearing: "une inquiétude du voile dans le temple avec des plis significatifs et un peu sa déchirure" (O.c. 360) ("an inquietude of the veil in the temple with significant folds and a little bit of tearing"). The affixing of the title "crisis" can thus be read as an attempt at deliberate over-statement, or perhaps even misstatement, especially when we note that in *Les Mots anglais* Mallarmé describes the *c* as a "consonne à l'attaque prompte et décisive" ("consonant with a prompt and deci-sive attack") and when used in initial position with the letter *r*, sig-naling words "d'éclat et de brisure" (O.c. 940) ("of bursting and breaking").

What "Crise de vers" in fact attests to is more in consonance with the etymological root of *crisis* from the Greek "to separate" and the Indo-European "to sift"; that is, a tranquil realignment and redistri-bution of existing elements rather than a jettisoning of the estab-lished for the new. The textual insistence on terms such as "scintil-lation," "libre disjonction," "retrempe," "dispersion volatile," and "éparpillement en frissons" ("scintillation," "free disjuncture," "rein-vigoration," "volatile dispersion," and "scattering in shivers") speaks more tellingly about the piece's significance than do its individual affirmations. The essay is, in point of fact, a verbal collage composed of disparate passages culled from previously published articles. As Leo Bersani has noted in his provocative reading of it, the piece has a "thrillingly frivolous speculative mobility" (*Death* 36) that "is per-haps the major 'statement' of Mallarmé's theoretical writing. . . . His essay never achieves the status of a secure and privileged statement *about* his work. It is an exemplification rather than a privileged sum-mary of his esthetic, and it therefore must be treated *nonreductively* but as a *symptomatic* text" (44–45). Bersani's thinking indicates that rather than searching for alternatives to the monumental dimension of Mallarmé's writing in the thematics of the late works, we ought to look for them in the examples of his textual performance.

At the antipodes to the disjunctiveness of "Crise de vers" lies the 1885 letter to Verlaine, the so-called "Autobiographie." Composing for the most part in exceedingly clear prose, Mallarmé reads his own life as a conventional narrative, from birth to education to marriage and to his ongoing work. The most frequently cited portions of the letter describe the "Grand Œuvre," which is envisioned as the prototype of the book ("un livre qui soit un livre, architectural et pré-médité, et non un recueil des inspirations de hasard fussent-elles merveilleuses" [*O.c.* 663] ["a book that would be a book, architectural and premeditated, and not a collection of chance inspirations however marvelous they may be"]). The structural implications of his thinking are unequivocally plain: the architectural and premeditated book is opposed to the haphazard collection or "album" of verse. As I have shown in the preceding chapter, the second term of this opposition modulates from an emphasis on *hasard* or chance to an underscoring and proliferation of terms describing the deficient architecture of the album: "fragments," "bits and pieces," "shreds," and "portions."

The self-contradictory nature of this characterization of the "Grand Œuvre" is obvious to anyone familiar with Mallarmé's late works and especially with the collection of notes for *Le Livre* published by Jacques Scherer. Although it would be unfair to attribute the qualifier "haphazard" to the organization of a text such as "Crise de vers," it would appear that remarking on the text's fragmentary nature constitutes a considerably more apt description of it than the application of the terms "architectural and premeditated." That is, in the polarity Mallarmé establishes between the architectural and premeditated book on one hand and on the other, the "album" ("ce mot condamnatoire" ["this condemnatory word"]), it is clearly the latter term that best describes the fragmented and performative aspects of not only "Crise de vers" but the majority of the late works and especially, as I shall show in the following pages, the *Vers de circonstance* and *Le Livre* itself. I make these observations less to point out an instance of Mallarmé's poetic blindness than to propose the plausibility of dismissing portions of the invective in his pronouncements of poetic theory against the circumstantial and the disconnected.

Among the writings of the later period then, the conventional architectural and premeditated style that Mallarmé evidences in the "Autobiographie" is something of an anomaly. Even his depiction of the attitude the poet should take toward his contemporaries can be seen in retrospect to emanate more from Romantic notions of the incompatibility of the poetic genius with the tenor of modern times than from a realistic appraisal of his emerging role as a preeminent *homme de lettres* in Parisian literary circles. The solitude he invokes

as necessary to establish and maintain a salubrious and literarily pro-
ductive distance from society may be less an inconvenient imposition
from within or without than the adoption of a strategic stance from
which to conduct a radical renovation of the literary enterprise:

Au fond je considère l'époque contemporaine comme un interrègne pour le
poëte qui n'a point à s'y mêler: elle est trop en désuétude et en effervescence
préparatoire pour qu'il ait autre chose à faire qu'à travailler avec mystère en
vue de plus tard ou de jamais et de temps en temps à envoyer aux vivants sa
carte de visite, stances ou sonnet, pour n'être point lapidé d'eux, s'ils le soup-
çonnaient de savoir qu'ils n'ont pas lieu. (*O.c.* 664)

Basically, I consider that for the poet, our times are an interregnum in which
he should not get involved: they are marked by too much obsolescence and
by too great an anticipatory effervescence for there to be anything else for
the poet to do than to work mysteriously with regard to later or never and
from time to time, send to the living his calling card, stanzas or a sonnet, in
order not to be stoned by them, were they to suspect him of knowing that
they don't exist.

   This passage, when juxtaposed (as I have done in my Introduction)
with other citations such as the response proffered in an interview in
1891 with Jules Huret in which Mallarmé disclaims the title of *chef
d'école* of the young symbolists ("L'attitude du poëte dans une époque
comme celle-ci, où il est en grève devant la société, est de mettre de
côté tous les moyens viciés qui peuvent s'offrir à lui" [*O.c.* 870] ["The
attitude of the poet in times such as these, when he is on strike before
society, is to put aside all the vitiated resources that are offered to
him"]) would seem to evidence a profoundly asocial and apolitical
Mallarmé, uninterested in, even ironically disdainful of the world of
his contemporaries and the affairs of the Third Republic. Both "in-
terrègne" and "grève" represent an interval of the cessation of activ-
ity and imply a temporal translation of the willed opening of a spatial
gap. The separation between the poet and "les vivants" thus becomes
an open field, a kind of void or vacuum, a blank space. And yet, in
borrowing vocabulary from the very political and economic spheres
he professes to scorn, Mallarmé would seem to compromise the dis-
tancing he intends to secure. This antilogy has important parallels
with the model of structurality implicated in Mallarmé's use of the
carte de visite as a metaphor to describe the relationship between him-
self and the world. Employed to span the gap between the artist and

Paris, Juillet [1892] (Arnold Goffin)

Merci, cher poëte, pour ces pages, où le blanc final même est précieux,

STÉPHANE MALLARMÉ

car la rêverie longtemps les continue; mais que d'absolues choses y sont dites, et sur un ton varié et

89, RUE DE ROME

MNR Mp 425

adéquat ! Le Fou raisonnable (ce qu'il faut être !) ne représente pas un titre inscrit au hasard, ici où les impressions subtiles et fuyantes sont par vous ramenées à leur logique et originel groupement presque toujours. votre SM

Carte de visite with message of thanks to the poet Arnold Goffin for sending his book, *Le Fou raisonnable*, 1892 (Bibliothèque Littéraire Jacques Doucet). The message begins on the front of the card (*top*) and concludes on the back (*bottom*).

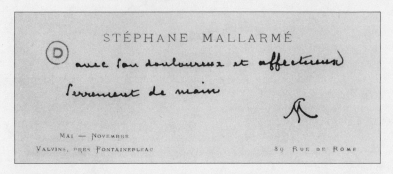

Carte de visite with brief message (Bibliothèque Littéraire Jacques Doucet).

society, the calling card paradoxically defines their distance by bridging it. In Derridean terms the *carte de visite* operates in the "écart" or interval, as a placeholder, inhabiting philosophical (binary) opposition, resisting and disorganizing it, without ever constituting a third term (*Positions* 43). Thus the *carte de visite* sets up a system of reversible relationships, sender to receiver, visitor to visited, writer to reader, absent to present, and so on, in its hypothetical movement across the space between the poet and his contemporaries.

On initial consideration a certain irony might be said to inform Mallarmé's choice of the *carte de visite*, the very emblem of decorum and social graces, to mark his alienation from society. By the end of the nineteenth century the practice of leaving calling cards had developed into a veritable institution with rules governing not only the card's proper format (size, choice of paper, style of engraving, disposition of names and titles) but also its correct usage (how many to leave, at what times and under what circumstances, when the card should be "cornée,"[2] who should call on whom). In her 1884 etiquette manual, *Manners and Social Usages*, Mrs. John Sherwood summed up the importance of the calling card in these predictably ethnocentric terms: "The card may well be noted as belonging only to a high order of development. No monkey, no 'missing link,' no Zulu, no savage, carries a card. It is the tool of civilization, its 'field-mark and device' . . . it cannot be dispensed with under our present environment" (81).

But if the *carte de visite* was then considered an invaluable "tool of civilization," it can today be read as an instrument of questionable technological progress. As one correspondence book notes, "the advantage procured by a calling card is the gain in time it affords" (Dournon 71). The card came to be regarded as a means of replacing the tedium of paying endless visits. Mallarmé's scornful use of the *carte de visite* as the emblem of his estrangement is more comprehensible when we note the degree to which by the end of the century the card began to supplant the individual. Within the regulated structure of the social system, a person became replaceable by his or her card. This was considered not only socially acceptable but was, increasingly, expected.

The ease of this form of token self-dissemination was considerably accelerated in 1857 by a revolution in the field of photography.[3] The daguerreotype received its deathblow with the invention of a process enabling the production of multiple exposures on an individual negative. Whereas a single print had previously cost from fifty to one hundred francs, A. A. E. Disdéri's new collodion technique ushered in the mass production of portraits, making them readily available to the bourgeoisie at only twenty francs for twelve photographs (Freund 56). Either because of their resemblance in size to the calling card, or because they were actually used as calling cards,[4] the miniature portraits became universally known as *carte de visite* photographs.

The resonances of Mallarmé's use of the term *carte de visite* may therefore be even greater than we suspected, especially when we consider the overwhelming popularity of the small photos[5] and the fact that a number of the *Vers de circonstance* were composed for photographs that were probably of the *carte de visite* format. The popularization of photography occasioned an unprecedented proliferation of what William M. Ivins, Jr., terms "exactly repeatable pictorial statements" (2), changing our modes of perception and ultimately, our very understanding of the nature of reality. As Walter Benjamin has shown, the technology of miniaturization ushered in by photography has irrevocably transformed the entire nature of art and our understanding of subjectivity. Both the calling card and the *carte de visite* photograph undoubtedly played an important role in what Elizabeth McCauley has called the "insidious transformation of the individual into a malleable commodity. Direct human intercourse was in a sense supplemented by the interaction with a machine-generated and therefore irrefutably exact alter-ego, a fabricated 'other'" (224).[6] McCauley quotes the French nineteenth-century caricaturist Mar-

celin who humorously chronicled the degradation of the *carte de visite*
as follows:

Originally one left a card when the person called upon was absent; then "one
dispensed with the visit and sent the card by an errand boy or valet"; and at
last one sends it by mail without paying a visit at all. Substituting a photo-
graph for a visit, he notes, allows the sender to choose a flattering pose but
results in nightmares for the postman, who is overburdened with cartes each
New Year's Day. (46)

The *carte de visite* thus contributes to three distinct but interrelated
cultural transformations that have important implications for the lit-
erary questions we shall be considering: a shift from the immobile to
mobile, from the monumental to its trivialization, and from tradi-
tional to contemporary conceptions of art.

The essential mobility of the calling card as a theoretical model of
one pole of occasional poetry is thus a first point of contrast with the
other pole, the monument. Whereas the monumental connotes the
static and the immobile, the durable, and the permanent by marking
death, the eternal absence, the *carte de visite* bespeaks the peri-
patetic, the changeable, the ephemeral, and the demountable by
marking a temporary absence, a having-been-and-gone that is subject
to reappearance. The monument consecrates, memorializes, and
reifies the occasion by promoting the idea that representation can
secure an idealized re-presentation by substituting a presence for
the marked absence. The *carte de visite* stresses rather the suppleness,
the accommodation, and the flexibility of the occasion by calling at-
tention to the fact that in its very mobility, it eludes these categories,
for the perpetually mobile is always simultaneously both absent and
present.

In the "Autobiographie" the distribution of the *cartes de visite*
serves as a buffer between ⁺he poet and the living, carving out an
adversarial zone that can be traversed only by the poet's stanzas or
sonnets in one direction and, in their absence, the presumably met-
aphorical retaliatory stones thrown by the public ("pour n'être point
lapidé d'eux"). But it is interesting to note that among the many
verses Mallarmé *was* sending forth were the distichs written on small
stones gathered at Honfleur. Here the institution of literature is de-
picted in a rather gruesomely bellicose fashion as a rock fight or sense-
less mutual stoning. Indeed, one of the poems written on "galets,"

like the "bond hagard" ("haggard bound") of the "Cantique" or the "bond extérieur" ("exterior bound") of the "Tombeau" for Verlaine (and in contrast to the stability of the tombstone of "Toast funèbre"), operates precisely on the oblique rebound of the pebble ricocheting at the beach: "Avec ceci Joseph, ô mon élève / Vous ferez des ricochets sur la grève" (*O.c.* 172) ("With this, Joseph, O my pupil / You will make ricochets on the beach"). The disciple-like relationship between the poet and Joseph that is the legacy of the inscribed rock suggests the desire for the institution and continuance of a poetry whose performative trajectory is that of the skipping stone: it strikes surfaces and bounces off at an unpredictable (that is, specifically *un*-premeditated) angle. Here the movement and capriciousness of the "galet" are the very antithesis of the fixity of the monument. Another of the "galets" seems to offer a metacommentary on the polarities of Mallarmé's poetics of the occasion. The weighty, obstinate stone is contrasted with a "winged writing" (*O.c.* 173):

> Pierre ne va pas, zélée
> Par ton poids qui s'obstina
> Couvrir l'écriture ailée
> Que signe ce nom Dinah.

> Stone, do not go, zealously
> By your weight that insists
> To cover the wingèd writing
> That signs this name: Dinah.

A parallel opposition can be read in the second of the epigraphs above where Mallarmé shifts his hopes for the destination of the "quatrain réussi" ("well-turned quatrain") from the weighty "tombe" to the frivolous "bonbon," much like one of the quatrains accompanying glazed fruits (cf. "Ces vils fruits ne sont que mensonge" [*O.c.* 117] ["These paltry fruits are but lies"]) that years later he was to accompany with verse and send out at New Year's.

The English usage of the term "ricochet" derives from the French *fable du ricochet*, a story in which the narrator constantly evades the hearer's questions. The deviant trajectories of the *fable du ricochet* (similar to the oblique reflection in the "Tombeau" for Verlaine in which the question *who* looks for Verlaine is perversely answered by *where* and followed by an echolalic repetition of his name: "Verlaine?

Il est caché parmi l'herbe, Verlaine") when read in terms of paradigms of communication offers a somewhat aberrant model. Rather than reading communication as a continuing exchange of information, the *fable du ricochet* offers a pattern of the "response" as metonymic swervings to the side of questions posed, suggesting the impossibility of meaningful exchanges.

A different but equally questionable communication model can be deduced from the peculiar mobility evidenced by another section of Mallarmé's *Vers de circonstance*, "Les Loisirs de la poste." These quatrains containing the names and addresses of Mallarmé's correspondents were inscribed on envelopes and sent through the mail. Here poetry is emblematized not as that which is communicated but rather as the vehicle of communication. The poetic is an excess: located on the envelope, it is at once that which attempts to make contact and the remainder of that effort. Destined to be discarded once the letter reaches its destination, the verse is significant only as the trace of a movement of meaning. On these *feuilles volantes* we have an extraordinary example of literature in motion, in transit *toward, vers des* "circonstances." The "Loisirs" exhibit a verbal art that does not require the direct object to complete its message. Poetry provides here an availability to movement that subverts the immobilization of meaning.

We have not yet finished with the question of mobility in the *carte de visite* model of literature. If the "galets" seemed to subvert traditional concepts of communication in their display of an erratic metonymic rebounding; and the "Loisirs" in an undirected movement outward, a sheer disseminatory force; the quatrains Mallarmé penned on fans and offered as gifts likewise inhibit communication, not by skewing or eliminating the reply, but by making the reply equivalent to and therefore indistinguishable from the question. The contours carved out by the specular trajectory of the "éventail," the to and fro fluttering of the fan, is a metaphoric repetition of the same, guaranteeing that the message will always be identical and, consequently, null. In the "Eventails" as elsewhere in the *Vers de circonstance* the deployment of rhyme and homophony projects equivalences so extensively that the quatrains nearly self-destruct in the play of reciprocal projections.[7] Tautology would seem to be the principal message in the first "Eventail," which opens with a quite literally "arresting"

"Eventail" quatrain inscribed on a fan to Madeleine Roujon (Bibliothèque Littéraire Jacques Doucet).

rhyme: "Aile quels paradis élire." The strength of the initial sound equivalence works to buffet the reader back and forth, catching one in the infinite rebound of "aile quels." The effect is such that we become implicated in the "délire" of the impossible choice of the first two verses (*O.c.* 107):

> Aile quels paradis élire
> Si je cesse ou me prolonge au
> Toucher de votre pur délire
> Madame Madier de Montjau.

> Wing, sing what paradise to choose
> If the touch of your sheer madness
> Causes me to cease or continue
> Madame Madier de Montjau.

Like the speaker of the poem, we cannot decide whether the web of the rebounding rhyme represents a cessation or prolongation of activity. The verse projects the perfect enactment of the dilemma: we vacillate deliriously in the verses' peculiar stasis in movement.

In quatrain 6 the reflexive operation becomes even more pervasive. The "Eventail" for Nelly Marras features not only the unexpected *rime riche* of "par taire" and "parterre" but also a thematics of comparison and similitude on two levels, that of grammar and rhetorical wordplay (O.c. 108):

> Autour de marbres le lys croît—
> Brise, ne commence par taire,
> Fière et blanche, son regard droit,
> Nelly pareille à ce parterre.

> Around the marble the lily grows—
> Breeze, do not begin by silencing
> Proud and white, looking straight ahead
> Nelly resembles this flower bed.

By the time the final verse tells us that Nelly resembles the flower bed, the message is already redundant: the resemblance has hitherto been twice conveyed, in the repetition of the sound "par" (*par* taire, *par*-eille, and *par*terre: the truncated sequence spells out its own meaning [i.e., "par taire" est pareille à (is similar to) "parterre"]) and in the "hidden" phonic planting of the "lys" in "Nelly."

A number of the "Eventails" function specifically in terms of a hinged motion or a mirrorlike reflection. Verses 2 and 3, which share the same rhyme scheme, stress a kind of give and take that I have highlighted here in italics, the "return" portion elaborated in the second half of each quatrain (O.c. 107):

> . . . Aile ancienne, *donne-moi*
> L'horizon dans une bouffée.

> . . . Ancient wing, *give me*
> The horizon in a puff of air.

> . . . Avec cette aile ouverte *amène-moi*
> Quelque éternelle et rieuse bouffée.

> . . . With this open wing *bring me*
> Some eternal and laughing puff of air.

The verbs "amener," "reployer," and "ramener" ("to bring," "to fold back," and "to bring back") are similarly used in quatrains 9, 12, and 15. A most clever use of the mirroring theme can be seen in an "Eventail" not included in the Pléiade collection, but numbered 19 in the Flammarion edition. The first verse plays out the "reflection" of the swan's image in a lake (reminiscent of the sonnet "Le vierge, le vivace") by juxtaposing the homonyms "signe" and "cygne": "Fleur, signe et, sur le lac, cygne" (555) ("Flower, sign and, on the lake, swan").

Perhaps the most striking use of the theme of the repetition of the same occurs in quatrain 7, one of the many Mallarméan offerings of an *art poétique* in miniature. The "flight" of the fluttering fan is hinged on the quatrain's middle word, "vers" (there are eleven words in the first two verses and eleven in the final two) (*O.c.* 108):

> Là-bas de quelque vaste aurore
> Pour que son vol revienne vers
> Ta petite main qui s'ignore
> J'ai marqué cette aile d'un vers.

> Down there from some vast dawn
> So that its flight returns toward [as verse]
> Your dainty hand that does not know
> I marked this wing with verse.

"Revienne vers," of course, plays on the two meanings of "vers": to return *toward* as well as to return *as verse*. The fact that the word "vers" itself returns in the last line further emphasizes the specular imaging of the fan's repeated movements.

In the foregoing I have attempted to show how the various forms of mobility inherent in the *carte de visite* model of literature are linked to the problematization of communication in poetry. For Laurence Porter, who opens his article "The Disappearing Muse: Erasure of Inspiration in Mallarmé" with the sweeping statement, "the history of nineteenth-century French poetry needs to be redefined" (389), part of the problem lies in the fact that critics blur the distinctions between Symbolism and Modernism, assuming that the former develops into the latter. Porter locates the specificity of French Symbolism precisely in a "crisis" of communication: "rather than merely challenging the reader's preconceptions regarding what poetry should say, it disrupted the very communicative axis linking sender to message to receiver, thus questioning whether any communication was possible" (390). Porter explores Mallarmé's role in this crisis in terms of the revisions made in the early poems where he finds evidence that

Mallarmé "makes the virtual axis of communication more tenuous" (391) by erasing references to muselike figures.

Porter's findings are relevant to the present study in that in many cases the "erasure of inspiration" involves a suppression of anecdote that is, quite simply, a version of the elision of the occasion discussed above in Chapter 3. In "Mallarmé," Derrida shows this same process at work in the poet's rewriting of a prose piece, "Or," originally published in 1893 in the *National Observer* under the title "Faits-Divers." The first version names its referent, its pre-text, its real historical occasion: the Panama affair. However, Derrida notes that

in the final version, the process of extraction and condensation keeps only the glimmer of gold; it effaces the referent: there is no longer a proper noun. . . . An entire thematic configuration . . . explores the vein of gold, in all of its senses, but it is first of all in order to foreground the signifier *gold*: gold inasmuch as, from a natural substance, it turns into a monetary sign, but also the linguistic element, letters, a syllable, a word. (376)

The systematic upstaging of the more conventional components of the communicative axis by the very materiality of language itself (the erasure of the referent, the subversion of address caused by the skewing of the structural propriety of sender and receiver as distinguishable entities, the blatant trivialization of the message, the problematization of the possibility of establishing contact), which is treated only obliquely in this early article, will become the principal concern of Derrida's *Post Card*. There the vast question of "communication" is taken up in terms of the postal system as the emblem of the logocentric era. Derrida writes, "the post is no longer a simple metaphor, and is even, as the site of all transferences and all correspondences, the 'proper' possibility of every possible rhetoric" (65). Because of its deliberate banality, its mobility and ephemerality, its subversion of the polarities outside/inside (in that it has only a recto and a verso) and public/private, the postcard functions in Derrida's text as the debunker of the now becoming obsolete era of communication and the harbinger of a new era of technology.

Derrida's treatment of the postcard offers a number of productive comparisons and contrasts with the *carte de visite* model I have been discussing and with the *Vers de circonstance* (especially "Les Loisirs de la poste") in terms of alternative modes of writing. Like the *carte de visite*, the postcard is viewed as antimonumental: "I immediately wanted to erect a monument, or a house of cards, sumptuous and fragile . . . barely durable . . . light" (*Post Card* 17–18). The foundation of logocentric thought, like Freud's "edifice of 'speculative' hypotheses," is glimpsed in all its fragility before its always imminent demise: "There are nothing but post cards, anonymous homeless fragments, without legitimate addressees, open letters, but open like crypts. Our entire library, our entire encyclopedia, our words, our pictures, our figures, our secrets, all an immense house of post cards" (53; translation modified). As Gregory Ulmer has noted in his discussion of *The Post Card*, "from the deconstructive point of view, the essence of the postal is not that letters arrive (the functionalist view) but that they (sometimes) *fail to arrive*. In terms of distance, spacing, rather than destiny, 'the post is nothing but a little fold . . . a relay to mark that there is never anything but relays'" ("The Post Age" 42). The notion of the *relay* serves to bring together a number of terms I have discussed above, such as the "interrègne" or "grève" and the gap opened up between the sender/receiver or visitor/visited with the spatial and temporal coordinates of literature. That is, the relaying of correspondence is always subject to the treachery of the space across which it moves, just as the written text is vulnerable to the white space that separates words and the margins that border them. Conventional forms of writing span the gap by trying to erase it, by devaluing or disguising it so that the semblance of continuity and unified meaning is fostered, allowing for the sense of developing anecdote and the illusion of unbroken narrative. But the "writing" of the calling card shatters the possibility of an accumulation of sense: the *carte de visite* does not bear any message except the card itself and that message is always the same. If the exchanging of letters permits a "real" correspondence in that the letter is addressed and signed, directed and destined, and bears its message inside, the *carte de visite* bears only a name, occasionally an address: not the name of the *destinataire*, however, but of the sender! One cannot communicate anything to another except to name oneself. And the possibility of attaining even this minimal degree of communication is dependent not on a notion of words as signification but on *positioning* as meaning. The *carte de visite* tucked away in the calling card case can "mean" nothing at all, but is merely a potentiality whose meaning can only be deployed when the card is left at the home of the absent one visited.

Ulmer notes that the postcard is "both readable and unreadable—the post card circulates, its message exposed to anyone who looks, but, whether because of the excess or poverty of the message, it is meaningless (without interest) to all, even to the signer and recipient, who understand it to say no more than 'I am here'" (42). Thus Ulmer reads the postcard not exactly as an example of positioning as meaning but as always producing a meaning about positioning. With all due respect to Ulmer, however, we ought to note that conventionally the postcard says not only "I am here" but "wish you were here." That is, it not only states a fact but posits a desire as well, conflating the indicative and subjunctive aspects of language. Communication does succeed, even if its message is always the same. In contrast, however, the function of the *carte de visite* is to say, "I was here and you were not." The positioning of the *carte de visite* is thus always the mark of the unintercepted relay. Leaving one's calling card refers one to a possible future visit (which may also be waylaid); that is, it refers only to another relay. It is essential to see, however, that communication, even in its most rudimentary form, *is* operative, even if the "message" is only proclaiming the fact of its own failure.

The tension between the communicative and noncommunicative properties of the *carte de visite* is perhaps best exemplified by "Les Loisirs de la poste." Mallarmé's extraordinary project of sending forth hundreds of envelopes, the intransitive addressing of himself outward, can be read as an art of derivation in the term's original sense of turning the stream away from its channel. The white envelope, once set adrift in an ocean of letters between *expéditeur* and *destinataire*, is sheer virtuality held in suspense just as the white water lily in the prose poem of that name marks both the distance separating the rower from "l'inconnue à saluer" ("the unknown one to be greeted") and their ideal encounter. Yet in spite of their de-rivation, the purpose of the "Loisirs" is to make the letter ar-rive at its destination. In the now (in)famous polemic about Poe's "Purloined Letter," it is Lacan who insists that the letter always arrives at its destination whereas it is Derrida who stresses the structural possibility of the letter's not arriving. In "The Frame of Reference," Barbara Johnson contributes to the discussion by problematizing the entire question of derivation/emission and arrival/destination by effacing the difference between them:

Everyone who has held the letter—or even beheld it—including the narrator, has ended up having the letter addressed to him as its destination. The reader is comprehended by the letter: there is no place from which he can stand back and observe it. Not that the letter's meaning is subjective rather than objective, but that the letter is precisely that which subverts the polarity "subjective/objective," that which makes subjectivity into something whose position in a structure is situated by an object's passage through it. The letter's destination is thus *wherever it is read*: the place it assigns to its reader as his own partiality. Its destination is not a place, decided a priori by the sender, because the receiver is the sender, and the receiver is whoever receives the letter, including nobody. (*Critical Difference* 144)

This drama of ambiguity is played out repeatedly in the "Loisirs" through an oscillation between subject/sender and object/receiver in what appears to be a designed proliferation of the possible referents of the pronoun *tu*. Who writes and who is addressed? The second person pronouns refer variously to the letter's conventional addressee, to the sender himself, to his personified thought or desire (*O.c.* 86, 94):

> L'âge aidant à m'appesantir,
> Il faut que toi, ma pensée, ailles

> With age weighing me down,
> You, my thought, must go

> Cours, ô mon Désir! et te rue
> Chez tous nos libraires

> Run, O my Desire! and rush
> To all our booksellers

or to the letter of the poet's persona in search of the poet (*O.c.* 106):

> Monsieur Mallarmé. Le pervers
> A nous fuir pour le bois s'acharne
> Ma lettre, suis sa trace

> Monsieur Mallarmé. The perverse one
> Persists in fleeing from us for the woods
> My letter, follow his trace

and even to the postal service (*O.c.* 92):

> Prends ta canne à bec de corbin
> Vieille Poste
>
> Take up your bill-head cane
> Old Postal Service

In still other cases the entire address becomes rerouted in that the address is to the act of addressing itself: that is, Mallarmé turns his back on the literal addressee to perform an apostrophe to literature, to the letter (*O.c.* 101):

> Ma lettre, ne t'arrête qu'à
> La main petite et familière
> De Gabrielle Wrotnowska
>
> My letter, do not stop but at
> The petite and familiar hand
> Of Gabrielle Wrotnowska

to the verse on the envelope (*O.c.* 99):

> Vers, s'il se peut qu'en son buvard
> Madame Seignobos vous glisse
>
> Verse, if it can be that in her blotter
> Madame Seignobos slips you

and even to the scrawled writing of the address (*O.c.* 104):

> Cette adresse si mal écrite
> Porte ou je te mène au collet
>
> This address so poorly written
> Bring or I will lead you by the collar

Moreover, the addressee sometimes functions as subject in that the verse carrying his address contains his own sketch or caricature, or even a parody of his art.

Mallarmé had planned to make a small book of the quatrains: its distribution would have infinitely expanded the space of play between *expéditeur* and *destinataire* since with publication an entirely new audience would have been drawn in through the multiplication of readers. The preface Mallarmé had prepared for the book was to

be signed not with his own name but rather with the deceptive sub-
scription, "Les Editeurs." This literary imposture enabled him to
achieve the distance necessary from his work to allow for disguised
self-irony. When in the guise of editor he thereby becomes his own
reader and critic, he has masterfully prepared the way for his most
ironic comment on the question of communication in literature and
correspondence: "Avec zèle nous avons remis la main peu à peu sur
l'ensemble de ces poëmes spéciaux et brefs que l'auteur espéra perdus"
(*O.c.* 1503) ("Zealously we have come into possession little by little
of the ensemble of these special and brief poems that the author had
hoped were lost"). So much for literature.

Just as, in their exterior trajectories, the "Loisirs" are adrift be-
tween sender and receiver, writer and reader, at the textual level they
vacillate between the poet's conflicting desires for structure and the
explosion of structure. In the preface Mallarmé also has his fictional
editors state that:

M. Stéphane Mallarmé en autorise l'impression, mentionnant que l'idée lui
vint à cause d'un rapport évident entre le format ordinaire des enveloppes
et la disposition d'un quatrain et qu'il fit cela par pur sentiment esthétique.
(*O.c.* 1503)

Mr. Stéphane Mallarmé authorizes their printing, mentioning that the idea
occurred to him because of the obvious relationship between the ordinary
format of envelopes and the disposition of a quatrain, and that he did this
out of a purely aesthetic sense.

This would seem to place the "Loisirs" squarely within a current
running through the entire oeuvre that seeks to establish a corre-
spondence between the subject of writing and its shape and ar-
rangement on the page, reaching its apogee in "Un Coup de dés."
In spite of Mallarmé's prefatory comment that "tout se passe, par rac-
courci, en hypothèse; on évite le récit" (*O.c.* 455) ("it all happens
by abridgment, hypothetically, narrative is avoided"), in that poem
structure itself, even at the level of the disposition of words on the
page, prepares and establishes a kind of narration preexisting and
steering content. The *Vers de circonstance* can be read as so many at-
tempts to play with the possibilities of the correspondence of medium
and message. The shape of the quatrain repeats the rectangle of the
envelope. In this regard Jean Royère has interestingly observed: "The

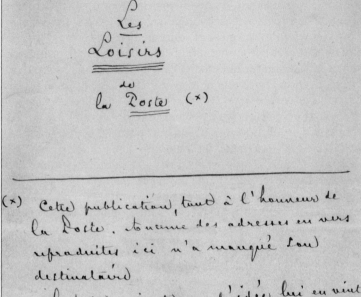

Les
Loisirs
de
la Poste (×)

(×) Cette publication, toute à l'honneur de
la Poste, étonnante des adresses en vers
reproduites ici n'a manqué son
destinataire

○ Le poëte ajoute que l'idée lui en vint
à cause d'un rapport évident entre
le format des enveloppes et la
disposition d'un quatrain — par
pur sentiment esthétique. Il les
multiplia au gré de   The Editor
ses relations

MNR Fol 20 (1)

Manuscript of the preface to "Les Loisirs de la poste" (Bibliothèque Littéraire Jacques Doucet).

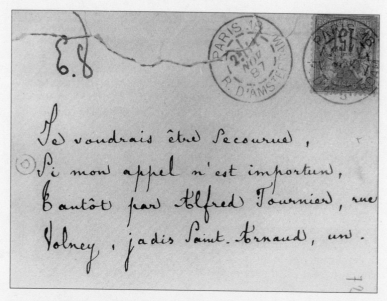

Stamped and postmarked manuscript of "Les Loisirs de la poste," "Je voudrais être secourue," to Alfred Fournier (Bibliothèque Littéraire Jacques Doucet).

envelope is the enclosure; it merits consideration. Those of ordinary format seem to demand that a quatrain imprint their destination at their center. After such a discovery, Mallarmé was no longer free not to write address quatrains!" (145). Because the structure of an address is a matter of convention, its recasting in the form of a quatrain seeks to combat its inherent arbitrariness through a will to structuralization. As such, the "Loisirs" install the fictional in the place of the gratuitous. In a mode analogous to Monet's water lily, haystack, or Rouen Cathedral studies, the one hundred and thirty odd quatrains are an attempt to explore and exploit the multiple structural possibilities of a minimal number of elements. The poetic act here consists in a creating of relationships; literature becomes a combinatory game. The relationship between proper name and address thus is explicitly motivated through fiction. The motivation, no matter how trivial, combats *le hasard* by instituting new structures, much as the freeing of poetry from the conventional alexandrine permits the emergence of subjacent structures and a freeplay of possible combinations:

Les fidèles à l'alexandrin, notre hexamètre, desserrent intérieurement ce mécanisme rigide et puéril de sa mesure; l'oreille, affranchie d'un compteur factice, connaît une jouissance à discerner, seule, toutes les combinaisons possibles, entre eux, de douze timbres. (*O.c.* 362)

Those loyal to the alexandrine, our hexameter, are internally loosening that rigid and puerile mechanism from its meter; the ear, freed from an artificial counting, experiences great pleasure in discerning, alone, all of the possible combinations, among themselves, of twelve tones.

In addition to the "Loisirs," Mallarmé experimented with the correspondence of writing and its shape in a number of the other *Vers de circonstance*. Indeed, in an 1897 letter to Camille Mauclair concerning the proofs for "Un Coup de dés," Mallarmé noted:

Je crois que toute phrase ou pensée, si elle a un rythme, doit le modeler sur l'objet qu'elle vise et reproduire, jetée à nu, immédiatement, comme jaillie en l'esprit, un peu de l'attitude de cet objet quant à tout. La littérature fait ainsi *sa preuve*: pas d'autre raison d'écrire sur du papier. (*Correspondance* 9:288)

I believe that any phrase or thought, if it has a rhythm, should model it on the object that it targets and should reproduce, cast nakedly, immediately, as if surging in the mind, a bit of the attitude of this object in all its aspects. In this way literature *proves itself*: there is no other reason to set pen to paper.

"Eventail" 15 is composed so as to imitate the contour of a fan being opened vertically (*O.c.* 110):

> Palpite,
>   Aile,
>   mais n'arrête
> Sa voix que pour brillamment
> La ramener sur la tête
> Et le sein
>   en diamant.

> Flutter,
>   Wing,
>   but do not stop
> Her voice but to brilliantly
> Bring it back over her head
> And breast
>   bedecked in diamonds.

The motif of expansion and contraction is further reinforced by the poem's accelerating and decelerating rhythm. The command to flutter, reified by the two syllables of the first verb, then slows with the vocative monosyllabic "aile," only to regain mobility with the second command not to stop, emphasized by a syntactical arrangement that obeys that command by making awkwardly impossible a pause after "arrête" and before its direct object.

A New Year's quatrain to Mme Whistler inscribed on one of Mallarmé's *cartes de visite* offered the opportunity to comment on the conventional sentiment of time passing with a reference to an hourglass. The expression is reinforced by the visual pun: the quatrain "thins" at the middle where the disposition of the third verse visually suggests sand falling gently but steadily from the upper bulb to the lower. The V-shaped top of the hourglass is accentuated by the emphatic capitalization of "Vous" in the second verse (*O.c.* 137):

> L'an s'en va quoique Whistler nie
> Ou par Vous on sache oublier
> Sourire
>   grâce
>   autre génie
> De renverser le sablier.

> The year goes by though Whistler denies
> Or thanks to You one knows how to forget
> Smile
>   grace
>   another genius
> To overturn the hourglass.

The series of verses inscribed on Easter eggs illustrate the correspondence of writing and surface as well. The roundness of the eggs suggested a circularity of meaning that could be attained through the virtually limitless number of permutations achievable by rotating the eggs. Mallarmé's daughter and son-in-law, the editors of the 1920 published version of the *Vers de circonstance*, prefaced the "Œufs de Pâques" with the following note:

Chaque vers était écrit à l'encre d'or sur un œuf rouge et précédé d'un numéro de manière à reconstituer le quatrain.—Une seule fois, le numérotage put être omis, et, en intervertissant les œufs, l'ensemble lu ainsi plusieurs fois de façon différente. (*O.c.* 139)[8]

Each verse was written in gold ink on a red egg and preceded by a number allowing one to reconstitute the quatrain. Only in one case was the numbering omitted, and, in inverting the eggs, the ensemble could thus be read several times each in a different way.

It is in Mallarmé's own arrangement of the "Loisirs," as they appear in the 1894 *Chap Book* edition where no particular grouping is evident, that we most strikingly sense the tension between the structuring thrust of the individual quatrains and the digressive tendency of the verse as a whole. The editors of the 1920 version of the *Vers de circonstance* had arranged the poems according to the profession of the correspondent. The Pléiade editors basically followed this grouping, striving to give the classification even "more rigor." But much as such attempts to experiment with structure make these editors ideal readers, such efforts actually betray the *Chap Book* version, which provides an extraordinary example of nonnarrativity. There the quatrains, merely juxtaposed on the page according to no discernible principle of order, provide no true foreground or background either in content or in typographical disposition. This would seem to evidence a literature incapable of development, unable to conclude, and yet constantly beginning anew. In the preface to this edition Mallarmé, referring to himself and to the rather undirected proliferation of quatrains, had noted: "Il les multiplia au gré de ses relations" ("He proliferated them as his relationships demanded"). The poems are thus mere improvisations, characterized by a nervous, directionless mobility. It is a superficial and constantly self-renewing movement of fits and starts, a kind of perpetual foreplay. Because of the brevity of the octo- or heptasyllabic lines, and of the quatrains themselves, their propositions are continually disrupted and the sense of the poems constantly deferred. As David H. T. Scott has noted in his discussion of Mallarmé's octosyllabic sonnets, the shortness of the verse line ensures a frequent appearance and dominance of rhyme, which, when combined with the *repli* of syntax, establishes the axis of the poems on the vertical as opposed to the horizontal (161). The phatic function of language predominates in that the verses constantly seek to open and establish communication. By virtue of their nature as mere *address* quatrains they cannot contain within them the narration of a completed communication. In this poem (*O.c.* 87),

Mon silence ne continue
Pas! un bonjour tente l'essor
Au cinquante-cinq Avenue
Bugeaud, qu'orne Monsieur Champsaur.

My silence does not continue
No! A greeting attempts to soar
At fifty-five Avenue
Bugeaud, decorated by Monsieur Champsaur.

the phatic moment of "un bonjour tente l'essor" recalls the contours of the upward movement suggested by the last quatrain of the "Cantique de Saint-Jean," where we see the severed head of John the Baptist "penche un salut." The "Pas!" placed in a position of emphasis (*rejet* from the previous line) further suggests the "rupture franche" of the decapitation and simultaneously recalls the other similarly placed *rejet* exclamations throughout Mallarmé's works such as "Palmes!" in "Don du poëme," "Lys!" in "L'Après-midi," and "Hyperbole!" from "Prose pour des Esseintes." The juxtaposition of the energetic "Pas!" (both final moment and absolute beginning in one swift vertical erection) with the pregnant moment of "tente l'essor" is formally analogous to a number of the poems that express little more in addition to the name and address of the *destinataire* than the thrust of a subjunctive, a desire as soon formulated as abandoned. Quatrain 88 fuses the sensuous desires of the poet with the romantic portrait of the femme fatale (evoked by her "ongles diaphanes") lost in reverie (*O.c.* 98):

Que la Dame aux doux airs vainqueurs
Qui songe 9 Boulevard Lannes
T'ouvre, mon billet, comme un cœur
Avec ses ongles diaphanes.

May the lady with the sweet conquering air
Who daydreams at 9 Boulevard Lannes
Open you, my letter, like a heart
With her diaphanous nails.

The third verse features the verb on which the quatrain pivots, the ically charged "ouvre," subtly positioned between "te" and "mon," the pronouns representing the principals in this delightfully enticing

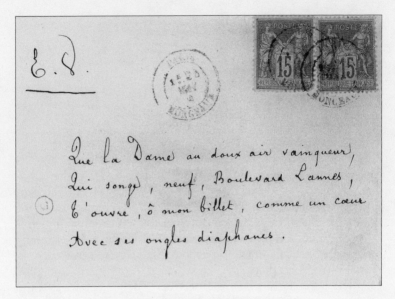

Manuscript of the stamped and postmarked original version of "Que la Dame . . ." of "Les Loisirs de la poste" to Méry Laurent (Bibliothèque Littéraire Jacques Doucet). The transcription of this appears on p. 177.

drama. The combination of the centrally placed "billet" of the third verse with the correspondingly positioned "doux" of the first yields the "secret" identity of the quatrain as love letter, *billet doux*.

The specific antinarrativity of the *Vers de circonstance* derived from their proliferation of incompleted anecdotes has important implications not only in terms of providing a new model of writing but also as imposing certain demands on the reader. Curiously contradicting their frivolous character, the more than 450 *Vers de circonstance* (distributed, as in the Pléiade edition, on the average with five poems per page for one hundred pages) are extremely taxing to read. To borrow Richard Poirier's terms, if not exactly his meaning, it is an exercise in "grim reading." Poirier's definition of Modernism as "the phenomenon of grim reading" actually refers to the "degree of textual intimidation felt in the act of reading" and the idea that Modernist texts are necessarily and rewardingly difficult (272). But unlike that of Mallarmé's "major" works of the late period, which undoubtedly would fall into Poirier's categories, the "difficulty" of the *Vers de cir-*

Cache dans un manchon de martre . . .
Ô Poste ou tends d'un doigt mutin
Sept, Impasse Guelma, Montmartre,
Ce mot pour André Desboutin
9 Cité Véron

Stamped and postmarked manuscript of "Les Loisirs de la poste," "Cache dans un manchon de martre . . ." to André Desboutin (Bibliothèque Littéraire Jacques Doucet).

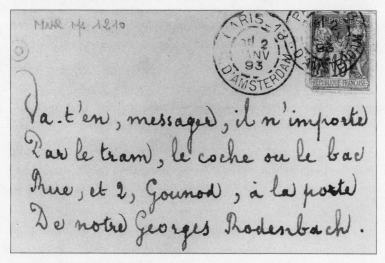

Va-t-en, messager, il n'importe
Par le tram, le coche ou le bac
Rue, et 2, Gounod, à la poste
De notre Georges Rodenbach.

Stamped and postmarked manuscript of "Les Loisirs de la poste," "Va-t-en, messager, il n'importe" to Georges Rodenbach (Bibliothèque Littéraire Jacques Doucet).

constance lies not in hermeticism or unconventional syntax but in a boredom created by fragmentation, repetition, and sheer volume. Unlike the difficult Modernist texts of, say, Joyce, Eliot, or Williams, which, as Poirier correctly perceives, work paradoxically to *reinvoke* the connections between artist and audience *severed* by the growth of mass culture, the example of literature offered by the *Vers de circonstance* read as an ensemble can only further alienate the reader: there is no promise standing within or behind the work that the connections he might labor to produce will eventually surface as a reward for his efforts. In stark contrast to the fourth from last verse of Eliot's *Waste Land*, "These fragments I have shored against my ruins" (69) (which is, paradoxically but tellingly, a perfect line of iambic pentameter), and unlike Williams's verses opening the preface to *Paterson*, which both state an *art poétique* and prescribe a method of reading, "To make a start, / out of particulars / and make them general, rolling / up the sum, by defective means—" (3), the pieces of the *Vers de circonstance* are not extracted from a larger whole that one might work toward reassembling. Instead, the white space that separates them is given full value and not designed to be trespassed on. The *Vers de circonstance* are neither the mere "debris of a very lofty hope" as Robert Vivier has claimed (207) nor quite the "fragile microcosms of a crisis in poetry" (Sonnenfeld 72), because, in spite of their fragmentary appearance, they presuppose no broken unities. In this refusal of integration lie the elements of a radically new concept of literature.

Up to this point I have explored the *carte de visite* model in terms of its mobility and a number of concepts such as communication and antinarrativity that cluster around it. I would like to turn now to another aspect of the *carte de visite* that emerges when it is contrasted with the monument, that is, its triviality. As we have seen, "occasional verse" is a term that covers a wide spectrum of poetic behavior from the highly respected elegy or epitaph to the largely spurned or ignored "nonserious" (and often unpublished) pieces that occupy the fringes of the work of major and minor literary figures alike. When these pieces *are* recognized by the critical establishment, they are viewed as documents to be perused and plundered and not as monuments to be read. The *Vers de circonstance* are a prime example of this tendency. Critics such as Richard and Davies who make ample use of the minor works tend, however, to see through these texts and avoid actually seeing them. The circumstantial pieces are served up as evidence used to underscore insights about the major works. When, as in the deconstructive strategies discussed at the opening of this chapter, minor texts are treated as monuments, that is, discussed in and of themselves at least to some degree before being sacrificed to (usually radical) claims about the major works, they are necessarily promoted to undue literary stature by virtue of that very treatment, despite claims to the contrary. It is difficult to cite instances of studies of the literary fringe proper because of their tendency to transform peripheries into centers.

Is it then possible to critically address oneself to the marginal without "corrupting" it into respectability? Perhaps not, because of the institutionalizing nature of critical attention, or perhaps for an even more basic reason: *Why* treat the nonserious seriously, if not to show its underlying seriousness or its capacity for making serious statements? One might claim, of course, that the author himself recognized the importance of a so-called minor text. This has been the strategy of an increasing number of critics who are writing on Mallarmé's fashion magazine, *La Dernière Mode*. There would appear to be a tacit agreement that it is de rigueur to open one's discussion by quoting at least the last phrases of Mallarmé's autobiographical "confession" about the journal:

J'ai . . . tenté de rédiger tout seul, toilettes, bijou, mobilier, et jusqu'aux théâtres et aux menus de dîner, un journal la *Dernière Mode*, dont les huit ou dix numéros parus servent encore quand je les dévêts de leur poussière à me faire longtemps rêver. (*O.c.* 664)

I . . . tried to write, by myself, attire, jewel, furniture, even including the theater and dinner menus, a journal, the *Latest Fashion*, whose eight or ten issues that appeared still serve, when I dust them off, to set me daydreaming a long while.

Mallarmé, of course, made explicit no such claims about the *Vers de circonstance*, although the fact that he recopied the vast majority of them in his private notebooks, that he published seven of the dedicatory quatrains written on copies of the published version of "L'Après-midi d'un faune" in the student journal *Au Quartier latin*, and that he so actively pursued the never-realized plans for the book form publication of the "Loisirs" would seem to attest to a certain degree of commitment to them and a more than sentimental appreciation of their value.

In any case, I would hope that this chapter could strive toward the unlikely goal of treating a marginal, trivial body of work as such. Unable to find suitable models in literary criticism, I turned to the social sciences and to Michael Thompson's provocative book, *Rubbish Theory*, which is a semiotic study of the dynamics of rubbish in contemporary society. For Thompson, objects in our culture are assigned to one of two overt categories, the "transient," whose values decrease over time, and the "durable," whose values increase (7). In between the regions of fixed assumptions established by these categories is a region of flexibility inhabited by objects of zero and unchanging value that constitute the covert category Thompson labels "rubbish." The attractiveness of Thompson's model is its ability to account for change, as when, in one of his primary examples, the woven silk pictures called Stevengraphs, touristic souvenirs from the Victorian era that had practically no market, suddenly became valued collector's items in the 1960's. Thompson accounts for the transformation as follows:

My hypothesis is that this covert rubbish category . . . is able to provide the path for the seemingly impossible transfer of an object from transience to durability. What I believe happens is that a transient object gradually declining in value and in expected life-span may slide across into rubbish. . . . It just continues to exist in a timeless and valueless limbo where at some later date . . . it has the chance of being discovered. . . . The delightful consequence of this hypothesis is that, in order to study the social control of value, we have to study rubbish. (9–10)

The process has interesting though limited congruencies with deconstructive practices in that it posits a third category that throws neat dualisms into imbalance. Thompson's models operate by a making visible of the covert third category just as Derrida does with the trace, the supplement, the pharmakon, the parergon, or any of the numerous "undecidables." But for my purposes the initial attraction of rubbish theory was the extent to which the parallel between ordinary rubbish and "literary rubbish" might be drawn. Certainly, if literary rubbish exists, the trivial pole of occasional literature would be a worthy contender for inclusion in the category. Furthermore, the kind of revaluation I have previously analyzed as the move from the trivial to the monumental (as with the Ben Jonson invitation poem that becomes an anthology piece) could perhaps be accounted for in a somewhat more rigorous manner. And third, I wondered if rubbish theory could further our understanding of Mallarmé's *Vers de circonstance*, which can, for the most part, accurately be described as verse inscribed on what otherwise, once used, would have been destined for the rubbish pile: (emptied) jugs of Calvados, pebbles gathered at the beach, envelopes, or Easter egg shells (the "Eventails" would have to be exempted from this category).

It is when Thompson shifts away from ordinary rubbish to a consideration of the relationship between rubbish and the contemporary arts that his argument is most pertinent to the present study. He portrays the conceptualist movement of the late 1960's and 1970's as iconoclastic, its practitioners as monument destroyers, in a vein similar to the way in which I have been trying to highlight what I take to be Mallarmé's most radical ventures. Thompson states that it is "the importance of the non-importance of the art object [that] is possibly the central tenet of conceptual art, certainly . . . the most important politically." Though objects are still produced, they are not important as objects. "Conceptual artists tend to see their work as a kind of superior art theory: a neutral, logical, even austere, meta-art" (125). Lucy Lippard, in *Six Years: The Dematerialization of the Art Object from 1966 to 1972*, notes that although "dematerialization" is an inaccurate term because of the persistence of the object in recent art production, there tends to be a deemphasis on its material aspects such as uniqueness, permanence, and decorative attractiveness (5). These are precisely the traits that characterize the traditional monument.

Thompson's acute observations about the intimacy between rubbish and art and the recent deemphasis on the monumental qualities of the art object provide a site on which we may develop certain parallels between conceptual art forms and Mallarmé's *Vers de circonstance*. As I suggested at the end of the previous chapter, it will be necessary as well to switch the focus of my study away from architecture and toward the sculptural avant-garde, although the conceptualists would probably resist such categorization. It is not my intention to enter into the polemic, but it appears that until quite recently the architectural community has been viewed as conservative in comparison with avant-garde movements in the other arts. Critics have claimed that the rad-

ical innovations we have witnessed in recent years in the arts have no
parallels in architecture.[9] Furthermore, I am interested in pursuing the
move from the monumental to the trivial in Mallarmé, which directly
poses the question of the object as opposed to that of the monument.
Recent innovations in architecture helped me to account for a crisis of
the monumental staged in "Un Coup de dés," but if we are to go beyond
this we must shift focus accordingly.

In his article "The Expanding and Disappearing Work of Art," the
American art critic Lawrence Alloway notes a fundamental change
that has occurred in art theory in recent years: "The minimum re-
quirement of esthetic identity in a work of art has been legibility as
an object, a degree of compactness (so that the object is united, com-
posed, stable). In the sixties, a number of non-compact art forms (dif-
fuse or nearly imperceptible) have proliferated" (207). It is precisely
this move away from the locatable and colossal integrity of the object
that I have traced in my discussion of Mallarmé's displacement of the
monumental. But in doing so it was necessary to come up with an
alternative model, a radically different conception of artistic prac-
tice, which I found in the *carte de visite*. The artistic avant-garde
would seem to have reached strikingly parallel conclusions. In the
following somewhat cryptic excerpt from a 1970 radio symposium,
critic Lucy Lippard discussed the importance of the *context* of the art
object with artists Dan Graham and Carl André:

DG: The artist is defined by the product he makes, but not necessarily by
    himself. I was interested in a system that is tied into a medium rather
    than in my saying I am an artist.
LL: A sort of giver and receiver situation.
DG: That's very important. The recipient effect is as important as the giver
    part. The object is just a cause.
CA: I think the object is just a locus, embodying some sort of transaction
    which is between all those things we are talking about—the reader,
    the recipient, the sender, the social situation, the art, whatever. (*Six
    Years* 155–56)

It is this notion of the object demoted from full presence to a mere
locus that interests me as a starting point for a comparison of trends
in contemporary art and Mallarmé's *Vers de circonstance*. A great deal
has been written about the status of the object in Mallarmé's poetry.
The most perceptive commentators have noted a rich, even produc-

tive ambivalence in his attitude toward the material object. I would like to open my discussion by citing Richard, however, who unlike Bersani, de Man, or Blanchot[10] appears to be unaware of the contradictory stances he notes in Mallarmé and therefore states them all the more emphatically, attributing to Mallarmé both a Sartrean nausea and a Freudian fixation in regard to the object. In separate chapters Richard paradoxically notes: "at the starting point of his entire esthetic one finds an existential refusal of *matter*" (376) and "the strange material fetishism that dominates an entire zone of Mallarméan creation" (345). In the first citation Richard would seem to be referring to the question of the abolition of the object I discussed in Chapter 1 and relying on his analyses of the major poems, particularly those of the Tournon crisis period. In the second instance, however, the citation concerns the later poetry and particularly the *Vers de circonstance*. He continues as follows:

So many little poems inscribed on stones, on handkerchiefs, on candies, or on reed pipes reveal, beyond their playfulness, the obsession with a material support, the search for a solid base to be given to the operation of the imagination. The stone testifies in its own way for the poem written on the stone; it constitutes its guarantee, its ballast. Thus a poetry of lace prefers to lean concretely on the same reality that it nevertheless proposes . . . to volatize and to reduce to emptiness, to the abstract, to language. (345)

What most intrigues me in Richard's analysis is the concept of the object as "ballast." Evidently he conceived of the relationship between Mallarmé's circumstantial verse and its objects as one of dependency, the "lightweight" verse depending on the "substance" of the object to anchor it, to give it (in the terms of the present study) a certain degree of monumental stability. This is, of course, the principal function of ballast, which is anything heavy carried in a moving vehicle to balance it. But ballast can be thought of in a more abstract way as a supplement to be added to or subtracted from the mobile; as such it is neither an integral part of the vehicle nor clearly separable from it, but somehow inhabits an indeterminate space between the vehicle and the other.

It is rather in this sense that I see the object operating in Mallarmé's *Vers de circonstance*. It functions as a placeholder, and can be conceived of as both lending weight to the verse and, as in the expression "jeter du lest," as that which can be thrown overboard or sacrificed to avoid a catastrophe. The implications of the concept are playfully significant with regard to Mallarmé's "naufrage" poems, and especially for "Un Coup de dés," where we might speculate that the discarding of jetsam at the properly calculated moment might have kept the "navire" afloat. The "Maître," in fact, who previously grasped the helm, must abandon it and prepare himself to throw overboard "l'unique Nombre qui ne peut pas / être un autre / Esprit / pour le jeter / dans la tempête" (*O.c.* 462–63) ("the unique Number that cannot / be another / Spirit / to throw it / into the storm"), but he hesitates. The dice throw here is perhaps an analogue of the jettisoning of ballast that might have procured the ship's safety by averting disaster and allowing the vessel to "en reployer la division et passe fier" (*O.c.* 463) ("fold up division and pass by proudly").

Ballast (much like the *carte de visite*) is that which, having no intrinsic value or meaning of its own, acquires purpose and function through its installment or removal. The addition or subtraction of ballast is only significant in terms of its (dis)placement. It is in this light that it seems to me not only possible but profitable to compare the functioning of Mallarmé's *Vers de circonstance* with the conceptual art movement, although the projects might at first seem contradictory. For whereas the conceptualists propose the elimination or the devaluation of the object as a means of attacking established notions of art, Mallarmé can be seen to shake the very foundation of literature (already a "conceptual" art to the extent that it does not depend on the unique art object) by *attaching* it to the object. It is not the question of the art object as entity, of its appearance or disappearance per se, but the conception of it as a semiotic placeholder that forms the basis for comparison.

One way in which artists have sought to undermine the sacredness of the art object is through an embracing of the self-destructing or self-terminating "object." Among the most outstanding examples we might cite Robert Smithson's *Partially Buried Woodshed* erected at Kent State University in Ohio. Smithson piled twenty cartloads of earth on the already partially ruined structure until the central beam cracked. The work shows the centrality of the notion of entropy to current art theory, which James Wines defines as follows:

Entropy, as a measure of phenomenology, may bring to mind the unpleasant specter of disaster. In science entropy concerns the irreversible degradation of matter and energy in the universe. With respect to art, the psychological

Above. Robert Smithson. *Partially Buried Woodshed.* Kent, Ohio. January 1970. (Photograph by Robert Smithson, courtesy of the John Weber Gallery, New York.)

At left. Marcel Duchamp. *The Bride Stripped Bare by Her Bachelors, Even (The Large Glass).* 1915–23. Oil, lead wire, foil, dust, and varnish on glass, 8′11″ × 5′7″. (Philadelphia Museum of Art: Bequest of Katherine S. Dreier.)

and cultural intensity of this natural catastrophe suggests an "aesthetic of chance" approaching heroic and ritual dimensions. The artist's conventional response to nature has usually been attracted to those stable and inert manifestations which offer reassurance of an objectified, rational, world— evidence of the importance of man's own physicality. As science has substituted its theories of relativity, infinity, dematerialization, and implosion, the artist and architect have been gradually forced to accept a less orderly view of their environment. (269–70)

It is the notion of an "aesthetic of chance" and the prominent place of the aleatory in art that may offer the most interesting parallels with the *Vers de circonstance*. Note that the term in question does not refer to art forms lacking design or purpose. Rather, such art opens itself to external forces and welcomes their intervention. One project, by Arakawa, featured a painting displayed at the Dwan Gallery inscribed with the challenge: "If possible, steal any one of these drawings including this sentence." The subsequent stealing of the sentence and other drawings displayed was seen not as a derailment of the exhibition but simply as its natural outcome. In this case the "art object," if we can still use such terminology, involved not only the artist, Arakawa, but also the group who stole the paintings, who became coartists through the very intervention of their illegal action. One further example will suffice to illustrate this aspect. James Wines describes Duchamp's *Bride Stripped Bare by Her Bachelors, Even (The Large Glass)* as art that forfeits the "mythology of the artist's 'hand' and the specific nature of objects [by implying] that these objects were never meant to be looked *at* or contain an intrinsic message in themselves; but rather, to function as semaphores in space which changed the spectator's attitudes towards the immediate surroundings. . . . The periphery became the art and the object only a shadow" (270). Duchamp's own characterization of the glass as a "projection of an invisible fourth dimension" was confirmed and perhaps clarified when *The Large Glass* was accidentally broken returning from an exhibition. Duchamp's response was a welcoming of the aleatory as an improvement: "It's better with the breaks, a hundred times better. It's the destiny of things" (quoted in Wines 271).

All of the *Vers de circonstance* function, like the *carte de visite*, like Carl André's object as locus, in the interval between giver and receiver. Especially as Mallarmé's celebrity grew, the verses, in spite of their often undeniably frivolous nature and sometimes questionable artistic (or even technical) merit, came to be regarded as the ultimate gift from the master poet.[11] They may be seen in conjunction with the Freudian notion of the interrelations of the series faeces, penis, child, gift, money (see "On the Transformation of Instincts with Special Reference to Anal Erotism") as the detachable object that defines the space of the abstract concept "relationship" itself. The analogy is not quite as far-fetched as it might at first seem, especially when we consider the nonprecious, even rubbishlike character of the majority of the gift objects Mallarmé wrote poetry on or used it to accompany. Whereas it would be an exaggeration to qualify the *Vers de circonstance* as a self-destructing art, we must note the verse's undeniable tendency toward the ephemeral. In the "Loisirs," the surface that the poetry is inscribed on is discardable in that it is normally the envelope that is thrown away once the communication has been received. A similar logic can be seen in the inscription of poetry on the jug of Calvados: here it is the container and not the contained that receives the valued poetic inscription. The poems on Easter eggs take advantage of the egg as a traditional symbol of fragility and point to the association of poetry and the ephemeral in spite of the gold ink that was used to engrave them. The poetry that accompanied the gifts of candied fruits often invokes an implicit contrast between the ephemerality of the consumable gift fruits and the constancy of Mallarmé's yearly poetic offering, as in these two quatrains (O.c. 120, 123):

> Si par un regard de fée haute
> Ou lasse seuls voilà mangés
> Mes fruits constants, c'est votre faute
> A vous qui non plus ne changez.

> If by a high or tired fairy's look
> Behold there now are eaten only
> My constant fruits, it's your fault,
> You, who are unchanged too.

> Grâce aux fruits humble stratagème,
> Amie on peut nous envier
> Un souhait proféré le même
> Depuis tant de premiers Janvier.

> Thanks to the fruits, humble strategy,
> Friend, one could envy us
> A wish proferred, always the same,
> Since so many first of Januaries.

The problematics of Mallarmé's poetics in terms of its relation to the question of the "aesthetic of chance" mentioned above are far too complex to detail here. Certainly the major thrust of most readings of *Igitur* and "Un Coup de dés" has been to attempt to account for the predicament of man faced with the unpredictable forces of the natural universe. What I would hope to do in this space is simply to pose the question of the validity of the traditional readings of these texts by describing what I perceive as an aesthetic of chance in the *Vers de circonstance*. Once the "Loisirs" are delivered into the hands of the post office, for example, their destiny is indeed left to chance, and as we have shown, constantly threatened with nondelivery and the possibility of ending up in the dead-letter office. Mallarmé's recognition of the verse's susceptibility to "dérivation" provides the major thematic thrust of this quatrain (*O.c.* 95):

> Lettre, va, le plus tôt c'est
> Le mieux sans que l'on t'égare
> Chez Monsieur Pierre Sosset,
> Ruette, Belgique—en gare.

> Letter, go, the earlier the better
> Without being led astray
> Chez Monsieur Pierre Sosset,
> Ruette, Belgique—at the train station.

The "égarement" or straying of the expression "le plus tôt c'est le mieux," that is, the unnatural break it receives when divided by the exigencies of the octosyllabic line, portends the potentiality of failure. In a similar fashion the trajectory of the stone skipping across the sea, a felicitous image, is nevertheless threatened at every moment with falling into irretrievable oblivion at the bottom of the ocean. In the following "galets" the fear of shipwreck, the result of the unpredictable inconstancy of the seas, dominates (*O.c.* 172, 174):

> Le seul rêve qui dans vos yeux purs navigua
> Ne naufrage jamais Mademoiselle Helga.

May the only dream that sails in your pure eyes
Never shipwreck, Mademoiselle Helga.

Monsieur Fraisse n'a la frousse
Que si la mer se courrouce.

Monsieur Fraisse is only in a funk
When the sea becomes enraged.

In the preceding quatrain and distichs chance would appear to be not only a prospectively destructive force, ready to sabotage man-made structures, and especially syntax, the structurality of literature itself, but also the supreme "space" of creative potential. That is, it is only at the point where the poetic offering enters the no-man's land between sender and receiver that it constitutes itself as poetry. This quatrain (one of the "Dons de fruits glacés") obliquely expresses on several levels a concern for the "in between" as the unchartable space of the poetic (*O.c.* 129):

> Un an qui succède à l'autre
> Toujours nous tend
> > pensez-y
> Ce fruit par le froid saisi
> Comme mon cœur ni le vôtre.

> A year that follows another
> Always offers us
> > think of it
> This fruit seized by the cold
> Unlike my heart or yours.

Thematically the verse opposes the same and the other as a perpetual problem: this year and the succeeding as always creating anew the hazardous space of an unspecifiable temporality. This year and the next or this year and the last are not locatable polarities but rather shifting markers in a continuum. Similarly, the space between "mon cœur" and "le vôtre" is the very definition and possibility of difference, posed here not in temporal but in human terms. The "toujours" marks the inescapability of the "in between" and the verb "tend," which signals the act of offering, hypostatizes the space between linking not only year to year and my heart to yours but also the temporal dimension to the human: the years are linked to "us," "Un an . . . /

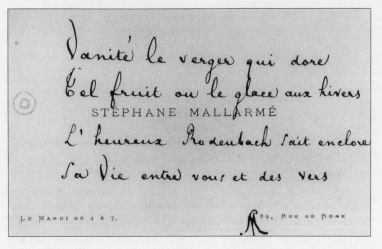

Carte de visite with "Dons de fruits glacés" manuscript, "Vanité le verger qui dore . . ." (Bibliothèque Littéraire Jacques Doucet).

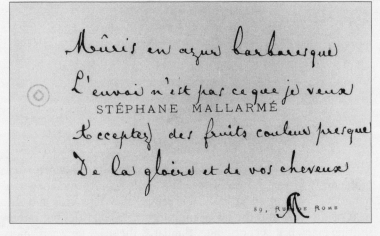

Carte de visite with "Dons de fruits glacés" manuscript, "Meuris en azur barbaresque . . ." (Bibliothèque Littéraire Jacques Doucet).

Toujours *nous* tend." The fruit is the concretization of the gift, both the actual object offered and the literature (quatrain) that accompanies it, the fruit of the creative space. This thematic play is then reinforced doubly by the verse's arrangement on the page. In order to emphasize the play between inner and outer, same and different, Mallarmé chose here to use the *rime embrassée a b b a* rhyme scheme rather than the *rime croisée a b a b*, which is the overwhelmingly preferred form in the *Vers de circonstance*. The separation of the second verse into two levels to create a stanza of five instead of four lines allows for a more precise articulation of the middle. "Pensez-y," the verb placed in emphatic position, further suggests the space in between through the employment of the hyphen, the syntactical emblem of the bridge, as well as through its command linking the human to the poetic proposition itself.[12]

We can pursue this valorization of the space of chance in yet another context. As Wines so perceptively notes, the avant-garde must strive toward a definition of art *as* space and not of art *in* space (268). One step toward achieving this goal is a problematization of the perimeters of the artwork. In the art gallery or museum, he notes, the sanction of *context* predetermines the reaction of the spectator to *content*. But in open spaces "distractions abound, perimeters are nonexistent except by implication, visual access is uncontrolled, and the focality of the exhibition sanctuary is unavailable" (273). The frame that we conventionally put around the art object is both the confirmation of a desire to perceive the object as integral and unassailable and the means of doing so. One artist who experiments in interesting ways with the question of the boundaries of the artwork is Robert Smithson. He developed a series of "Sites/Nonsites" that consisted in the visiting of an actual geographical site, often a New Jersey industrial waste area, and collecting a number of relics such as rocks, ore, and other matter that are then displayed in bins in the gallery or the museum as the Nonsite. The result is that both Site (the actual geographical location) and Nonsite (the museum or gallery piece) are simultaneously present and absent, inevitably invoking each other. The Site frames the Nonsite as a macrocosm to the microcosm, whereas the Nonsite "frames" the Site as representation to the represented. The perimeters of the work are expanded (or contracted) *en abyme*:

Robert Smithson. *Nonsite, Oberhausen, Germany.* 1968. (Courtesy of the John Weber Gallery, New York.)

The land or ground from the Site is placed *in* the art (Nonsite) rather than the art placed *on* the ground. The Nonsite is a container within another container—the room. The plot or yard outside is yet another container. Two-dimensional and three-dimensional things trade places with each other in the range of convergence. Large scale becomes small. Small scale becomes large. A point on a map expands to the size of the land mass. A land mass contracts into a point. Is the site a reflection of the Nonsite (mirror), or is it the other way around? (Smithson, quoted in Hobbs 105)

Smithson's work provides a curious critique of representation (with striking parallels to my analysis of "La Déclaration foraine" in Chapter 3) in that Site and Nonsite become so implicated in each other as to appear ultimately indistinguishable. Like the occasional poem, Smithson's work questions the very viability of the notion of an autonomous work of art. Both the Nonsite and the occasional poem point unerringly to extratextual events or extramural sites, making them dependent on that which is "exterior" to the work. But at the same time, the Nonsite quite literally contains the Site within its frame much as the occasional poem "contains" the occasion within its verse.

Whereas a monumental occasional poetry necessarily participates in just such an interdependent relationship with the circumstances that occasion it, it nevertheless imposes itself as a completely autonomous construction, entirely self-present and self-contained. The writing model that emerges from the *Vers de circonstance*, however, implicates a whole network of interrelated and to some extent indistinguishable components. Like Derrida's "Envois," that part of *The Post Card* that is dedicated to his unnamed correspondent ("the entire book is *for* you, but for this very reason dedicated to 'to' [dédié à "à"], devoted to the dative" [78]) is also an art in movement toward its indirect object, an art of the asymptote, in transit and intransitive, indicating always the approach *toward*. The dative, of course, implies its Latin roots in the verb "to give." In contrast to the monument, this gift poetry is never self-sufficient. At once dependent on the object it is engraved on or that it accompanies and pending toward a potential receiver, it is always directed, never autonomous, always between *expéditeur* and *destinataire*.

Viewed within Mallarmé's entire oeuvre, the *Vers de circonstance* become a comment on the very circumstantiality of literature; it is an art always to the side of its target. In the "Loisirs" especially we see Mallarmé's refusal to give a privileged place to poetry: its place is no longer *in* the envelope, hermetically sealed within a three-dimensional frame, but instead *on* the envelope. Once the palpable frame of the envelope is dispensed with as container and becomes itself the place of inscription, the peripheries of the message become indeterminate. These peripheries, rather than acting as a stabilizing frame like the controlled establishment context of the art object, allow for the intervention of distractions, much as the open air site prevents the formation of a specific focality. The "Loisirs" are paradoxically "at home" in the nonsite between the addresser and the addressee and decidedly out of place in the controlled environment of the anthology.

The "Loisirs" are thus an art inscribed on a surface that promises

no depths, no hidden messages, nothing *sous-entendu*. Like the pun
implied in Site/Nonsite, where the seen and the unseen are both al-
ways visible and hidden, where represented and representation are
always displacements of one another, Mallarmé's quatrains conflate
the level of the phatic and the message: the move toward establishing
contact *is the message itself*. The writing points not to the three di-
mensionality of the object but to itself as it plays along its surfaces.
The *Vers de circonstance* are an art that functions on the empty en-
velope, on the yolkless egg, on the empty jug. In fact, we might read
it as a kind of graffiti, a nonsacred writing that defaces public surfaces.
The public becomes a place for unauthorized private expression and
the message becomes blatantly available for all to see. In their cir-
culation the *Vers de circonstance* attest to an extraordinary sociability,
a de-solemnizing and democratizing of literature, making poetry a
suitable vehicle for even the most trivial of circumstances.

In a notebook in which Mallarmé recopied and reworked most of
the address quatrains of the "Loisirs" he wrote, "à ajouter pour com-
pléter les 80" (*O.c.* 1504) ("to be added in order to make 80"), fol-
lowed by fifteen names, which indicates that this verse was intended
to serve a purpose beyond assuring the delivery of his mail. The col-
lection of quatrains can thus be read as a parody of the poetic apos-
trophe, a theatrically self-conscious addressing of society and culture.
If he had published the projected "plaquette," Mallarmé would have
set up a pantheon, a real, although deeply ironic tribute to his friends
and the intellectual elite of his time who serve, by virtue of their
names and addresses, as the material for verbal skill (*adresse*) in
rhyme. Receiving top honors: the post office. The first paragraph of
the projected preface reads: "Cette petite publication, tout à l'hon-
neur de la Poste. Aucune des adresses en vers collationnées ici n'a
manqué son destinataire" (*O.c.* 1503) ("This little publication, all
in honor of the Postal Service. None of the addresses in verse col-
lected here have missed their addressees"). It is the postman who is
the successful reader of this new poetry and thus is able to make the
letters arrive.[13] No interpretative violence need be done to the qua-
trains to read them; they are self-evident as is that letter left "face
down, address uppermost" on the table by the queen, or crumpled
and thrust carelessly in a division of a pasteboard cardrack by the min-
ister in Poe's short story, "The Purloined Letter." This is a marginal,
exterior, two-dimensional phenomenon rather than a poetry of

depth. Mallarmé has come full circle from the poetry outlined in the youthful manifesto "L'Art pour tous" ("Art for All") where he demanded that "toute chose sacrée et qui veut demeurer sacrée s'enveloppe de mystère" (*O.c.* 257) ("all things sacred that wish to remain sacred envelop themselves in mystery"). We witness here a demystification of the envelope. This is a poetry that points to itself rather than to some latent signification, a literature whose ideal reader is also its disseminator (*O.c.* 88):

> Sans t'étendre dans l'herbe verte
> Naïf distributeur, mets-y
> Du tien, cours chez Madame Berthe
> Manet, par Meulan, à Mézy.
>
> Without stretching out in the green grass
> Naive distributor, put a bit of yourself
> In it, run to Madame Berthe
> Manet's at Meulan, in Mézy.

Here it becomes clear that the proper name inscribed on the envelope is not necessarily the quatrain's proper addressee. Such literature does not need to arrive at its "destination" before being read; it is a literature not only read but written *en route*. As Barbara Johnson notes in her discussion of Lacan's statement that "une lettre arrive toujours à destination" ("a letter always arrives at its destination"), if the letter's destination is not its literal addressee, and if "destination" is not necessarily a place that preexists the letter's movement (144), then "destination" loses its sense as a terminus defining one point of a polarity and becomes instead any point in a continuum. Mallarmé's "Loisir" quoted above thus is the illustration par excellence of this concept: the *facteur* or postman, the very vehicle of literature's movement, is invited not only to relay the letter but to put a bit of himself into it ("mets-y du tien"). In so doing he proves himself to be at once writer, reader, and disseminator, effacing the difference between these functions.

As I have shown in the preceding pages, one can sabotage the art object as a political, economic, and aesthetic entity by destroying it, by making it unpossessable, or alternatively, by mass producing it so that possession is no longer the sign (in Thompson's terms) of a *durable*; its sheer numbers decree it a candidate for the rubbish pile. In this spirit a number of avant-garde movements have attacked the established order by trying to eliminate the scarcity of art. Rather than being revered for its longevity, art becomes just one more product to be consumed. One group of artists who best exemplify this aspect of contemporary aesthetics are those engaged in correspondence art. Because of the extreme diversity of the movement and the refusal of all conventional categories by the participants, mail or correspondence art is difficult to define. In general we might say that it is any art that uses the international postal system as support (in the sense that nonmail arts use canvas, paper, iron, and wood as support) and, as one commentator puts it, "as far as the mail art piece is concerned, the only thing that really counts is getting answers" (Crane and Stofflet xv–xviii). That is, the mail artist produces a "piece," often a postcard, a photocopied collage, a questionnaire, a concrete poem, a reproducible drawing, and so on, and mails it to at least one but generally to dozens, hundreds, or even thousands of potential receivers, often but not necessarily other mail artists. As Ulmer has remarked about On Kawara's postcards, mailing the piece activates a kind of "social sculpture" ("The Post-Age" 56). In other words, as with Mallarmé's "Loisirs," a contour of time and space is carved out when the piece is sent through the mail, establishing a network in which sender and receiver are linked in a system of social transactions by means of the mobile art. The posting of the piece opens it up to the vagaries of the aleatory, which are usually welcomed as with the Duchamp *Large Glass* discussed above. Like Mallarmé's *Vers de circonstance*, much mail art relies on the "found object" and revels in the very commonness of its materials. Thomas Albright notes that as correspondence art uses "ephemera, banalities, and disposables as its materials, it sometimes comes uncomfortably close to being trash or junk mail" (Crane and Stofflet 230). Correspondence art has been called "easy, cheap, unpretentious, and democratic" (xvii), although as many mail artists reject these categories as accept them. Some operate from a liberal or radical political stance, hoping to bring art into everyone's mail as well as into the street, and others see their enterprise as destined for a small elite.

Although, to my knowledge, the mail art community has not officially recognized Mallarmé as one of its forerunners, it is clear that his savvy manipulation of postal system technology through "Les Loisirs de la poste" and the other *Vers de circonstance* circulated through the mail constitutes an implicit critique and reinvention of the notion of address inherent to lyric poetry as it was articulated in the nineteenth century. If the conventions of the lyric invited us to read such poetry as an "I" addressed to a "you," in both Mallarmé's art and contemporary mail art the "address" is not merely posed as pronominal, is not merely constituted by the vocative, but is in fact inherent in the postal system. Mallarmé's inundation of the post office with his "mail art" contributes to the modernist problematization of the lyric by replacing a tradition of personalized address with the anonymity of the modern institution.

Perhaps the best-known "organization" of mail artists is Ray Johnson's New York Correspondance School. In an article on / manifesto of the school, A. M. Fine describes the network as "a permanent monument to the essence of the transitory" (Crane and Stofflet 122). In taking up and repositioning some of the terms we have been discussing, this label points to one current of much contemporary art that seeks to reverse the established hierarchies of the art world simply by inverting traditionally opposed values such as the permanent and the transitory, the monumental and the trivial, the essential and the contingent. An example is the enterprise of retitling as an act of art conferral. In Smithson's "Tour of the Monuments of Passaic," a New Jersey suburb is suggested as a candidate for replacing Rome as the Eternal City. The "zero panorama" of the banks of the Passaic River and the new construction under way suggest *"ruins in reverse . . . the opposite of the 'romantic ruin' because the buildings don't fall into ruin after they are built but rather rise into ruin before they are built"* (quoted in Holt 54). A sewage outlet is viewed as art when it is renamed "The Fountain Monument"; a pumping derrick with a long pipe attached to it becomes "The Great Pipes Monument." Comparable strategies can be seen in Claes Oldenburg's work. In the fall of 1967, when asked to participate in a city outdoor sculpture show, one of his suggestions was simply to call Manhattan a work of art. Oldenburg's series of proposed monuments rely on a similar principle: the ordinary, banal object is made "excruciatingly banal" when blown up to colossal size: the baked potato, the wing nut, the saw, the Good Humor Bar all propose themselves as artworks through a monumentalization of the quotidian.

But it seems to me that to read Mallarmé's *Vers de circonstance* in these terms would be misguided. Most traditional poetry (including

Robert Smithson. *The Fountain Monument: Side View.* 1967. (Instamatic snapshot by Robert Smithson, courtesy of the John Weber Gallery, New York.)

Robert Smithson. *The Great Pipes Monument.* 1968. (Instamatic snapshot by Robert Smithson, courtesy of the John Weber Gallery, New York.)

Mallarmé's early work, the "Tombeaux," even "Un Coup de dés") would seem "at home" inscribed in stone, drafted on parchment, or printed on the pages of the poetry collection or anthology. But Mallarmé's singular practice of inscribing the poetic on pebbles, fans, envelopes, Easter eggs, and jugs; on copies of his poems or on calling cards or stationery accompanying gifts of teapots, mirrors, handkerchiefs, bonbons, flowers, photographs, and postcards; and for "occasions" such as returning a fish net, celebrating Méry Laurent's intimates in verse entwined around a pole ("Autour d'un mirliton"), sending thanks for a gift of prunes, presenting a sample of his handwriting, apropos of the exclamation point, and proving that there are rhymes in French ending in -or, appears to be a willful misplacement of the poetic, an unconventional juxtaposition of poetry and the quotidian. The established view of poetry as a product of high culture makes even the enumeration of such poetic practices either comical or disturbing. Unlike Picasso's appropriation of the found object in, for instance, the mounting of an old bicycle seat on handlebars to represent a bull's head placed on the walls of a museum, the *Vers de circonstance* do not produce a monumentalization of the quotidian (this is not to confuse the notion of monumentalization with the production of a "durable": I would imagine that the surviving "manuscripts" of the "Eventails" would command a fortune at a literary auction). Perhaps if Mallarmé had produced only one "Eventail," the novelty of the enterprise might have worked toward a monumentalizing of the found object. But the sheer magnitude of Mallarmé's enterprise, the more than four hundred verses assiduously written and gleefully dispatched (consider that Mme Léopold Dauphin received at least twelve of the "Dons de fruits glacés," presumably each New Year for twelve consecutive years!), suggests that his interest was aimed more at displacing the poetic than at elevating rubbish to the level of art.

In most accounts of Mallarmé's literary output the *Vers de circonstance* would be considered at the antipodes of his great projected work, the "Grand Œuvre," known to us only in the form of the fragmentary notes published by Jacques Scherer. Given Mallarmé's references to the never-to-be-completed Book, his statement that such a work would be unique, that it would be "l'explication orphique de la Terre" ("the orphic explanation of the Earth"), that its very rhythm "impersonnel et vivant, jusque dans sa pagination, se

"Autour d'un mirliton" pole given to Méry Laurent with verses inscribed in spiral fashion (Bibliothèque Littéraire Jacques Doucet).

Detail of the "Mirliton" with verses 1–4:

Tous de l'amitié. Sans ça l'on
Ne saurait orner mon salon

J'ai, sur ce mirliton rêveur
Ma devise "Evans for ever"

Of friendship, to all. Without friendship, one
Could not possibly decorate my parlour

I have written, on this whimsical mirliton
My motto "Evans for ever"

Detail of the "Mirliton" with the following verses:

Portalier un cœur; mais de seins
Pas plus que tous les médecins

Je m'accoude dans le bain
Aimant entendre Robin

Quelquefois je nomme Adrien
Marx mon docteur, quand je n'ai rien

Je crois, sans qu'on m'en ait conté
Plaire à Rosine Labonté

For Portalier, a heart; but no chest
No more than what all physicians get

I lean on my elbow in the bath
Loving to hear Robin

Sometimes I name Adrien
Marx my physician, when nothing is the matter

I believe, without having been told
That Rosine Labonté likes me

juxtapose aux équations de ce rêve, ou Ode" (*O. c.* 663) ("impersonal and living, even in its pagination, is juxtaposed with equations of this dream, or Ode"), one might expect the Book to be a symphonic orchestration, an encyclopedic text, a metaphysical work; all of which would certainly be interpretations in line with the standard literary history's version of Mallarmé adumbrated at the opening of this chapter.

In fact, however, the notes for *Le Livre* are considerably more illuminating about the physical circumstances of the production of the Book than about what its content might be. A full 90 of the 202 "manuscript" sheets assembled contain little more than mathematical calculations about the number of copies to be printed, number of participants in attendance, or designs for the physical layout of the ceremonies. Except for the minutely calculated aspect of the Book, it appears as if the actual presentation of *Le Livre* would have had more in common with a Kaprow "happening" than with conventional notions of printed books. The Book reads more like a series of stage directions for a theatrical production with a number of possible variants than like a work of poetry. Mallarmé would have been "in attendance" as a kind of operator, facilitating the interaction between written material and participants rather than appearing in the traditional guise of poet.

Given the various myths surrounding and enshrining the poet and his work, Scherer's ability to read the fragments and to see them for what they are was not only remarkable but frankly courageous in 1957. He notes that Mallarmé's correspondence, after the first volume (1862–71) in which he was primarily concerned with difficult aesthetic problems, "is almost uniquely filled with descriptions of events. One sees there a Mallarmé surrounded by his family and his very numerous literary friends, happy to live life to the fullest, and not at all scorning the circumstantial as much as has been said" (xiv). In the first chapter of his analysis of the Book, entitled, curiously enough, given the concrete aspect of the fragments, "Metaphysics of the Book," he devotes at least twelve pages to a remarkably acute account of the role of the circumstantial in Mallarmé's work, noting that "One must attribute to specific occasions the greater part of the *Poésies* and the totality of *Divigations*" (17).

Scherer even acknowledges that the notes for *Le Livre* are more circumstantial than "metaphysical," and it is therefore with dismay that we read his conclusion: "in order to write the Book, he will have to free himself completely from the circumstantial" (17).

Speculation about what the Book really would have been, based on the incomplete and perhaps misleading evidence of the notes, seems hazardous, and it is not my intention to try to offer an alternative version to Scherer's. What I would like to do, however, is to point to a number of the fragments to show how they are harmonious with the analysis of the *Vers de circonstance* I have provided above. The first and most obvious point of comparison would be the most minimal element of the Book, the *feuillet* or sheet. Scherer sees each one as being, in its materiality, constant, but when rearranged within the book, able to take on new values in its juxtaposition with different pages (85). The assembled *feuillets* might have resembled a notebook without a binding and no definitive order of presentation. We have already seen this notion of a combinatory literature in Mallarmé's "Œufs de Pâques" and in the "Rondels"; there, however, recombination is restricted to the disposition of a limited number of verses. With the large number of pages Mallarmé was contemplating (20 volumes of 384 pages each is the most frequently mentioned figure), however, the possibilities of recombination approach the infinite. This, in fact, is the principal source of poetic play operative in the "Loisirs," where the permutations on the relationship of name and address constitute the very challenge of the literary enterprise.

The most frequently referred-to attribute of the Book is its mobility, to be activated by the reshuffling of the *feuillets*: "le volume, malgré l'impression fixe, devient par ce jeu, mobile—de mort il devient vie" (191A) ("the volume, in spite of the fixed print, becomes by this game, mobile—from death it becomes life"). Presumably, like the *carte de visite* and like the *Vers de circonstance*, the Book would reject the static impact of the monument, projecting rather a more supple, even ludic assemblage of variously interlocking fragments: "chaque séance ou pièce étant un *jeu*, une représentation fragmentaire, mais se suffisant de cela" (93A) ("each performance or piece being a *game*, a fragmentary and yet self-sufficient representation"). The concordance of its elements, however, would be decidedly lacking in anecdotal continuities. Like those attending Mallarmé's famous "mardis," the weekly gatherings of the master poet and his young disciples, the ideal "readers" of (participants in) the Book would not be subject to narrative or even descriptive renderings of extratextual phenomena: "deux *alternatives* d'un même sujet—ou ceci, ou cela—(et non pas traitées par suite, historiquement—mais toujours intelluectellement [sic])" (147A) ("two *alternatives* of the same subject—either this, or that—[and not treated successively, historically—but always intellectually]"). The model is precisely that described above with reference to the episodic, erratic "format" of the *Chap Book* version of the "Loisirs": the illusion of a perpetual foreplay is created by constantly denying the participants the gratification of conventional narrative contours. No climax can be reached, no denouement cathartically released because the Book is forever in progress, perpetuating itself through a pretense whereby it mimics but eludes traditional bookish properties: "un livre ne commence ni ne finit: tout au plus fait-il semblant" (181A) ("a book neither begins nor ends: at most, it pretends to").

The Book therefore erects a flexible, demountable, highly public social sculpture whose supple materiality consists of its mobile *feuillets*, its operator, and, perhaps most important, a rotating series of participants who, more than the readers of even the more radically experimental contemporary novels (say, Cortázar's *Hopscotch* or Sollers's *Nombres*)[14] and much like the "spectators" of avant-garde theater, become implicated in the performance. Mallarmé's plans for the Book invoke a vast arena of theatrical space projected over an indefinite period of time. It appears as if the Book would have been a celebration of sorts through poetry, an aesthetically satisfying communion marked not by the sharing of specific contents but by the sharing of contexts.

It would obviously be foolhardy (though I confess, powerfully tempting) to push the correspondences between the Book and the *Vers de circonstance* so far as to suggest that Mallarmé's ongoing engagement with the composition and dissemination of the quatrains and distichs represents his most authentic enactment of the Book. Certainly, however, a strong case might be made in this direction, and one wonders if the myriad commentators who have confidently concluded along with Michaud that "the 'Coup de dés' is clearly, then, a fragment of the Book glimpsed in the manuscript notes published by Scherer" (155) ought not have exercised similar reserve. The point, of course, is not to debate the radicality of the *Vers de circonstance* as an ensemble relative to Mallarmé's undeniably masterly "Un Coup de dés" but instead to appreciate the contribution a speculative reading of the *Vers de circonstance* can make toward an understanding of the new poetics of *Le Livre*.

In Chapter 3 I explored "La Déclaration foraine" as an allegory of the situation of the occasional text. The prose poem was shown to be central to my thesis in that the model of writing it proposes can be read as a foundation for a new poetics of the occasion. There the occasion of writing (that is, the prose frame text, the anecdote about a man and a woman out for a drive who stop at a fairground and recite a poem) is itself "framed" by the very poem the occasion produces. In its hermeticism, the verse poem in turn "produces" the prose poem anecdote as a kind of self-explication, as its pre-text, as *its* occasion. The resulting reciprocity, in a *mise en abyme* symbolized by the frame within a frame, ultimately dislodges conventional conceptions of representation in that that which represents and its representation become interchangeable, neither able to claim temporal or causal priority over the other. Nor is the occasion ultimately effaced—precisely because it is constantly being effaced. After each attempt at elision, the occasion reasserts itself as the very vehicle of elision. But if the model of the *mise en abyme* usually leads to a stalemate and the reaching of an undecidable, here instead the vacillation between framed and frame becomes richly productive. It is, in fact, the source and product of both the prose and the poetry of "La Déclaration foraine" and, as such, emblematizes literature itself. The production of literature is posed in this text in terms of a man confronting a public whose demand for a show is what finally produces (in Barbara Johnson's comically brilliant term) a "toothpaste-tube-like" self-expression.

This model varies only nominally from that self-portrait featured in Mallarmé's "Autobiographie" of the reticent poet who relishes his solitude: "Au fond je considère l'époque contemporaine comme un interrègne pour le poëte qui n'a point à s'y mêler. . . . La solitude accompagne nécessairement cette espèce d'attitude" (*O.c.* 664) ("Basically I consider that for the poet, our times are an interregnum in which he should not get involved. . . . Solitude necessarily accompanies this type of attitude"). We may compare this, Mallarmé's self-depiction, with the male speaker of "La Déclaration foraine" who leads us to believe that he would have preferred never to have left the "conjoint isolement par exemple de [leur] voiture" ("joint isolation

for example of [their] carriage"). Both, however, are forced to relin-
quish silence and solitude alike and to confront society, which for the
poet is in a most regrettable state ("trop en désuetude et en efferves-
cence préparatoire" ["too much obsolescence and in preparatory ef-
fervescence"]) and for the prose poem's gentleman sonneteer is sym-
bolized by the "rire strident ordinaire des choses et de leur cuivrerie
triomphale" ("usual strident laughter of things and their triumphal
brassiness") of the fairgrounds. Like this poetic persona who is
obliged to speak by the "coup de poing brutal à l'estomac que cause
une impatience de gens auxquels coûte que coûte et soudain il faut
proclamer quelque chose" ("brutal punch to the stomach that the
impatience of people to whom one must suddenly proclaim some-
thing at any cost"), Mallarmé paints himself as obligated to send out
his *carte de visite* ("stances ou sonnet") in order not to be stoned by
members of the public if they suspected him of knowing they don't
exist (in "La Déclaration foraine": to secure "la certitude pour chacun
de n'être pas refait" ["the certitude for each one not to get taken in"]).

   This is precisely the model of writing we have evidenced as well in
the *Vers de circonstance*: the poet is continually seduced into expres-
sion on the most trivial of occasions, simply because there is a public
that must be addressed. Between the writing of the "Autobiographie"
and the practice of the *Vers de circonstance*, however, there would ap-
pear to be a certain disparity: the "real" Mallarmé, unlike his auto-
biographical or poetic counterparts, accedes to the demands of such
occasions with a disarming proclivity, an unmatched prolixity, and
a graciousness born not of pressure but of pleasure.

   In its general outlines, this model is also comparable to that of the
production of literature in *Le Livre*. We may speculate that Mallarmé
devoted so many hours to calculating the ceremonial and theatrical
features of the Book and gave so little thought to its content because,
in a sense, content was irrelevant. Any occasion is capable of pro-
ducing poetry, even the simple recombination of already proffered
text. If "everything in the world exists to end up in a book" it is be-
cause the importance of the book is the modulation of textual per-
formance itself and not the specificity of the communication. Liter-
ature is simply people addressing each other, the improvising son-
neteer in "La Déclaration foraine," the "operateur" in *Le Livre*, the
poet sending out his *cartes de visite*, and Mallarmé disseminating over
450 *Vers de circonstance*. If there is a public to buy or simply to receive,

there is literature: "Le fait: que la foule achètera [est une] preuve ré-ciproque" (*Le Livre* 114A) ("The fact: that the crowd will buy [is a] reciprocal proof").

Thus, addressing the occasion by employing the poetic forms sanc-tified by the institution of literature is no longer a cultural priority. In fact, it corrupts the very nature of literature as a readiness to ad-dress in that our preoccupation with the monumental forces us to fix-ate on certain events and exclude others. The monumental circum-stances that poetry traditionally takes as its occasions, deaths, his-toric events, and affairs of state, cause us to become obsessed with the past, and the only way to access that past is by opening the space between text and world that we call narrative. The "tombeau" (to the extent that it invokes the inscription on a tombstone), in fact, presents the ideal narrative in miniature. It figures, by the birthdate, date of decease, and the hyphen that conventionally intervenes, the span of a human life as the three entities necessary to storytelling: beginning, middle, and end; or birth, life, and death.

But if the poet can make himself open to the mobility of the oc-casion, that is, refusing to lend the kind of attention to it that im-mobilizes it, then the space intervening between text and world closes down and the occasion as pre-text is abolished. Mallarmé's writing of the *Vers de circonstance* reflects his abdication of the im-mobilizing "regard" that is narration. Writing and occasion instead become collapsed into one: writing about occasions *is* the occasion for writing. The occasion is not prior to the text; it is the performance of the text itself, in the act of addressing. Mallarmé's poetics of the occasion performs literature as an addressing of the act of addressing, abolishing the occasion by its exclusive attention to occasion.

Does this mean that Mallarmé's poetry is, finally, an exercise in intransitive language? That by addressing itself in the act of address-ing, literature is nothing more than a self-reflexive exercise? Clearly not. In the first place, the art of address necessarily presupposes a pub-lic and a strategy not only of writing but also of reading. This was amply demonstrated by "La Déclaration foraine" and the three-way dynamic of speech and silence that manifested itself as seduction among the speaker, his female companion, and their audience. But if we limited the question of who, ultimately, was the seducer and who the seducee at that point in our discussion to the male and female principals, we had not yet had the example of the *Vers de circonstance* to reveal the full importance of the audience and its contribution to the stage of literature, the shared "lieu commun." As surely as the principals reciprocally seduce each other, they are further seduced into performance (she into her silent self-exhibition, he into language) *by the audience.* The question raised at that point was: What, if anything, is communicated between speaker and audience in this privileged "lieu commun"? What place does a hermetic art have in the "lieu commun"? We are now, I believe, in a position to answer. We must do so by re-posing the question of the object in Mallarmé's poetry.

Mallarmé's poetic career may be read, from this perspective, as a protracted attempt to perform a dismissal of objects. Beginning with the early "Ses purs ongles" and the "Ouverture ancienne," the text manifests an attempt to abolish the object either by negating its presence with annihilating adjectives or by concealing or veiling the object within the folds of language. In the Poe, Baudelaire, and Verlaine sonnets, poetry appears to enact the dismissal of the ultimate object, the "tombeau," by tampering with its monumentality. In the *Vers de circonstance*, Mallarmé becomes involved in a vast project that takes on the dissemination of real objects: poetry may be read as the vehicle for the dispersal of envelopes, pebbles, fans, eggs, jugs, candies, and so on.

But in all these instances of the circulation of objects, what appears to be the most interesting aspect is the degree to which the object is *nevertheless conserved.* In "Ses purs ongles," the "aboli bibelot" phonically restores the object it referentially denies. Even in the Verlaine sonnet, the "tombeau" is never effaced; it is simply converted into that mobile "bribe," the "noir roc courroucé." And in the *Vers de circonstance*, the sending out of poetry on objects assures that the word will never quite abolish the world or the world the word; the object lends ballast to language just as language bolsters reality. Like Derrida's postcards, the *Vers de circonstance* not only say "I am here" or "Wish you were here," but they also posit a "Here it is for you." The object substitutes a kind of dumb presence for the absence that is language.

What is then "communicated" in the "lieu commun" between speaker and audience is that dumb presence. The object can be read, as the token of the address, the token that finally breaks down the supposed "double état de la parole" ("dual state of the word") whereby language is divided into its two functions: "brut ou immédiat ici, là essentiel" ("crude or immediate here, there essential"). If "brut" or "immédiat" language is that for which it suffices "peut-être pour échanger la pensée humaine, de prendre ou de mettre dans la main d'autrui en silence une pièce de monnaie" (O.c. 368) ("perhaps to exchange human thought by taking or placing in the hand of others, silently, a coin"), so, then, is the language of the poetics of the occasion, for it also operates through the exchange of a token object.

Appendix

Appendix:
Texts and Translations

Ouverture ancienne d'Hérodiade

La Nourrice

   (*Incantation*)

Abolie, et son aile affreuse dans les larmes
Du bassin, aboli, qui mire les alarmes,
Des ors nus fustigeant l'espace cramoisi,
Une Aurore a, plumage héraldique, choisi
Notre tour cinéraire et sacrificatrice,   5
Lourde tombe qu'a fuie un bel oiseau, caprice
Solitaire d'aurore au vain plumage noir . . .
Ah! des pays déchus et tristes le manoir!
Pas de clapotement! L'eau morne se résigne,
Que ne visite plus la plume ni le cygne   10
Inoubliable: l'eau reflète l'abandon
De l'automne éteignant en elle son brandon:
Du cygne quand parmi le pâle mausolée
Ou la plume plongea la tête, désolée
Par le diamant pur de quelque étoile, mais   15
Antérieure, qui ne scintilla jamais.
Crime! bûcher! aurore ancienne! supplice!
Pourpre d'un ciel! Etang de la pourpre complice!
Et sur les incarnats, grand ouvert, ce vitrail.

La chambre singulière en un cadre, attirail   20
De siècle belliqueux, orfèvrerie éteinte,
A le neigeux jadis pour ancienne teinte,
Et sa tapisserie, au lustre nacré, plis
Inutiles avec les yeux ensevelis
De sibylles offrant leur ongle vieil aux Mages.   25
Une d'elles, avec un passé de ramages

Sur ma robe blanchie en l'ivoire fermé
Au ciel d'oiseaux parmi l'argent noir parsemé,
Semble, de vols partis costumée et fantôme,
Un arôme qui porte, ô roses! un arôme,   30
Loin du lit vide qu'un cierge soufflé cachait,
Un arôme d'os froids rôdant sur le sachet,
Une touffe de fleurs parjures à la lune
(A la cire expirée encor s'effeuille l'une),
De qui le long regret et les tiges de qui   35
Trempent en un seul verre à l'éclat alangui.
Une Aurore traînait ses ailes dans les larmes!

Ombre magicienne aux symboliques charmes!
Une voix, du passé longue évocation,
Est-ce la mienne prête à l'incantation?   40
Encore dans les plis jaunes de la pensée
Traînant, antique, ainsi qu'une toile encensée
Sur un confus amas d'ostensoirs refroidis,
Par les trous anciens et par les plis roidis
Percés selon le rythme et les dentelles pures   45
Du suaire laissant par ses belles guipures
Désespéré monter le vieil éclat voilé
S'élève: (ô quel lointain en ces appels celé!)
Le vieil éclat voilé du vermeil insolite,
De la voix languissant, nulle, sans acolyte,   50
Jettera-t-il son or par dernières splendeurs,
Elle, encore, l'antienne aux versets demandeurs,
A l'heure d'agonie et de luttes funèbres!
Et, force du silence et des noires ténèbres
Tout rentre également en l'ancien passé,   55
Fatidique, vaincu, monotone, lassé,
Comme l'eau des bassins anciens se résigne.

Elle a chanté, parfois incohérente, signe
Lamentable!
    le lit aux pages de vélin,
Tel, inutile et si claustral, n'est pas le lin!   60
Qui des rêves par plis n'a plus le cher grimoire,
Ni le dais sépulcral à la déserte moire,
Le parfum des cheveux endormis. L'avait-il?
Froide enfant, de garder en son plaisir subtil
Au matin grelottant de fleurs, ses promenades,   65
Et quand le soir méchant a coupé les grenades!

Le croissant, oui le seul est au cadran de fer
De l'horloge, pour poids suspendant Lucifer,
Toujours blesse, toujours une nouvelle heurée,
Par la clepsydre à la goutte obscure pleurée,   70
Que, délaissée, elle erre, et sur son ombre pas
Un ange accompagnant son indicible pas!
Il ne sait pas cela le roi qui salarie
Depuis longtemps la gorge ancienne et tarie.
Son père ne sait pas cela, ni le glacier   75
Farouche reflétant de ses armes l'acier,
Quand sur un tas gisant de cadavres sans coffre
Odorant de résine, énigmatique, il offre
Ses trompettes d'argent obscur aux vieux sapins!
Reviendra-t-il un jour des pays cisalpins!   80
Assez tôt? Car tout est présage et mauvais rêve!
A l'ongle qui parmi le vitrage s'élève
Selon le souvenir des trompettes, le vieux
Ciel brûle, et change un doigt en un cierge envieux.
Et bientôt sa rougeur de triste crépuscule   85
Pénétrera du corps la cire qui recule!
De crépuscule, non, mais de rouge lever,
Lever du jour dernier qui vient tout achever,
Si triste se débat, que l'on ne sait plus l'heure
La rougeur de ce temps prophétique qui pleure   90
Sur l'enfant, exilée en son cœur précieux
Comme un cygne cachant en sa plume ses yeux,
Comme les mit le vieux cygne en sa plume, allée
De la plume détresse, en l'éternelle allée
De ses espoirs, pour voir les diamants élus   95
D'une étoile mourante, et qui ne brille plus. *

Ancient Overture to Hérodiade

The Nurse

   (*Incantation*)

Abolished, and its ghastly wing in the tears
Of the abolished basin, which mirrors the alarms,
Of the naked gold whipping the crimson space
A Dawn has, of heraldic plumage, chosen

---

* Where the Pléiade edition differs from Gardner Davies's version of the "Ouverture" in his *Les Noces d'Hérodiade* (lines 29, 32, 42, and 74), I have adopted Davies's readings.

Our cinerary and sacrificial tower   5
Weighty tomb that a beautiful bird has fled,
Solitary caprice of the dawn with vain black plumage . . .
Ah! the manor of fallen and sad lands!
No splashing! The mournful water is resigned,
That neither the feather nor the unforgettable swan still visit   10
The water reflects the abandonment
Of the autumn extinguishing its torch in it:
Of the swan when about the pale mausoleum
Or the feather [swan] plunged its head, grieved
By the pure diamond of some star, but   15
Anterior, that never twinkled.
Crime! Pyre! Ancient dawn! Torment!
Crimson of a sky! Pool, accomplice of the crimson!
And on the rose tints, wide open, this window of stained glass.

The strange room in a frame, trappings   20
Of a bellicose century, lustreless gold ware
Has for its former hue the snowy yesteryear
And its tapestry, pearly lustred, useless
Folds with the buried eyes
Of sybils offering their aged fingernail to the Magi.   25
One of them, with a past of floral patterns
On my bleached dress closed in ivory
In the sky full of birds strewn amidst the black silver,
Seems, garbed in flights taken and phantom
An aroma that carries, O roses! an aroma,   30
Far from the empty bed that a snuffed out candle hid,
An aroma of cold bones prowling on the sachet,
A bunch of flowers unfaithful to the moon
(In the light of the expired candle one still drops its petals)
Of which the long regret and the stems of which   35
Steep in a single glass of languid luster.
A Dawn dragged its wings in the tears!

Magic shade with symbolic charms!
A voice, a long evocation of the past,
Is it mine ready for incantation?   40
Still in the yellow folds of thought
Dragging, antique, like a perfumed cloth
Over a confused pile of cold monstrances,
Through the ancient holes and the stiffened folds
Pierced according to the rhythm and the pure lacework   45
Of the shroud letting through its beautiful guipures

To rise, desperate, the old veiled brilliance,
It rises: (O how far off in these calls hidden!)
The old veiled brilliance of an unusual vermilion,
Of the languishing voice, null, without acolyte,   50
Will it throw off its gold in final splendors,
It, still, the hymn of questioning verses,
At the hour of agony and of funereal struggles!
And, by dint of the silence and the black darkness
All returns equally to the ancient past   55
Fateful, vanquished, monotonous, weary,
As the water of ancient basins grows resigned.

She sang, at times incoherently, lamentable
Sign!
      the bed of vellum pages
Such, useless and so claustral, is not the linen!   60
Which no longer has the cherished writing of folded dreams
Nor the sepulchral dais with the deserted moire
The perfume of sleeping hair. Did it have it?
Cold child, to indulge her subtle pleasure
In the morning shivering with flowers, her walks,   65
And when the malevolent evening has cut the pomegranates!
The crescent moon, yes it alone is on the iron dial
Of the clock, suspending Lucifer as a weight,
Always wounds, always a new striking of the hour
By the water clock with a dubious drop wept   70
That, left alone, she wanders, and on her shade, no
Angel accompanying her unspeakable step!
He does not know this, the king who hires
That since long ago the ancient and dried up breast
Her father does not know that, nor does the fierce glacier   75
Reflecting the steel of his arms,
When, on a pile of cadavers without coffins,
Odorous of resin, enigmatic, he offers
His trumpets of somber silver to the old firs!
Will he return one day from the cisalpine countries!   80
Soon enough? Because all is foreboding and bad dreams!
To the fingernail that rises amidst the stained-glass windows
According to the memory of trumpets, the old
Sky burns, and changes a finger into an envious candle.
And soon the redness of the sad crepuscule   85
Will penetrate the body of the wax that shrinks!
Of the crepuscule, no, but the red dawn,

Dawn of the last day that comes to end all
So sadly it flounders, that one no longer knows the hour
The redness of this prophetic time that weeps   90
Over the child, exiled in her precious heart
Like a swan hiding its eyes in its feathers,
As the old swan put them in its plumage, path
Of the sorrowful plumage, in the eternal passing
Of its hopes, in order to see the chosen diamonds,   95
Of a dying star, that no longer shines.

L'Après-midi d'un faune
Eglogue
   Le Faune

Ces nymphes, je les veux perpétuer.
                  Si clair,
Leur incarnat léger, qu'il voltige dans l'air
Assoupi de sommeils touffus.

                Aimai-je un rêve?
Mon doute, amas de nuit ancienne, s'achève
En maint rameau subtil, qui demeuré les vrais   5
Bois mêmes, prouve, hélas! que bien seul je m'offrais
Pour triomphe la faute idéale de roses.
Réfléchissons . . .

          ou si les femmes dont tu gloses
Figurent un souhait de tes sens fabuleux!
Faune, l'illusion s'échappe des yeux bleus   10
Et froids, comme une source en pleurs, de la plus chaste:
Mais, l'autre tout soupirs, dis-tu qu'elle contraste
Comme brise du jour chaude dans ta toison?
Que non! par l'immobile et lasse pâmoison
Suffoquant de chaleurs le matin frais s'il lutte,   15
Ne murmure point d'eau que ne verse ma flûte
Au bosquet arrosé d'accords; et le seul vent
Hors des deux tuyaux prompt à s'exhaler avant
Qu'il disperse le son dans une pluie aride,
C'est, à l'horizon pas remué d'une ride,   20
Le visible et serein souffle artificiel
De l'inspiration, qui regagne le ciel.

O bords siciliens d'un calme marécage
Qu'à l'envi de soleils ma vanité saccage,
Tacite sous les fleurs d'étincelles, CONTEZ   25
"Que je coupais ici les creux roseaux domptés
Par le talent; quand, sur l'or glauque de lointaines
Verdures dédiant leur vigne à des fontaines,
Ondoie une blancheur animale au repos:
Et qu'au prélude lent où naissent les pipeaux   30
Ce vol de cygnes, non! de naïades se sauve
Ou plonge . . ."

     Inerte, tout brûle dans l'heure fauve
Sans marquer par quel art ensemble détala
Trop d'hymen souhaité de qui cherche le *la*:
Alors m'éveillerai-je à la ferveur première,
Droit et seul, sous un flot antique de lumière,
Lys! et l'un de vous tous pour l'ingénuité.

Autre que ce doux rien par leur lèvre ébruité,
Le baiser, qui tout bas des perfides assure,
Mon sein, vierge de preuve, atteste une morsure
Mystérieuse, due à quelque auguste dent;
Mais bast! arcane tel élut pour confident
Le jonc vaste et jumeau dont sous l'azur on joue:
Qui, détournant à soi le trouble de la joue,
Rêve, dans un solo long, que nous amusions
La beauté d'alentour par des confusions
Fausses entre elle-même et notre chant crédule;
Et de faire aussi haut que l'amour se module
Evanouir du songe ordinaire de dos
Ou de flanc pur suivis avec mes regards clos,
Une sonore, vaine et monotone ligne.

Tâche donc, instrument des fuites, ô maligne
Syrinx, de refleurir aux lacs où tu m'attends!
Moi, de ma rumeur fier, je vais parler longtemps
Des déesses; et par d'idolâtres peintures,
A leur ombre enlever encore des ceintures:
Ainsi, quand des raisins j'ai sucé la clarté,
Pour bannir un regret par ma feinte écarté,
Rieur, j'élève au ciel d'été la grappe vide
Et, soufflant dans ses peaux lumineuses, avide
D'ivresse, jusqu'au soir je regarde au travers.

O nymphes, regonflons des SOUVENIRS divers.
"Mon œil, trouant les joncs, dardait chaque encolure
Immortelle, qui noie en l'onde sa brûlure
Avec un cri de rage au ciel de la forêt;
Et le splendide bain de cheveux disparaît
Dans les clartés et les frissons, ô pierreries!
J'accours; quand, à mes pieds, s'entrejoignent (meurtries
De la langueur goûtée à ce mal d'être deux)
Des dormeuses parmi leurs seuls bras hasardeux;
Je les ravis, sans les désenlacer, et vole
A ce massif, haï par l'ombrage frivole,

35

40

45

50

55

60

65

70

De roses tarissant tout parfum au soleil
Où notre ébat au jour consumé soit pareil."
Je t'adore, courroux des vierges, ô délice   75
Farouche du sacré fardeau nu qui se glisse
Pour fuir ma lèvre en feu buvant, comme un éclair
Tressaille! la frayeur secrète de la chair:
Des pieds de l'inhumaine au cœur de la timide
Que délaisse à la fois une innocence, humide   80
De larmes folles ou de moins tristes vapeurs.
"Mon crime, c'est d'avoir, gai de vaincre ces peurs
Traîtresses, divisé la touffe échevelée
De baisers que les dieux gardaient si bien mêlée:
Car, à peine j'allais cacher un rire ardent   85
Sous les replis heureux d'une seule (gardant
Par un doigt simple, afin que sa candeur de plume
Se teignît à l'émoi de sa sœur qui s'allume,
La petite, naïve et ne rougissant pas:)
Que de mes bras, défaits par de vagues trépas,   90
Cette proie, à jamais ingrate se délivre
Sans pitié du sanglot dont j'étais encore ivre."

Tant pis! vers le bonheur d'autres m'entraîneront
Par leur tresse nouée aux cornes de mon front:
Tu sais, ma passion, que, pourpre et déjà mûre,   95
Chaque grenade éclate et d'abeilles murmure;
Et notre sang, épris de qui le va saisir,
Coule pour tout l'essaim éternel du désir.
A l'heure où ce bois d'or et de cendres se teinte
Une fête s'exalte en la feuillée éteinte: 100
Etna! c'est parmi toi visité de Vénus
Sur ta lave posant ses talons ingénus,
Quand tonne un somme triste ou s'épuise la flamme.
Je tiens la reine!

    O sûr châtiment . . .

              Non, mais l'âme
De paroles vacante et ce corps alourdi   105
Tard succombent au fier silence de midi:
Sans plus il faut dormir en l'oubli du blasphème,
Sur le sable altéré gisant et comme j'aime
Ouvrir ma bouche à l'astre efficace des vins!

Couple, adieu; je vais voir l'ombre que tu devins.   110

The Afternoon of a Faun
Eclogue
    The Faun

These nymphs, I want to perpetuate them.
                                    So clear,
Their light rosiness, that it hovers in the air
Drowsy with tufted slumbers.

                        Did I love a dream?
My doubt, accumulation of a former night, ends up
As many a subtle branch, that having remained the true   5
Woods themselves, proves, alas! that I offered myself alone
For triumph the ideal sin of roses.
Let us reflect . . .

                    or if the women that you tell
Represent a wish of your fabulous senses!
Faun, the illusion escapes from the blue and
Cold eyes, like a spring in tears, of the more chaste: 10
But, the other one all sighs, do you say she contrasts
Like a warm day's breeze in your fleece?
But no! by the immobile and weary swoon
Suffocating with heat the cool morning if it struggles,   15
It does not murmur water but that my flute pours
In the grove drenched in chords; and the wind alone
Out of the two pipes prompt to exhale before
It disperses the sound in an arid rain,
It is, on the horizon unstirred by a wrinkle,   20
The visible and serene artificial breath
Of inspiration, that returns to the sky.

O Sicilian banks of a calm marsh
That my vanity plunders with a multitude of suns,
Tacit under the flowers of sparks, TELL   25
"That I was cutting here the hollow reeds, tamed
By talent; when, on the dull gold of the far off
Foliage dedicating their vine to the fountains,
Undulates an animal whiteness at rest:
And at the slow prelude where the reed-pipes are born   30
This flight of swans, no! of water nymphs escapes
Or plunges . . ."

                Inert, everything burns at the tawny hour
Without indicating by which art together ran off

Too much hymen wished for by he who seeks the *la*:
Then I will awake to the primal fervor,   35
Erect and alone, under an antique flood of light,
Lilies! and one of you all for ingenuity.

Other than this sweet nothing by their lips made known,
The kiss, that hushedly secures the perfidious ones,
My breast, virgin of proof, attests a bite   40
Mysterious, due to some august tooth;
But enough! such mystery chose for confident
The vast and twin reed played under the azure:
Which, turning toward itself the cheek's turmoil,
Dreams, in a long solo, that we will entertain   45
The beauty of the surroundings by false
Confusions between itself and our credulous song;
And to make as high as love modulates itself
Vanish from the ordinary dream of a back
Or a pure flank followed by my closed looks,   50
A sonorous, vain and monotonous line.

Try then, instrument of flights, O mischievous
Syrinx, to flower again by the lakes where you await me!
I, proud of my noise, I will speak for a long while
Of the goddesses; and by idolatrous paintings,   55
I will lift still more girdles from their shadows:
Thus, when from the grapes I have sucked the brightness,
In order to banish a regret put aside by my pretense,
Laughing, I raise to the summer sky the empty cluster
And, blowing in its luminous skins, avid   60
For drunkenness, I gaze through them until evening.

O nymphs, let us swell again with diverse MEMORIES.
"My eye, piercing the reeds, darted each immortal neckline
That drowns its burning in the wave
With a cry of rage to the sky of the forest;   65
And the splendid bath of hair disappears
In the lights and the shivers, O precious stones!
I run over; when, at my feet, are intertwined (bruised
By the languor felt at this hurt of being two)
Some sleeping women among their haphazard arms;   70
I ravish them, without untangling them, and fly
To this clump of trees, hated by the frivolous shade,
Of roses drying up all perfume in the sun.
May our playfulness be like the day consumed."

I adore you, wrath of virgins, O ferocious   75
Delight of the sacred naked burden that slips
To escape my burning lips drinking, as a flash of lightning
Trembles! the secret terror of the flesh:
From the feet of the inhuman one to the heart of the timid one
Who is at the same time forsaken by innocence, wet   80
With passionate tears or less sad vapors.
"My crime, is to have, gay to vanquish these treacherous
Fears, divided the dishevelled tuft
With kisses, that the gods kept so well entangled:
Because, hardly did I hide an ardent laugh   85
Under the happy folds of one alone (keeping
By a single finger, in order that her featherlike candor
Take on the hue of the excitement of her sister, which was beginning to
     catch fire,
The little one, naive and not blushing:)
When from my arms, undone by vague deaths,
This prey, forever ungrateful, frees herself   90
Without pity for the sob with which I was still drunk."

Too bad! toward happiness others will draw me
By their locks knotted to the horns of my brow:
You know, my passion, that, purple and already ripe,   95
Each pomegranate bursts and murmurs with bees;
And our blood, in love with she who will seize it,
Flows for all the eternal swarm of desire.
At the hour when this wood takes on tints of gold and ashes
A celebration exults in the extinguished foliage: 100
Etna! It is among you, visited by Venus
Posing her ingenuous heels on your lava,
When a sad slumber thunders or when the flame goes out.
I hold the queen!
                    O sure punishment . . .

                                        No, but the soul
Empty of words, and this weighed down body   105
Succumb late to the proud silence of noon:
Without further ado one must sleep in the forgetting of blasphemy,
On the sand, parched, lying, and how I love
To open my mouth to the efficacious star of wines!

Couple, adieu; I will see the shadow that you became.   110

Toast funèbre

O de notre bonheur, toi, le fatal emblème!

Salut de la démence et libation blême,
Ne crois pas qu'au magique espoir du corridor
J'offre ma coupe vide où souffre un monstre d'or!
Ton apparition ne va pas me suffire: 5
Car je t'ai mis, moi-même, en un lieu de porphyre.
Le rite est pour les mains d'éteindre le flambeau
Contre le fer épais des portes du tombeau:
Et l'on ignore mal, élu pour notre fête
Très simple de chanter l'absence du poëte,   10
Que ce beau monument l'enferme tout entier.
Si ce n'est que la gloire ardente du métier,
Jusqu'à l'heure commune et vile de la cendre,
Par le carreau qu'allume un soir fier d'y descendre,
Retourne vers les feux du pur soleil mortel!   15

Magnifique, total et solitaire, tel
Tremble de s'exhaler le faux orgueil des hommes.
Cette foule hagarde! elle annonce: Nous sommes
La triste opacité de nos spectres futurs.
Mais le blason des deuils épars sur de vains murs   20
J'ai méprisé l'horreur lucide d'une larme,
Quand, sourd même à mon vers sacré qui ne l'alarme
Quelqu'un de ces passants, fier, aveugle et muet,
Hôte de son linceul vague, se transmuait
En le vierge héros de l'attente posthume.   25
Vaste gouffre apporté dans l'amas de la brume
Par l'irascible vent des mots qu'il n'a pas dits,
Le néant à cet Homme aboli de jadis:
"Souvenirs d'horizons, qu'est-ce, ô toi, que la Terre?"
Hurle ce songe; et, voix dont la clarté s'altère,   30
L'espace a pour jouet le cri: "Je ne sais pas!"

Le Maître, par un œil profond, a sur ses pas,
Apaisé de l'éden l'inquiète merveille
Dont le frisson final, dans sa voix seule, éveille
Pour la Rose et le Lys le mystère d'un nom.   35
Est-il de ce destin rien qui demeure, non?
O vous tous, oubliez une croyance sombre.
Le splendide génie éternel n'a pas d'ombre.
Moi, de votre désir soucieux, je veux voir,

A qui s'évanouit, hier, dans le devoir   40
Idéal que nous font les jardins de cet astre,
Survivre pour l'honneur du tranquille désastre
Une agitation solennelle par l'air
De paroles, pourpre ivre et grand calice clair,
Que, pluie et diamant, le regard diaphane   45
Reste là sur ces fleurs dont nulle ne se fane,
Isole parmi l'heure et le rayon du jour!

C'est de nos vrais bosquets déjà tout le séjour,
Où le poëte pur a pour geste humble et large
De l'interdire au rêve, ennemi de sa charge: 50
Afin que le matin de son repos altier,
Quand la mort ancienne et comme pour Gautier
De n'ouvrir pas les yeux sacrés et de se taire,
Surgisse, de l'allée ornement tributaire,
Le sépulcre solide où gît tout ce qui nuit,   55
Et l'avare silence et la massive nuit.

Funeral Toast

O of our happiness, you, the fatal emblem!

Greeting of madness and pale libation,
Do not believe that to the magic hope of the corridor
I offer my empty cup where suffers a golden monster!
Your apparition will not suffice me: 5
For I put you, myself, in a place of porphyry.
The rite is for hands to put out the torch
Against the thick iron of the gates of the tomb:
And we cannot ignore, chosen for our very simple
Celebration to sing the absence of the poet,   10
That this beautiful monument encloses him altogether.
If it isn't that the ardent glory of our profession,
Until the common and vile hour of ashes,
Through the windowpane that an evening, proud to wind down,
    illuminates,
Returns toward the fires of the pure mortal sun!   15

Magnificent, total, and solitary, such
The false pride of men trembles to exhale.
This haggard crowd! It announces: We are
The sad opacity of our future specters.

But the blazon of mourning scattered on vain walls   20
I scorned the lucid horror of a tear,
When, deaf even to my sacred verse that does not alarm him,
One of those passing, proud, blind, and mute,
Inhabitant of his vague shroud, was transformed
Into the virgin hero of posthumous expectation.   25
Vast abyss brought into the mass of fog
By the irascible wind of words he has not spoken,
Nothingness to this man abolished of yore (says):
"Memories of horizons, what, O thou, is Earth?"
This dream cries out; and, voice whose clarity fades,   30
Space has as its plaything the cry: "I do not know!"

The Master, through a profound eye, has in his wake,
Appeased the restless marvel of Eden
Whose final quiver, in his voice alone, awakens
For the Rose and the Lily the mystery of a name.   35
Is there of this destiny nothing that remains, no?
O you all, forget a somber belief.
The splendid eternal genius has no shadow.
I, solicitous of your desire, I want to see,
Him who, yesterday, vanished in the ideal duty   40
That the gardens of this star impose on us,
[I want to see] Survive for the honor of the tranquil disaster
A solemn agitation through the air
[A solemn agitation] Of words, drunken purple and great
    white calyx,
That, rain and diamond, the diaphanous look   45
Remains there on those flowers of which none wilt,
Isolates among the hour and the rays of day!

That already is all the sojourn of our true groves,
In which the pure poet has as a gesture humble and large
To ward off dreaming from it, enemy of his charge: 50
In order that the morning of his lofty repose,
When ancient death and as for Gautier
Not to open his sacred eyes and to be silent,
[In order that] Rise up, from the path, tributary ornament,
The solid sepulcher in which lies all that blights,   55
Both the avaricious silence and the massive night.

Prose

pour des Esseintes.

(1) Hyperbole! de ma mémoire
Triomphalement ne sais-tu
Te lever, aujourd'hui grimoire
Dans un livre de fer vêtu:

(2) Car j'installe, par la science,   5
L'hymne des cœurs spirituels
En l'œuvre de ma patience,
Atlas, herbiers et rituels.

(3) Nous promenions notre visage
(Nous fûmes deux, je le maintiens)   10
Sur maints charmes de paysage,
O sœur, y comparant les tiens.

(4) L'ère d'autorité se trouble
Lorsque, sans nul motif, on dit
De ce midi que notre double   15
Inconscience approfondit

(5) Que, sol des cent iris, son site,
Ils savent s'il a bien été,
Ne porte pas de nom que cite
L'or de la trompette d'Eté.   20

(6) Oui, dans une île que l'air charge
De vue et non de visions
Toute fleur s'étalait plus large
Sans que nous en devisions.

(7) Telles, immenses, que chacune   25
Ordinairement se para
D'un lucide contour, lacune,
Qui des jardins la sépara.

(8) Gloire du long désir, Idées
Tout en moi s'exaltait de voir   30
La famille des iridées
Surgir à ce nouveau devoir,

(9) Mais cette sœur sensée et tendre
Ne porta son regard plus loin

Que sourire et, comme à l'entendre   35
J'occupe mon antique soin.

(10) Oh! sache l'Esprit de litige,
A cette heure où nous nous taisons,
Que de lis multiples la tige
Grandissait trop pour nos raisons   40

(11) Et non comme pleure la rive,
Quand son jeu monotone ment
A vouloir que l'ampleur arrive
Parmi mon jeune étonnement

(12) D'ouïr tout le ciel et la carte   45
Sans fin attestés sur mes pas,
Par le flot même qui s'écarte,
Que ce pays n'exista pas.

(13) L'enfant abdique son extase
Et docte déjà par chemins   50
Elle dit le mot: Anastase!
Né pour d'éternels parchemins,

(14) Avant qu'un sépulcre ne rie
Sous aucun climat, son aïeul,
De porter ce nom: Pulchérie!   55
Caché par le trop grand glaïeul.

Prose
                              for des Esseintes.

(1) Hyperbole! from my memory
Triumphantly do you not know
How to rise up, today a book of spells
Clad in a book of iron:

(2) For I install, by means of science,   5
The hymn of spiritual hearts
In the work of my patience,
Atlases, books of herbs, and prayer books.

(3) We promenaded our faces
(We were two, I so maintain)   10
Along many a landscape charm,
O sister, comparing them to yours.

(4)   The era of authority becomes troubled
      When, with no reason, they say
      About this south land that our double   15
      Unconsciousness fathomed

(5)   That, land of a hundred irises, its site,
      They know if it really existed,
      Bears no name that cites
      The gold of the trumpet of Summer.   20

(6)   Yes, on an isle that the air charges
      With insight and not visions
      Every flower displayed itself more grand
      Without us talking about it.

(7)   Such were they, immense, that each one   25
      Ordinarily adorned itself
      With a lucid contour, lacuna,
      That separated it from the gardens.

(8)   Glory of long desire, Ideas
      Everything in me exalted to see   30
      The family of irises
      Rise up to this new task,

(9)   But this sister, sensible and tender
      Carried her look no further
      Than to smile, and in order to hear her   35
      I dedicate my ancient care.

(10) Oh! let the Spirit of litigation know,
      At that hour in which we are silent,
      That with multiple lilies the stem
      Grew too much for our reason   40

(11) And not as the bank weeps,
      When its monotonous game lies
      In wishing that abundance arrives
      Among my young surprise

(12) To hear all the sky and the map   45
      Unendingly attested in my wake,
      By the very wave that ebbs away,
      That this country did not exist.

(13)   The child abdicates her ecstasy
       And already learned in ways   50
       She says the word: Anastase!
       Born for eternal parchments,

(14)   Before a sepulcher laughs
       In no climate, its ancestor,
       At bearing this name: Pulchérie!   55
       Hidden by the too tall gladiolus.

La Déclaration foraine

Le Silence! il est certain qu'à mon côté, ainsi que songes, étendue dans un berchement de promenade sous les roues assoupissant l'interjection de fleurs, toute femme, et j'en sais une qui voit clair ici, m'exempte de l'effort à proférer un vocable: la complimenter haut de quelque interrogatrice toilette, offre de soi presque à l'homme en faveur de qui s'achève l'après-midi, ne pouvant à l'encontre de tout ce rapprochement fortuit, que suggérer la distance sur ses traits aboutie à une fossette de spirituel sourire. Ainsi ne consent la réalité; car ce fut impitoyablement, hors du rayon qu'on sentait avec luxe expirer aux vernis du landau, comme une vocifération, parmi trop de tacite félicité pour une tombée de jour sur la banlieue, avec orage, dans tous sens à la fois et sans motif, du rire strident ordinaire des choses et de leur cuivrerie triomphale: au fait, la cacophonie à l'ouïe de quiconque, un instant écarté, plutôt qu'il ne s'y fond, auprès de son idée, reste à vif devant la hantise de l'existence.

"La fête de . . ." et je ne sais quel rendez-vous suburbain! nomma l'enfant voiturée dans mes distractions, la voix claire d'aucun ennui; j'obéis et fis arrêter.

Sans compensation à cette secousse qu'un besoin d'explication figurative plausible pour mes esprits, comme symétriquement s'ordonnent des verres d'illumination peu à peu éclairés en guirlandes et attributs, je décidai, la solitude manquée, de m'enfoncer même avec bravoure en ce déchaînement exprès et haïssable de tout ce que j'avais naguères fui dans une gracieuse compagnie: prête et ne témoignant de surprise à la modification dans notre programme, du bras ingénu elle s'en repose sur moi, tandis que nous allons parcourir, les yeux sur l'enfilade, l'allée d'ahurissement qui divise en écho du même tapage les foires et permet à la foule d'y renfermer pour un temps l'univers. Subséquemment aux assauts d'un médiocre dévergondage en vue de quoi que ce soit qui détourne notre stagnation amusée par le crépuscule, au fond, bizarre et pourpre, nous retint à l'égal de la nue incendiaire un humain spectacle, poignant: reniée du châssis peinturluré ou de l'inscription en capitales une baraque, apparemment vide.

A qui ce matelas décousu pour improviser ici, comme les voiles dans tous les temps et les temples, l'arcane! appartînt, sa fréquentation durant le jeûne n'avait pas chez son possesseur excité avant qu'il le déroulât comme le gonfalon d'espoirs en liesse, l'hallucination d'une merveille à montrer (que l'inanité de son famélique cauchemar); et pourtant, mû par le caractère frérial d'exception à la misère quotidienne qu'un pré, quand l'institue le mot mystérieux de fête, tient des souliers nombreux y piétinant (en raison de cela poind aux profondeurs des vêtements quelque unique velléité du dur sou à

sortir à seule fin de se dépenser), lui aussi! n'importe qui de tout dénué sauf
de la notion qu'il y avait lieu pour être un des élus, sinon de vendre, de faire
voir, mais quoi, avait cédé à la convocation du bienfaisant rendez-vous. Ou,
très prosaïquement, peut-être le rat éduqué à moins que, lui même, ce men-
diant sur l'athlétique vigueur de ses muscles comptât, pour décider l'engoue-
ment populaire, faisait défaut, à l'instant précis, comme cela résulte souvent
de la mise en demeure de l'homme par les circonstances générales.

"Battez la caisse!" proposa en altesse Madame . . . seule tu sais Qui, mar-
quant un suranné tambour duquel se levait, les bras décroisés afin de signifier
inutile l'approche de son théâtre sans prestige, un vieillard que cette cama-
raderie avec un instrument de rumeur et d'appel, peut-être, séduisit à son
vacant dessein; puis comme si, de ce que tout de suit on pût, ici, envisager
de plus beau, l'énigme, par un bijou fermant la mondaine, en tant qu'à sa
gorge le manque de réponse, scintillait! la voici engouffrée, à ma surprise de
pitre coi devant une halte du public qu'empaume l'éveil des ra et des fla as-
sourdissant mon invariable et obscur pour moi-même d'abord. "Entrez, tout
le monde, ce n'est qu'un sou, on le rend à qui n'est pas satisfait de la repré-
sentation." Le nimbe en paillasson dans le remerciement joignant deux
paumes séniles vidé, j'en agite les couleurs, en signal, de loin, et me coiffai,
prêt à fendre la masse debout en le secret de ce qu'avait su faire avec ce lieu
sans rêve l'initiative d'une contemporaine de nos soirs.

A hauteur du genou, elle émergeait, sur une table, des cent têtes.

Net ainsi qu'un jet égaré d'autre part la dardait électriquement, éclate
pour moi ce calcul qu'à défaut de tout, elle, selon que la mode, une fantaisie
ou l'humeur du ciel circonstanciaient sa beauté, sans supplément de danse
ou de chant, pour la cohue amplement payait l'aumône exigée en faveur d'un
quelconque; et du même trait je comprends mon devoir en le péril de la sub-
tile exhibition, ou qu'il n'y avait au monde pour conjurer la défection dans
les curiosités que de recourir à quelque puissance absolue, comme d'une Mé-
taphore. Vite, dégoiser jusqu'à l'éclaircissement, sur maintes physionomies,
de leur sécurité qui, ne saisissant tout du coup, se rend à l'évidence, même
ardue, impliquée en la parole et consent à échanger son billon contre des
présomptions exactes et supérieures, bref, la certitude pour chacun de n'être
pas refait.

Un coup d'œil, le dernier, à une chevelure où fume puis éclaire de fastes
de jardins le pâlissement du chapeau en crêpe de même ton que la statuaire
robe se relevant, avance au spectateur, sur un pied comme le reste hortensia.
Alors:

> La chevelure vol d'une flamme à l'extrême
> Occident de désirs pour la tout déployer

Se pose (je dirais mourir un diadème)
Vers le front couronné son ancien foyer

Mais sans or soupirer que cette vive nue
L'ignition du feu toujours intérieur
Originellement la seule continue
Dans le joyau de l'œil véridique ou rieur

Une nudité de héros tendre diffame
Celle qui ne mouvant astre ni feux au doigt
Rien qu'à simplifier avec gloire la femme
Accomplit par son chef fulgurante l'exploit

De semer de rubis le doute qu'elle écorche
Ainsi qu'une joyeuse et tutélaire torche

Mon aide à la taille de la vivante allégorie qui déjà résignait sa faction, peut-être faute chez moi de faconde ultérieure, afin d'en assoupir l'élan gentiment à terre: "Je vous ferai observer, ajoutai-je, maintenant de plain pied avec l'entendement des visiteurs, coupant court à leur ébahissement devant ce congé par une affectation de retour à l'authenticité du spectacle, Messieurs et Dames, que la personne qui a eu l'honneur de se soumettre à votre jugement, ne requiert pour vous communiquer le sens de son charme, un costume ou aucun accessoire usuel de théâtre. Ce naturel s'accommode de l'allusion parfaite que fournit la toilette toujours à l'un des motifs primordiaux de la femme, et suffit, ainsi que votre sympathique approbation m'en convainc." Un suspens de marque appréciative sauf quelques confondants "Bien sûr!" ou "C'est cela!" et "Oui" par les gosiers comme plusieurs bravos prêtés par des paires de mains généreuses, conduisit jusqu'à la sortie sur une vacance d'arbres et de nuit la foule où nous allions nous mêler, n'était l'attente en gants blancs encore d'un enfantin tourlourou qui les rêvait dégourdir à l'estimation d'une jarretière hautaine.

—Merci, consentit la chère, une bouffée droit à elle d'une constellation ou des feuilles bue comme pour y trouver sinon le rassérènement, elle n'avait douté d'un succès, du moins l'habitude frigide de sa voix: j'ai dans l'esprit le souvenir de choses qui ne s'oublient.

—Oh! rien que lieu commun d'une esthétique . . .

—Que vous n'auriez peut-être pas introduit, qui sait? mon ami, le prétexte de formuler ainsi devant moi au conjoint isolement par exemple de notre voiture—où est-elle—regagnons-la:—mais ceci jaillit, forcé, sous le coup de poing brutal à l'estomac, que cause une impatience de gens auxquels coûte que coûte et soudain il faut proclamer quelque chose fût-ce la rêverie . . .

—Qui s'ignore et se lance nue de peur, en travers du public; c'est vrai. Comme vous, Madame, ne l'auriez entendu si irréfutablement, malgré sa réduplication sur une rime du trait final, mon boniment d'après un mode primitif du sonnet,* je le gage, si chaque terme ne s'en était répercuté jusqu'à vous par de variés tympans, pour charmer un esprit ouvert à la compréhension multiple.

—Peut-être! accepta notre pensée dans un enjouement de souffle nocturne la même.

The Fairground Declaration

Silence! It is certain that at my side, just like a dream, stretched out in cradling rocking of the drive under the wheels hushing up the interjection of flowers, any woman, and I know one who sees clearly here, exempts me from the effort of uttering a word: to compliment her out loud on some interrogative attire, almost an offer of herself to the man in whose favor the afternoon is drawing to a close, able only, counter to all this fortuitous rapprochement, to suggest the distance of her features that ends up in the dimple of a witty smile. To this reality does not consent: because there was mercilessly, except for the rays of sun that one luxuriously felt expire in the varnish of the landau, a sort of vociferation, among too much tacit felicity for the fall of day on the outskirts of town, with a storm, in all directions at once and without motive, of the usual strident laughter of things and their triumphal brassiness: in fact, a cacophony to anyone's ear, anyone having for an instant moved away rather than becoming one with it, now stands by his ideas, remains exposed, vulnerable to the obsession of existence.

"The fair at . . ." and I don't know what out of town rendez-vous! said the child transported in my distractions, her voice clear of any annoyance; I obeyed and stopped the carriage.

Without compensation for this jolt except for a need of plausible figurative explication for my mind, as lamps little by little light up and arrange themselves symmetrically in garlands and emblems, I decided, having failed to find my solitude, to throw myself bravely into this willed and odious outburst of all that I had heretofore fled in gracious company: ready and showing no surprise at the change in our plans, she rested on me with her ingenuous arm, while we traversed, our eyes on the line of booths, the path of confusion that divides fairgrounds into an echo of that same hubbub and permits the crowd for a time to enclose therein the universe. Subsequent to the assaults of a mediocre dissoluteness with regard to whatever diverts our stagnation en-

*Usité à la Renaissance anglaise.

tertained by the twilight, in the back, bizarre and purple, a human spectacle, poignant, caught our eye as did the incendiary clouds: a fair booth, apparently empty, repudiated by the loudly painted framework or the inscription in capital letters.

To whomever belonged this mattress ripped up for the purpose of improvising here the arcane, like the veils of all times and all temples, its use during the fast had not excited in its possessor before he unfurled it like the banner of revelling hopes, the hallucination of a marvel to be shown (except for the inanity of his starving nightmare); and nevertheless, moved by the fraternal character of exception to quotidian misery that a meadow, when the mysterious word of festival introduces there, has from the numerous shoes trampling it (for this reason in the depths of clothing sprouts some unique passing fancy of the hard coin to emerge with the single aim of being spent), he also! anyone at all, stripped of everything except the notion that there was a chance to be one of the chosen ones, if not to sell, to show, but what? had yielded to the summoning of the beneficent rendez-vous. Or, very prosaically, perhaps the trained rat at least, himself, this beggar counted on the athletic vigor of his muscles in order to win over the public, he was absent at that precise instant, as it often happens as a result of man's being summoned by general circumstances.

"Beat the drum!" proposed her highness Madame . . . only you know Who, pointing out an antiquated drum from which rose, his arms uncrossed in order to indicate the uselessness of approaching his prestigeless theater, an old man whose camaraderie with a noisy instrument of summons, perhaps seduced by her unformulated plan; then, as if, from that which one could envisage as most beautiful, the enigma scintillated, in the form of a jewel enclosing the worldly one, just like the lack of a response at her throat! there she was engulfed, to my surprise of a silent clown before a stopping of the public caught by the waking of the double beat of the drum deafening my invariable and at first obscure even for myself: "Everyone, enter, it's only one sou, it will be returned to whoever is not satisfied with the show." The halo of a straw hat joining in gratitude two senile palms emptied, I waved its colors as a signal, from far off, and I put on the hat, ready to elbow my way through the masses standing in the secret of that which the initiative of a fashionable lady contemporary of our evenings had known how to do with this dreamless place.

She was emerging, on a table, her knees level with the height of a hundred heads.

As clear cut as a beam strayed from elsewhere darting her forth electrically, a reckoning burst forth for me that lacking everything, she, according to fashion, a fantasy or the humor of the sky circumstanced her beauty, without supplement of dance or song, amply paid for the crowd the alms demanded for the favor of anyone; and in the same flash I understand my duty in the peril of the subtle exhibition, that there was no way in the world to conjure away defection from these curiosities than to resort to some absolute power, like a Metaphor. Fast, spout off until seeing, upon many a face, the elucidation of their security that, not grasping everything all at once, renders itself to the evidence, even though with difficulty, implied in their speech, and consents to exchange his base coin for exact and superior presumptions, in brief, the certitude for each one not to get taken in.

A glance, the last, at a head of hair on which smokes and then lights up with the pomp of gardens the paleness of the crepe hat of the same color as the statuesque dress, being lifted above the foot, advancing toward the spectator, purple like the rest.

Then:

> Hair, flight of a flame to the extreme
> Occident of desires to unfurl it all
> Perches (to die a diadem I would say)
> Toward the crowned forehead, its former hearth
>
> But without gold to sigh that this live cloud
> The ignition of the always interior fire
> Originally the only one, continues
> In the jewel of the veracious or laughing eye
>
> A nakedness of tender hero slanders
> Her who neither moving star nor fires on her finger
> Nothing but to simplify the woman with glory
> Accomplishes the feat with her lightning head
>
> To sow with rubies the doubt that she flays
> Like a joyous and tutelary torch

To gently soften her jump off the stage, I offered my aid to the waist of the living allegory who was already resigning her watch, perhaps because of my lack of further loquacity: "Ladies and gentlemen, I will have you notice," I added, now on the level of the understanding of our visitors, cutting short their astonishment before this dismissal by affecting to return to the authenticity of the spectacle, "that the person whose honor it was to submit herself to your judgment does not require a costume or any customary theater props to communicate to you the intelligence of her charm. Her naturalness adapts itself to the perfect allusion that attire furnishes one of the primordial reasons of woman, and suffices, as your kind approbation convinces me."

There was a suspension of appreciative reaction except for a few mingled "Of course!" or "That's it" or "Yes" from their throats like several bravos lent by pairs of generous hands, which led us to the exit through a lack of trees and the night and the crowd with which we were going to mingle, if it had not been for the waiting of a childish soldier in white gloves who dreamed of warming them up in the estimation of a high garter.

—Thank you, consented the dear woman, a puff of air drunk in that had come straight to her from a constellation or from leaves as if to recover, if not her serenity, she had not doubted success, at least the customary coolness of her voice: I have in mind the memory of things that are not forgotten.

—Oh! it was nothing but the commonplace of an aesthetic . . .

—That you would perhaps not have introduced, who knows? my friend, the pretext of formulating thus before me in the joint isolation for example of our carriage—Where is it?—let's get back to it.—But it came out, forced, caused by the brutal punch to the stomach that the impatience of people to whom one must suddenly proclaim something at any cost, even if it is only reverie . . .

—She who forgets herself and dashes, naked with fear, among the public, it's true. Just as for you, Madame, who would not have heard it so irrefutably, in spite of its reduplication on a rhyme of the final part, my charlatanry in the form of the primitive mode of a sonnet,* I bet, if each term did not reverberate back to you off various eardrums, to charm a mind open to multiple understandings.

—Perhaps! accepted our thought in a playfulness of night breath, the same.

*Used during the English Renaissance.

Reference Matter

Notes

Introduction

1. Texts providing the broadest-based discussions of the problem of occasional poetry include Hardison 107–22; Kamholtz (on Ben Jonson); Oppenheimer (on Goethe); Leighton (eighteenth-century German); and Thayer (on Klopstock).

2. O. B. Hardison's comment that "a very large percentage of Jonson's poetry is *frankly* occasional" (112; emphasis added) evidences lingering prejudice against occasional verse even in those who most seek to eradicate it.

3. Other critics who have already begun investigating this other Mallarmé include Virginia A. La Charité, whose article "Mallarmé and the Plastic Circumstances of the Text" offers a remarkably perceptive discussion of the importance of the *Vers de circonstance* and the dominance of plasticity in the so-called pure poetry (her 1987 book *Un Coup de dés: The Dynamics of Space* is also noteworthy in this respect); Alison Fairlie, who labelled her work on Mallarmé's thank-you letters as a study of a form "on the fringe of 'literature proper' "; Jacques Michon, who has written a book-length study of *Les Mots anglais*; John Porter Houston, who perceptively describes Mallarmé's new conception of drama as that which separates him from the negative *l'art pour l'art* social thought of his youth and from the usual Symbolist emphasis on an elite; Barbara Johnson, who, writing on performative language, reads Mallarmé's prose poem "La Déclaration foraine" as the story of the recitation of an occasional poem, and whose article, "Erasing Panama: Mallarmé and the Text of History," characterizes Mallarmé as a "mild-mannered reporter sending us delayed dispatches from nineteenth-century Paris" (59); and Vincent Kaufmann, whose fine chapter on Mallarmé in *Le Livre et ses adresses* also acknowledges the importance of the circumstantial aspects of Mallarmé's oeuvre and considers the question of "address" in literature based on a compelling reading of *La Dernière Mode*, the "poëmes critiques," *Le Livre*, and certain of the *Vers de circonstance*. In this context I would also like to mention Ross Chambers's article, "An Address in the Country: Mallarmé and the Kinds of Literary Context." The article, though not specifically *about* Mallarmé, nevertheless brilliantly uses one of Mallarmé's "Loisirs de la poste" to make its point. The pieces by Kaufmann and

Chambers were brought to my attention by Ann Smock and Pat Merivale, respectively, after I had completed the original draft of this study.

It is, however, Leo Bersani's book, *The Death of Stéphane Mallarmé*, that develops the most innovative approach to Mallarmé studies in years. Bersani's great merit is to have considered, nonexegetically, the whole of the Mallarméan enterprise. The result is the uncovering of a Mallarmé radically opposed to the by now "official" versions of him, one whose writing is "at once impossible to read and extremely easy to read" in its mobile representations of the eroticized mental text (ix). Fully acknowledging the occasional nature of the later works, Bersani contends that Mallarmé's manner of attending to occasions consists in his leaving them, and that this displaced attentiveness is crucial for an understanding of his difficulty (56–57). But Bersani is less interested in conventional notions of difficulty that require interpretation and exegesis as an antidote than in difficulty as the product of Mallarmé's movement away from the circumstances that occasion his poems. Thus his emphasis is not on interpretation but on a description of the performance of the text.

Chapter One

1. In *Virtual Theater from Diderot to Mallarmé*, Evlyn Gould provides excellent in-depth discussions of the "Ouverture ancienne" and "L'Après-midi." She gives a more nuanced account of the seeing, speaking subject of these poems, showing how like all narrators of what she terms *virtual theatre*, the Nurse and the Faun are also spectators. In the case of the "Ouverture ancienne," Gould notes: "the facts reported in the finished past tense by a theoretically objective narrator are confused with the subjective present-tense impressions of a spectator. As in all virtual plays, the text works to insure the distance of narrative objectivity so as to illustrate the mobility of subjectivity across that distance" (150).

2. See Bersani's discussion of Mallarmé's "Triptych" (*Death* 67–73) for a persuasive argument about the eroticization of perception.

3. In "Mallarmé's 'Sonnet en yx': The Ambiguities of Speculation," Ellen Burt discusses the problem of a literal point of view in the sonnet, comparing Mallarmé's description of the scene in his letter to Cazalis that "provides a description of the space seen from outside of the room" with the final version that "appears, at least initially, to depend on a spectator located within" (58). Robert Cohn (*Toward* 59) states that in the first stanza of the "Ouverture," the "scene is set outdoors, and as in a cinematic pan-in, we enter, through the frame of the window, Hérodiade's abandoned room" in the second stanza.

4. It is not my purpose to suggest that the sonnet be read in terms of this letter, but it is curious to note the extent to which correspondences can be

drawn between them. The letter also features a view of a Mallarméan inte-
rior, "ma chambre à moi, seule, pleine de ma pensée, les carreaux bombés
par les Rêves intérieurs comme les tiroirs de pierres précieuses d'un riche
meuble, les tapisseries tombant à plis connus" ("my own room, alone, full
of my thought, the window panes bulging with my inner Dreams like the
drawers of precious stones in a rich piece of furniture, the tapestries falling
in familiar folds"), with a "miroir ancien" ("old mirror"). Mallarmé fears
that "Ces quelques lignes seront défaites comme mon décor" ("These few
lines will be undone like my decor"). He goes on to mention "l'œuvre des
gens qui pensent à côté, ni même ne s'extravase en cadre, mais se fige en le
contour coupé là où il cesse d'être" (*Correspondance* 1:233–34) ("the work
of people who miss the point, which does not flow out into the framework,
but which is fixed in a sharp contour cut off there where it ceases to be").

5. Another masterful use of a parenthetical expression that comes im-
mediately to mind is in the "Time Passes" section of *To the Lighthouse* in
which we are informed of the main character's death by a series of subordi-
nated phrases figured within the space of brackets: "[Mr. Ramsay, stumbling
along a passage one dark morning, stretched his arms out, but Mrs. Ramsay
having died rather suddenly the night before, his arms, though stretched
out, remained empty]" (194). Mrs. Ramsay's death is curiously hypostatized
as the empty space between her husband's arms.

6. See Bersani's *Death of Stéphane Mallarmé* (7–17) for a perceptive ac-
count of these repetitions.

7. In "Toward the Poetics of Juxtaposition: *L'Après-midi d'un faune*" (33),
Roseline Crowley described the structure of the text as tripartite: (1) a pre-
text that represents a phenomenon prior to the act of writing, designated
from the first verse, (2) the Fable, the three italicized sections, and (3) a
framing discourse, set in roman type.

8. For an excellent discussion of the problematic status of narrative in this
poem, see Nathaniel Wing's chapter on Mallarmé in *The Limits of Narrative*:
"The poem both produces and suspends narrative; it describes and speculates
and blurs the distinction between decor and thought: a lyric 'voice' 'speaks'
and this becomes fragmented and depersonalized. An allegory of desire and
esthetic production, the poem allegorizes its own production of meaning
without ever achieving a totalizing, transfiguring moment; it is a deferring
of intentionality and interpretation" (98).

Chapter Two

1. Austin specifically mentions "I salute you" on pages 71 and 81 and, as
"behabitives," the verbs "toast" and "drink to" on page 160.

2. Although there are no explicit performative utterances in the *Poésies*,
there are several in the *Vers de circonstance*. Among those we might note:

Non comme pour étinceler
Aux immortels dos de basane
Tard avec mon laisser-aller
Je vous salue, Octave Uzanne.
   ("Envois divers," *O.c.* 155)

Not as if to sparkle with wit
At the immortal bronzed backs
Late with my letting-go
I salute you, Octave Uzanne.

J'atteste ici pour votre œil enchanté
Que James est en parfaite santé.
   ("Envois divers," *O.c.* 156)

I attest here for your delighted eye
That James is in perfect health.

Ployé devant la Vierge élue
Un ange autrefois la pria
Avec ces mots je vous salue
Marie, en latin Maria.
   ("Envois divers," *O.c.* 160-61)

Wings spread before the chosen Virgin
In bygone days an angel prayed to her
With these words, I greet you,
Marie, in Latin, Maria.

Je fais le vœu que ma liqueur
Vous coule douce jusqu'au cœur.
   ("Sur des cruches de Calvados," *O.c.* 175)

I make a vow that my liqueur
Flows sweetly to your heart.

The relative abundance of explicit performative utterances in the *Vers de circonstance* can perhaps be accounted for by three principal reasons: (1) the fact that, generally speaking, the syntax of the *Vers de circonstance* is less dislocated than that of the later *Poésies*; here the conjugated verb is not consistently avoided; (2) the posited *address* of the verses (see the mention of the "dialogic situation" of occasional verse in the main text of this chapter); and (3) the simple fact that most occasional verse *is* itself performative. Note the specific reference to the speech acts of greeting or salutation, avowing, stating, saying, and so on, in the above quoted examples.

3. Austin also considered the proper procedure for the orthodox execution of the performative in written utterances: "In written utterances (or 'inscriptions'), *by his* [the person doing the uttering, and so the acting] *appending his signature* (this has to be done because, of course, written utterances are not tethered to their origin in the way spoken ones are)" (60–61). I am not considering the question of the signature in the poems, which obviously are not signed in a manner analogous to legal documents. Thus the criteria for the explicit performative in Mallarmé's poetry are essentially the same as those established by Austin for verbal utterances. For discussions of the question of the signature as it relates to the performative, see J. Derrida's "Signature Event Context" (193–97) and his "Limited Inc."

4. Kristeva notes that Mallarmé's texts show a preference for the category of nouns over that of verbs and quotes P. Guiraud's calculation (iv) of the distribution of the parts of speech in Mallarmé's poems: "46% nouns, 24% verbs, 20% adjectives, 5.5% adverbs and 4.7% function words [*sic*]" (274).

5. In the *Poésies* there are a number of other locutions that approximate the force of the performative without fulfilling the requirements for the explicit performative. In the late poems, for instance, there is a curious negation of performance in the sonnet "Mes bouquins refermés sur le nom de Paphos" in the verse "Je n'y hululerai pas de vide nénie" ("I will not ululate an empty funeral dirge"). This is not an explicit performative, both because of the use of the future tense and the negation of the verb, but I would argue that the verse actually accomplishes phonically what it denies grammatically: the onomatopoetic verb "hululer" in fact "performs" the wailing of the dirge. See my discussions of the verses "Aboli bibelot d'inanité sonore" and "Pas de clapotement" in Chapter 1 for parallel arguments.

6. Mallarmé's collected toasts provide a veritable primer for the novice toastmaster. In four of the six prose "Toasts" gathered in the Pléiade edition the action appears unequivocally in the first person present indicative (*O.c.* 862–65):

"Discours à Catulle Mendès": "Je lève, pour tous ici, mon verre à Catulle Mendès" ("I raise, for all here, my glass to Catulle Mendès").

"Toast à Gustave Kahn": "Je tends une coupe privée de mousse ou mieux, à vous, Kahn, simplement la main" ("I hold out a cup deprived of bubbles or better, to you, Kahn, simply my hand").

"Toast au nom de Leconte de Lisle": "Je lève mon verre, au nom de Leconte de Lisle, à tous, à la poésie" ("I raise my glass, in the name of Leconte de Lisle, to all, to poetry").

"Toast à ses jeunes amis": "Je bois au bonheur de chacun" ("I drink to the happiness of each one of you").

In the other two toasts the verb is either absent or wayward. In the "Toast à Jean Moréas" the verb is elided: "Ce toast, Au nom du cher absent Verlaine" (*O.c.* 864) ("This toast, in the name of dear absent Verlaine"). In the "Toast à Emile Verhaeren," the verb is so deeply embedded in complex syntax that, separated from its object, its performative force is lost (*O.c.* 864):

> A Verhaeren . . .
>   pour toast
>   j'élève, avec une solennité
> intime
>   en le lisant, ce soir, dans
> les dix livres de *Poëmes* aux
> *Villes Tentaculaires*
>   ma joie du grandiose . . .
> . . . entre eux,
> selon un génie humain, son
> Vers.

> To Verhaeren . . .
>   as a toast
>   I raise, with an intimate solemnity
>   on reading, this evening, in
> his ten books of *Poems* to the
> *Tentacular Cities*
>   my joy of the grandiose . . .
> . . . among them
> according to a human genius, his
> Poetry.

(The irregularity of the verse lines is not a result of my ellipsis; Mallarmé's toast to Verhaeren is composed in an unusual composite of verse and prose.)

The combination "salut"/toast can also be found in an interesting poem collected in the *Vers de circonstance*, the "Toast" offered to M. Rousselot, Director of Collège Rollin, on the occasion of a banquet of Saint-Charlemagne, in February 1895. Here again the performative is implied without quite conforming to an orthodox expression of it. In this case the verb is indeed a first person singular ("je tends") but it acquires performative force only in its linking with the last line: "Je tends . . . la louange" or figuratively, as in my analysis of "Toast funèbre" in this chapter, in "je tends . . . haut notre Coupe." The unusual typographical disposition allows one to perform a series of permutations on the first and last octosyllabic lines quoted below and their "coupe" after four syllables (*O.c.* 178):

Aussi je tends
          avec le rire
Ecume sur ce vin dispos
Qui ne saurait se circonscrire
Entre la lèvre et des pipeaux

A Vous dont un regard me coupe
La louange
          haut notre Coupe

Thus I hold out
          with laughter
Sparkle on this wine
Which could not be circumscribed
Between the lip and the pipe

To You whose look cuts my
Praise
          high our cup

7. The "Quelqu'un" is usually taken either as a representation of Everyman, as in "Homme" (line 28), or as Gautier himself. Noulet reads "Quelqu'un" as "Gautier, and, by extension, all great poets" (22).

8. The Flammarion edition of the complete works presents the following version of this line, which by its shift of the question mark and the separation and capitalization of "Non" performs the negation even more emphatically: "Est-il, de ce destin, rien qui demeure? Non." (242) ("Is there, of this destiny, anything that remains? No.")

9. One example given by Davies is the following: "There are several examples of insertions . . . whose purpose is most often to restore the original sense to expressions that have become clichés. Cf. in *Ballets*, where the poet tries to avoid the use of the common expression *du fait de* (due to the fact that): '. . . elle paraît, appelée dans l'air, s'y soutenir, du fait italien d'une moelleuse tension de sa personne'" ("*Tombeaux*" 185).

10. There is a degree to which the verse, after undergoing its "monumentalization" as active performative, then, however, falls back into cliché once its performativity is played out. This, at least, has been the function of literary criticism. Through repeated exegesis of the line we have redomesticated it to the point where we no longer think about it as an aberrant construction. We simply accept it as the equivalent of "Je lève mon verre" and suppress any qualms we might have about the line's acceptability in that the difficulty of this phrase is negligible when compared to the problem posed by the second hemistich: "où souffre un monstre d'or."

11. The importance accorded to the poem's prepositions can be even more readily seen in the 1913 typesetting instructions Pound gave to Harriet Monroe:

> The apparition   of these faces   in the crowd:
> Petals   on a wet, black bough. (In Kenner 197)

12. See Mary Louise Pratt's *Toward a Speech Act Theory of Literary Discourse* (25–37) for an excellent discussion and critique of Jakobson's article.

13. One example of a performative moment par excellence in Mallarmé's prose would seem to be the famous "Je dis: une fleur! et, hors de l'oubli où ma voix relègue aucun contour, en tant que quelque chose d'autre que les calices sus, musicalement se lève, idée même et suave, l'absente de tous bouquets" (*O.c.* 368) ("I say: a flower! and, out of the forgetfulness to which my voice relegates no contour, as something other than the known calyxes musically arises the idea itself, sweet, the absent one from all bouquets"). But what happens when in criticism this particular quote has been used so often that it seems to lose its force? Is the performative force of an utterance inexhaustible, or can it slowly fade over time? Austin never addressed the question, but Benveniste indirectly did so when he deliberately excluded all conventional locutions from the performative. It might be instructive to see the function of criticism itself as contributing to an etiolation of the performative in that in hearing repeated so often the very same phrases we no longer are sensitive to their performativity. This would indicate that the iterability of a performative phrase is, paradoxically, at once its constituting factor and its deathknell.

Chapter Three

1. Note the contrast with de Man's earlier views on the problem of representation cited in Chapter 1.

2. See de Man (*Allegories* 106–10) and Culler (*On Deconstruction* 86–88) for discussions of Nietzsche's deconstruction of causality.

3. The structure I outline here is similar in many respects to that which I discussed in Chapter 1 in "L'Après-midi d'un faune," although in "Prose" the intervention of a third term, the "era of authority," to some extent skews the comparison.

4. For this discussion I am indebted to Jean Andrews, who generously shared with me her work on first person narration in Samuel Beckett's prose.

5. In a footnote Richard suggests (only to later reject because of its fragility) the possibility of distinguishing three distinct phases in the poem according to a framework of historical evolution, a "medieval youth"; a "noon" of sensation, thought, unconsciousness, and silence that devolves into "l'ère

d'autorité"; and a "modern epoch," the critical age of Mallarmé and des Esseintes (453).

6. In her essay "The Frame of Reference: Poe, Lacan, Derrida" in *The Critical Difference*, Barbara Johnson points out Derrida's critique of Lacan's reading of Poe's "The Purloined Letter" (one cannot help noticing a bit of "relational frenzy" in the successive "frame-ups" here as well) as stating that "Lacan has eliminated not the frame but the unframability of the literary text. But what Derrida calls 'parergonal logic' is paradoxical precisely because both of these incompatible (but not totally contradictory) arguments are equally valid. The total inclusion of the frame is both mandatory and impossible. The frame thus becomes not the borderline between the inside and the outside, but precisely what subverts the applicability of the inside/ outside polarity to the act of interpretation" (128). And later: "the frame is always being framed by part of its contents" (131).

7. In "A Poetry-Prose Cross" Robert G. Cohn has interestingly noted the importance of the *shape* of the prose poem: "The prose poem seems fated to a *croisée* (casement window) effect, partly by its shape on the page, which reflects the poetic brevity and density (vertically) combined with the horizontal lines of the narrative—despite their being broken up, they suggest the single line which could keep on going through a lengthy narration—and is kept limited this way. To a certain extent the symmetry dictates the shape, and we may say that a prose poem tends toward a balance between its horizontal and vertical elements. When, for example, Baudelaire's more garrulous pieces in the *Spleen de Paris* run on for a couple of pages, one is obscurely aware of a violation of the rules of the game" (140).

Chapter Four

1. The majority of these terms are taken from the architectural critic Henry-Russell Hitchcock's definition of the monumental in the symposium "In Search of a New Monumentality" in the British journal *Architectural Review* (123–24).

2. This terminology might be more suggestive for classifying the conventions of the traditional funeral elegy. See Hardison, chap. 6, "Varieties of Elegy."

3. See Paul de Man, "Lyric and Modernity" in *Blindness and Insight* (166–86) for a convincing refutation of Stierle's reading of Mallarmé's "Tombeau" as nonrepresentational.

4. The question of the nature of Mallarmé's tribute to Baudelaire is the subject of a polemic between Austin Gill ("Le Tombeau de Charles Baudelaire"), who believes the "Tombeau" expresses disapproval of Baudelaire and L. J. Austin, who contests this ("'Le Tombeau de Charles Baudelaire' by Stéphane Mallarmé: Satire or Homage?").

5. My own phrasing here reveals a certain irony in that it is highly paradoxical and highly suspect to do away with monumentality, the supreme expression of mastery, with a "masterstroke." Mallarmé does away with a poetry of monumentality without yielding his poetic mastery, in spite of his claims to the "elocutionary disappearance of the poet." As I am able to only broach the vast topic of the monument in this chapter, I plan to take up again the question of monumental representation in the nineteenth and twentieth centuries in a future book-length project.

6. An interesting parallel can be found in Henry James's short story, "The Altar of the Dead," in which James elaborates on Stransom's obsessive relationship with his "dead": "There were hours at which he almost caught himself wishing that certain of his friends would now die, that he might establish with them in this manner a connection more charming than, as it happened, it was possible to enjoy with them in life" (242). Mallarmé himself explicitly noted, after the departure of François Coppée: "Car ce n'est qu'après leur départ et quand ils sont redevenus des absents, que je suis avec mes chers hôtes hâtifs" (Mondor 287) ("Because it is only after their departure and when they have become absent ones again that I am with my dear hasty guests").

7. See Robert G. Cohn's *Toward the Poems of Mallarmé* (156–57) for Mallarmé's own translation of an earlier version of the sonnet.

8. According to Charles Chassé, who had written to Richard H. Hart, then head of the Humanities department of Baltimore's Enoch Pratt Free Library, neither description of the monument is entirely accurate. The base of the monument is of granite, and the upper part is of white marble drawn from local quarries (106).

9. See the stanza that begins with "M'introduire dans ton histoire" (O.c. 75) and the image of the Faun's finger, "*gardant / Par un doigt simple, afin que sa candeur de plume / Se teignît à l'émoi de sa sœur qui s'allume*" (O.c. 52) ("*keeping / By a single finger, in order that her featherlike candor / Take on the hue of the excitement of her sister, which was beginning to catch fire*"), which may share a certain resemblance with the casual but powerful "doigt" of "Sur les bois oubliés."

10. The term "cemetery of tradition" is borrowed from Caroline Newman, "Cemeteries of Tradition: The Critique of Collection in Heine, Nietzsche, and Benjamin." I am indebted to Caroline Newman for our richly productive discussions that helped me formulate many of the concepts elaborated here and in other chapters, and especially for her work on the museum, which sparked my interest in the monument.

11. The monumentality perceived as inherent in the column may, indeed, date back to the ancients. Gregor Paulsson notes that Classic Rome characterized its buildings with adjectives like *magnificus, splendidus, decorus,*

and nouns like *maiestas* and *dignitas*. Vitruvius describes a building without columns as purely functional, but with columns it is designated as *dignitas* ("In Search" 122).

12. Bowie's evaluation might be contested on the grounds that the text doesn't *look* "normal" and thus might allow one a certain comfort in not expecting it to be read in any normal fashion. I wonder if "Prose" or even "A la nue accablante tu" might not, in fact, be more disturbing in that the regularity of their stanzaic composition might lead one to expect a corresponding regularity in syntax and semantics.

13. I present a few representative examples of Mallarmé's use of the term "architecture": In an epigraph to *Divagations*, "Un livre comme je ne les aime pas, ceux épars et privés d'architecture" ("A book as I don't like them, scattered and deprived of architecture"). In a letter dated March 7, 1885, to René Ghil, "cette tentative de poser dès le début de la vie la première assise d'un travail dont l'architecture est sue dès aujourd'hui de vous; et de ne point produire (fût-ce des merveilles) au hasard" (*Correspondance* 2:286) ("this attempt to lay right from the beginning of one's life the first foundation for a work whose architecture is already known to you; and not to produce [however marvelous such works might be] at random"). Note the way in which the same thought is reformulated for the "Autobiographie" (quoted in the text) written seven months later. Other uses may be found in *O.c.* 732; *Divagations* 259–60; and in a letter to Cazalis, dated April 3, 1870.

The terms "monument" and "monumental" are used with similar resonances; see *O.c.* 298, 361, and 635.

These uses can be instructively contrasted with the following: From fragment 2 of *Le Livre*, "Eviter quelque réalité d'échafaudage demeuré autour de cette architecture spontanée et magique n'y implique pas le manque de puissants calculs et subtils" ("To avoid a certain reality of structure surrounding that spontaneous and magic architecture does not therefore imply a lack of powerful and subtle calculations"). And from a September 1897 letter to A. G. Khan, "Comme cela se groupe et se construit à la manière des architectures mobiles musicales, toutes les probabilités que contient une riche substance de rêve tour à tour s'érigeant, illuminant et souriant" (*Correspondance* 9:276) ("It is grouped and constructed like mobile musical architectures, all the probabilities that a rich substance of dream contains, self-erecting, illuminating, and smiling in turn"). It is tempting to read these last citations as evidence of Mallarmé's changing conception of the architectural monument.

14. In "Toast au nom de Leconte de Lisle" Mallarmé refers to the poet's "architectural skills": "Le maître dont apparaît l'œuvre comme une cité exclusive ou grandiose de palais et de temples" (*O.c.* 864) ("The master whose work appears as an exclusive or grandiose city of palaces and temples").

Chapter Five

1. A preliminary version of this chapter, entitled "Postplay: The Other Mallarmé," which focused on Mallarmé's *Les Loisirs de la poste*, was presented at the tenth annual meeting of the Colloquium in Nineteenth-Century French Studies at Duke University, November 1984.

2. Although nineteenth-century etiquette elaborated an intricate semiotic system with regard to the "cornée" by means of which the folding down of different corners of the *carte de visite* had distinct meanings, in France today formal etiquette dictates that the upper right hand corner of the card must be "cornée" only in the case of a personal visit (never through the mail) when the occupants are not at home or believed to be too ill to receive guests.

3. I thank Stanley Tick for bringing the subject of the *carte de visite* photograph to my attention.

4. There appear to be conflicting opinions as to whether the *carte de visite* photographs were actually used as calling cards. In his study *Cartes de Visite in Ninteenth-Century Photography*, William C. Darrah states that the Duke of Parma introduced the *carte de visite* photograph in 1857 when he placed his portrait on engraved visiting cards. But Darrah then goes on to say that despite their name, they were seldom used as visiting cards (4). In *A. A. E. Disdéri and the Carte de Visite Portrait Photograph*, however, Elizabeth Anne McCauley cites several instances of the *cartes* being used as calling cards (27–28) and states that "the photographic carte de visite began as a novel extension of the traditional calling card. The carte itself was created for an urban society in which people of rank, whose names might or might not be recognized, visited other people of rank, who demanded to know the identity of a caller before admitting him into their homes. The possession of a card was, then as now, a legitimization of identity and proof of a certain social standing, even if the claims and title printed on the card were bogus. With the addition of a small photograph, the card's expressive potential was hugely increased. The face and bearing of a caller or well-wisher could reveal much more about his character than a signature or a catalog of titles and decoration. In addition, the cartes of friends and famous visitors could be preserved and displayed later to guests as evidence of the family's prestige and connections" (30).

5. From 1860 to shortly after the turn of the century a huge industry burgeoned surrounding the production of the *carte de visite* photographs. Special albums in which families collected the portraits of friends and relatives became the rage; for the first time the likenesses of famous figures, of historical landmarks, and of great works of art became universally available.

6. In her study of Mallarmé's thank-you letters Alison Fairlie notes that Mallarmé himself used the *carte de visite* as a shortcut to avoid the tedium of responding to the innumerable manuscripts and offprints he received as his

recognition as poet and Maître increased: "One convention must have light-ened his task (from about 1876): that of the gracefully worded message on a visiting-card. It remains surprising how much, in his fine calligraphy, he can include, whether in this restricted space, or on the larger, but still limited, correspondence-cards he often uses" (184).

7. Mallarmé's oft-quoted statement about the reciprocity of the reflec-tions of independent words on the page perhaps bears repeating here: "Ce sera la Langue, dont voici l'ébat. —Les mots, d'eux-mêmes, s'exaltent à mainte facette reconnue la plus rare ou valant pour l'esprit, centre de suspens vibratoire; qui les perçoit indépendamment de la suite ordinaire, projetés, en parois de grotte, tant que dure leur mobilité ou principe, étant ce qui ne se dit pas du discours: prompts tous, avant extinction, à une réciprocité de feux distante ou présentée de biais comme contingence" (*O.c.* 386). ("Such is Language, whose revels I shall describe. Words, by themselves, exalt the many facets that are the most rare or valuable for the mind. The mind is a center of vibratory suspense, which perceives them independently of normal word order, as if projected on the walls of a cave, for as long as the mobility that is their principle lasts; in this they differ from discourse. All are quick before their extinction to show a reciprocity of fire, distant or presented obliquely, as if contingent.")

8. Mallarmé experimented with the recombination of verses as well in the "Rondels," and, as I will mention later, in the projects for *Le Livre*. The use of such permutations as a basis for poetic creation has had a great deal of popularity in recent years with the French Oulipo group. See Warren F. Motte, Jr., *Oulipo: A Primer of Potential Literature*, esp. pp. 115–25 and 143–53.

9. In "De-architecturization" James Wines criticizes the architecture of the past sixty years as being restrained by "Bauhaus maxims-cum-economy and reconciled to a level of innovation that is more technical than fundamental. Unlike the visual arts of the twentieth century, architecture has not undergone a total inversion or destruction of its aesthetic convictions; but, instead, has continued to thrive on those modest inventions which generally serve to confirm propriety. For example, architecture cannot claim a revolutionary figure of the stature of Duchamp. Even its most respected creative forces—Wright, Corbusier, Mies, Kahn—are appreciated primarily for their uncanny ability to manipulate form and process as extensions of traditions and not as purveyors of some cataclysmic change. There is no one personality who, like Duchamp, questioned every premise, every assumption, and who finally rejected historical precedent in order to establish an entirely new set of definitions" (268). I would argue that in literature it is Mallarmé who occupies the position parallel to Duchamp in the plastic arts.

10. For Bersani, Mallarmé's "doubt about the presence of objects, far

from being—as in Descartes—a deliberate tactical move designed to test the reality of thought and of the world, is itself the very movement of his belief in the world's reality." In the sonnets of the triptych, "it is as if an annihilating identification with objects took place . . . without being completed. *Mallarmé separates himself from his thought's negativizing power to separate itself from the world.* . . . In psychoanalytic terms, he de-realizes those spectral inner objects which, in the Freudian topology, are themselves de-realizations of external objects" (*Freudian Body* 103–5). In de Man's essay "Intentional Structure of the Romantic Image" Mallarmé is a poet in whom loyalty to language is so strong that "the object nearly vanishes under the impact of his words. . . . But . . . it would be a mistake to assume that the ontological priority of the object is being challenged. . . . Mallarmé . . . had always remained convinced of the essential priority of the natural object. The final image of his work, in *Un Coup de Dés*, is that of the poet drowned in the ubiquitous 'sea' of natural substances against which his mind can only wage a meaningless battle" (70–71). For Blanchot, in the essay "Le Mythe de Mallarmé": "The word has meaning only if it rids us of the object it names; it should spare us its presence or its 'concrete recall.' In authentic language, the word has a function, not only representative, but destructive. [But,] for the real absence of an object, it does not substitute its ideal presence. . . . On the contrary . . . we are again in contact with reality, but a more evasive reality, which is presented and evaporates, heard and vanishes, made of reminiscences and allusions, so that if on the one hand it is abolished, on the other it reappears in its most palpable form, like a succession of fugitive and unstable nuances, instead of the abstract meaning whose emptiness it pretends to fill" (37–38).

11. The Flammarion edition of Mallarmé's complete poetry recounts the circumstances of the writing of one of the "Offrandes à Divers du *Faune*" that illustrates this point. The quatrain is dedicated to Pierre René Hirsch, a young poet and pianist that Mallarmé had met at Rodenbach's home. Dying, the young man had expressed the desire to have a dedication from Mallarmé on his copy of "L'Après-midi d'un faune." Mallarmé readily complied, but the book arrived too late, as a letter from Rodenbach informed him: "Bien merci de ce que votre bon cœur vous avait suggéré, les exquis vers auraient fait la dernière joie du pauvre enfant et, arrivés trop tard, n'ont pu que joindre leurs rimes—comme des mains—à son chevet mortuaire" (573) ("Thank you very much for what your good heart suggested to you, the exquisite poem would have been the final joy of the poor child, and, having arrived too late, could only join its rhymes—like hands—on his death bed").

12. Another of the "Dons de fruits glacés" valorizes the creative space opened by chance through a classical allusion (*O.c.* 129):

Pâris qu'un jugement décore
Présenterait sur le chemin
Vers vous belle et plus simple encore
Une pomme de chaque main.

Paris whom a judgment decorates
Would present in his path
Toward [verse] you, beautiful and even more simple
An apple with each hand.

It is the goddess Eris (Strife) who avenges the slight paid her by throwing the golden apple into the midst of the guests attending the wedding of Peleus and Thetis. Paris must then award the apple to "the fairest," and his choice of Aphrodite, who in return has offered him Helen, is, of course, the precipitating cause for the war and the destruction of Troy. Here the positioning of the apple is of paramount importance. It is always "in between": first in the midst of the guests, then as Paris's offering, and finally, symbolized by Helen, it is the fruit stolen from Menelaus. Mallarmé capitalizes on the suggestive positioning of the apple by placing the word "vers" (again, as always, both "toward" and "verse") in the very center of the quatrain and by doubling the offering. Madeleine (Mme Henry Roujon), to whom the quatrain is dedicated, is offered not one but two apples "sur le chemin / Vers vous."

13. Bénichou recounts a marvelous anecdote from Mondor's biography of Mallarmé that has some bearing here. That Mallarmé may indeed have hoped his literature was addressed to the common man can be seen to some extent in the prose poem "Conflit" and in his response to Berthe Morisot, who received this reply when she asked why he didn't write in order to be able to be understood by his cook: "Comment? mais pour ma cuisinière, je n'écrirais pas autrement" (Bénichou 75) ("What? but I wouldn't write any differently for my cook"). Indeed, two of the "Galets d'Honfleur" are directed to "Françoise," evidently one of the domestics in the Mallarmé household (O.c. 174):

Françoise qui nous sert à table
Apporte maint plat délectable.

Françoise, who serves our dinner
Brings many a delectable dish.

Françoise, pareille au requin
Mange de baisers "paur tit quin."

Françoise, like the shark
Eats up "honey lambkins" with kisses.

14. One might note Marc Saporta's novel *Composition n° 1* here, which
is, to my knowledge, the only work of literature published by a major press
with unbound pages.

Works Cited

Abrams, M. H., et al., eds. *The Norton Anthology of English Literature*. Vol. 1. New York: Norton, 1974.

Agulhon, Maurice. *Marianne into Battle: Republican Imagery and Symbolism in France, 1789–1880*. Trans. Janet Lloyd. Cambridge: Cambridge UP, 1981.

Alloway, Lawrence. *Topics in American Art Since 1945*. New York: Norton, 1975.

Apollinaire, Guillaume. *Œuvres poétiques*. Ed. Marcel Adéma and Michel Décaudin. Paris: Gallimard, 1965.

Aristotle. *Poetics*. Trans. James Hutton. New York: Norton, 1982.

Auden, W. H. *Academic Graffiti*. New York: Random House, 1971.

Austin, John L. *How to Do Things with Words*. Ed. J. O. Urmson and Marina Sbisà. 2d ed. Cambridge: Harvard UP, 1962.

Austin, L. J. "'Le Tombeau de Charles Baudelaire' by Stéphane Mallarmé: Satire or Homage?" *Etudes baudelairiennes*. Vol. 3. *Hommage à W. T. Bandy*. Ed. James S. Patty and Claude Pichois. Neuchâtel: A la Baconnière, 1973. 185–200.

Barthes, Roland. *The Eiffel Tower and Other Mythologies*. Trans. Richard Howard. New York: Hill and Wang, 1979.

————. "Rhetoric of the Image." *Image, Music, Text*. Trans. Stephen Heath. New York: Hill and Wang, 1977. 32–51.

————. *Writing Degree Zero / Elements of Semiology*. Boston: Beacon Press, 1967.

Baudelaire, Charles. *Œuvres complètes*. Ed. Y.-G. le Dantec and Claude Pichois. Paris: Gallimard, 1961.

Beckett, Samuel. "Three Dialogues." *Disjecta: Miscellaneous Writings and a Dramatic Fragment*. Ed. Ruby Cohn. New York: Grove, 1984. 138–45.

Bénichou, Paul. "Mallarmé et le public." *L'Ecrivain et ses travaux*. Paris: José Corti, 1967. 69–88.

Benjamin, Walter. "Walter Benjamin's Short History of Photography." Trans. Phil Patton. *Artforum* (Feb. 1977): 46–51.

Benveniste, Emile. *Problems in General Linguistics*. Coral Gables, FL: U of Miami P, 1970.

Bersani, Leo. *The Death of Stéphane Mallarmé*. Cambridge: Cambridge UP, 1982.

———. *The Freudian Body*. New York: Columbia UP, 1986.

———. "Mallarmé in Mourning." *New York Times Book Review*, 15 Jan. 1984: 10.

Blanchot, Maurice. "Le mythe de Mallarmé." *La Part du feu*. Paris: Gallimard, 1949. 35–48.

Bosley, Keith, trans. *Mallarmé: The Poems*. By Stéphane Mallarmé. Harmondsworth, Eng.: Penguin, 1977.

Boulay, Daniel. *L'Obscurité esthétique de Mallarmé et la "Prose pour des Esseintes."* Paris: D. Boulay, 1960.

Bowie, Malcolm. *Mallarmé and the Art of Being Difficult*. Cambridge: Cambridge UP, 1978.

Bowra, C. M. *Poetry and Politics, 1900–1960*. Cambridge: Cambridge UP, 1966.

Brereton, Geoffrey. *A Short History of French Literature*. Harmondsworth, Eng.: Penguin, 1976.

Bronson, Bertrand Harris. *Facets of the Enlightenment*. Berkeley: U of California P, 1968.

Burt, Ellen. "Mallarmé's 'Sonnet en yx': The Ambiguities of Speculation." *Yale French Studies* 54 (1977): 55–82.

Chambers, Ross. "An Address in the Country: Mallarmé and the Kinds of Literary Context." *French Forum* 11 (1986): 199–215.

Chase, Cynthia. "Paragon, Parergon: Baudelaire Translates Rousseau." *Diacritics* 11 (1981): 42–51.

Chassé, Charles. *Les Clefs de Mallarmé*. Paris: Aubier, 1954.

Cohn, Robert Greer. "A Poetry-Prose Cross." *The Prose Poem in France: Theory and Practice*. Ed. Mary Ann Caws and Hermine Riffaterre. New York: Columbia UP, 1980. 135–62.

———. *Toward the Poems of Mallarmé*. Berkeley: U of California P, 1980.

Crane, Michael, and Mary Stofflet, eds. *Correspondence Art: Source Book for the Network of International Postal Art Activity*. San Francisco: Contemporary Arts, 1984.

Creighton, Thomas H. *The Architecture of Monuments: The Franklin Delano Roosevelt Memorial Competition*. New York: Reinhold, 1962.

Crowley, Roseline. "Toward the Poetics of Juxtaposition: *L'Après-midi d'un faune*." *Yale French Studies* 54 (1977): 33–44.

Culler, Jonathan. "Junk and Rubbish: A Semiotic Approach." *Diacritics* 15 (Fall 1985): 3–12.

———. *On Deconstruction: Theory and Criticism after Structuralism*. Ithaca: Cornell UP, 1982.

———. *The Pursuit of Signs—Semiotics, Literature, Deconstruction*. Ithaca: Cornell UP, 1981.

——. *Structuralist Poetics*. Ithaca: Cornell UP, 1975.

Darrah, William C. *Cartes de visite in Ninteenth-Century Photography*. Gettysburg, PA: W. C. Darrah, 1981.

Davies, Gardner. *Mallarmé et le drame solaire*. Paris: José Corti, 1959.

——. *Les Noces d'Hérodiade*. Paris: Gallimard, 1959.

——. *Les "Tombeaux" de Mallarmé*. Paris: José Corti, 1950.

——. *Vers une explication rationnelle du Coup de dés, essai d'exégèse mallarméenne*. Paris: José Corti, 1953.

de Man, Paul. *Allegories of Reading*. New Haven: Yale UP, 1979.

——. "Autobiography as De-facement." *MLN* 94 (1979): 919–30.

——. *Blindness and Insight: Essays in the Rhetoric of Contemporary Criticism*. New York: Oxford UP, 1971.

——. "Intentional Structure of the Romantic Image." *Romanticism and Consciousness: Essays in Criticism*. Ed. Harold Bloom. New York: Norton, 1970. 65–77.

Derrida, Jacques. "The Double Session." *Dissemination*. Trans. Barbara Johnson. Chicago: U of Chicago P, 1981. 173–285.

——. "Limited Inc." *Glyph* 2 (1978): 162–254.

——. "Mallarmé." *Tableau de la littérature française de Mme de Stael à Rimbaud*. Ed. Marcel Arland et al. Paris: Gallimard, 1974. 368–79.

——. "The Parergon." *October* 9 (1979): 3–40.

——. *Positions*. Trans. Alan Bass. Chicago: U of Chicago P, 1981.

——. *The Post Card: From Socrates to Freud and Beyond*. Trans. Alan Bass. Chicago: U of Chicago P, 1987.

——. "Signature Event Context." *Glyph* 1 (1977): 172–97.

Dournon, J. Y. *La Correspondance pratique*. Paris: Livre de Poche, 1977.

Draper, John W. *The Funeral Elegy and the Rise of English Romanticism*. New York: Octagon, 1967.

Eliot, T. S. *Collected Poems 1909–1962*. New York: Harcourt, 1970.

Fairlie, Alison. " 'Entre les lignes': Mallarmé's Art of Allusion in His Thank-you Letters." *Baudelaire, Mallarmé, Valéry: New Essays in Honour of Lloyd Austin*. Ed. Malcolm Bowie, A. Fairlie, and A. Finch. Cambridge: Cambridge UP, 1982. 181–201.

Felman, Shoshana. *The Literary Speech Act: Don Juan with J. L. Austin; or, Seduction in Two Languages*. Trans. Catherine Porter. Ithaca: Cornell UP, 1983.

Fischler, Alexander. "The Ghost-Making Process in Mallarmé's 'Le Vierge, le vivace,' 'Toast funèbre,' and 'Quand l'ombre menaça.' " *Symposium* 20.4 (Winter 1966): 306–20.

Foucault, Michel. *The Order of Things*. New York: Random House, 1970.

Franklin, Ursula. *An Anatomy of Poesis: The Prose Poems of Stéphane Mallarmé*. North Carolina Studies in Romance Languages and Literatures 16. Chapel Hill: U of North Carolina P, 1976.

Freud, Sigmund. "On the Transformation of Instincts with Special Reference to Anal Erotism." *Character and Culture*. Ed. Philip Rieff. New York: Collier, 1963. 202–9.

Freund, Gisèle. *Photography and Society*. Boston: David R. Godine, 1980.

Frey, Hans-Jost. "The Tree of Doubt." *Yale French Studies* 54 (1977): 45–54.

———. "Undecidability." *Yale French Studies* 69 (1985): 124–33.

Fuchs, R. H. "Monuments." *Claes Oldenburg: Large-Scale Projects, 1977–1980*. New York: Rizzoli, 1980. 96–97.

Gans, Eric. "Prose poétique." *Romanic Review* 65.3 (May 1975): 187–98.

Gautier, Théophile. *Emaux et camées*. Ed. George Matoré. Geneva: Droz, 1947.

Giedion, Sigfried. "The Need for Monumentality." *New Architecture and City Planning*. Ed. Paul Zucker. New York: Philosophical Library, 1944. 549–68.

Gill, Austin. "Le Tombeau de Charles Baudelaire." *Comparative Literature Studies* 4 (1967): 45–65.

Goethe, Johann Wolfgang von. *Conversations of Goethe with Eckermann and Soret*. Trans. John Oxenford. London: George Bell, 1882.

Goodkin, Richard E. *The Symbolist Home and the Tragic Home: Mallarmé and Oedipus*. Purdue University Monographs in Romance Languages 13. Amsterdam: John Benjamins, 1984.

Gould, Evlyn. *Virtual Theatre from Diderot to Mallarmé*. Baltimore: Johns Hopkins UP, 1989.

Guiraud, P. *Index du vocabulaire du symbolisme*. Vol. 3. Paris: Klincksieck, 1953.

Gundersheimer, Werner L. "Patronage in the Renaissance: An Exploratory Approach." *Patronage in the Renaissance*. Ed. Guy Fitch Lytle and Stephen Orgel. Princeton: Princeton UP, 1981. 3–23.

Hardison, O. B., Jr. *The Enduring Monument: A Study of the Idea of Praise in Renaissance Literary Theory and Practice*. Chapel Hill: U of North Carolina P, 1962.

Haskell, Barbara. *Claes Oldenburg: Object into Monument*. Pasadena: Pasadena Art Museum, 1971.

Hegel, G. W. F. *Aesthetics*. Trans. T. M. Knox. Vol. 2. Oxford: Clarendon P, 1975.

Hobbs, Robert. *Robert Smithson: Sculpture*. Ithaca: Cornell UP, 1981.

Holt, Nancy, ed. *The Writings of Robert Smithson*. New York: New York UP, 1979.

Horace. *Odes and Epodes*. Ed. Paul Shorey. New York: Sanborn, 1919.

Houston, John Porter. *Patterns of Thought in Rimbaud and Mallarmé*. Lexington, KY: French Forum, 1986.

Huysmans, J.-K. *A rebours*. Trans. Robert Baldick. Harmondsworth: Penguin, 1984. (Translated as *Against Nature*.)

"In Search of a New Monumentality." *Architectural Review* (Sept. 1948): 117–28.

Isaac, Bonnie J. "'Du fond d'un naufrage': Notes on Michel Serres and Mallarmé's 'Un Coup de dés.'" *MLN* 96 (1981): 824–38.

Ivins, William M., Jr. *Prints and Visual Communication.* Cambridge: Harvard UP, 1953.

Jakobson, Roman. "Closing Statement: Linguistics and Poetics." *Style in Language.* Ed. Thomas Sebeok. Cambridge, MA: Massachusetts Inst. of Technology P, 1960. 350–77.

James, Henry. *The Complete Tales of Henry James.* Ed. Leon Edel. Vol. 9. Philadelphia: Lippincott, 1964.

Johnson, Barbara. *The Critical Difference: Essays in the Contemporary Rhetoric of Reading.* Baltimore: Johns Hopkins UP, 1980.

———. "Erasing Panama: Mallarmé and the Text of History." *A World of Difference.* Baltimore: Johns Hopkins UP, 1987. 57–67.

Kamholtz, Jonathan Z. "Ben Jonson's Epigrammes and Poetic Occasions." *Studies in English Literature* 23 (1983): 77–94.

Kaufmann, Vincent. *Le Livre et ses adresses.* Paris: Méridiens Klincksieck, 1986.

Kenner, Hugh. *The Pound Era.* Berkeley: U of California P, 1971.

Kierkegaard, Søren. *Either/Or.* Trans. David F. Swenson and Lillian Marvin Swenson. Vol. 1. Princeton: Princeton UP, 1959.

Kristeva, Julia. *La Révolution du langage poétique.* Paris: Seuil, 1974.

La Charité, Virginia A. "Mallarmé and the Plastic Circumstances of the Text." *Pre-text, Text, Context: Essays on Nineteenth-Century French Literature.* Ed. Robert L. Mitchell. Columbus: Ohio State UP, 1980. 173–83.

———. *"Un Coup de dés": The Dynamics of Space.* Lexington, KY: French Forum, 1987.

Lawler, James R. *The Language of French Symbolism.* Princeton: Princeton UP, 1969.

Leighton, Joseph. "Occasional Poetry in the Eighteenth Century in Germany." *Modern Language Review* 78 (1983): 340–58.

Lemerre, Alphonse, ed. *Le Tombeau de Théophile Gautier.* Paris: Alphonse Lemerre, 1873.

Lipking, Lawrence. *The Life of the Poet: Beginning and Ending Poetic Careers.* Chicago: U of Chicago P, 1981.

Lippard, Lucy R., ed. *Six Years: The Dematerialization of the Art Object from 1966 to 1972.* New York: Praeger, 1973.

Mallarmé, Stéphane. *Correspondance 1862–1892.* Ed. Henri Mondor and Lloyd James Austin. Vols. 1–9. Paris: Gallimard, 1959–83.

———. *Le Livre.* Ed. Jacques Scherer. Paris: Gallimard, 1957.

———. *Œuvres complètes.* Ed. Carl Paul Barbier and Charles Gordon Millan. Paris: Flammarion, 1983.

————. *Œuvres complètes*. Ed. Henri Mondor and G. Jean-Aubry. Bibliothèque de la Pléiade. Paris: Gallimard, 1945.

————. *Œuvres de Mallarmé*. Ed. Yves-Alain Favre. Paris: Garnier, 1985.

————. *Pour un Tombeau d'Anatole*. Ed. Jean-Pierre Richard. Paris: Seuil, 1961.

————. *Propos sur la poésie*. Ed. Henri Mondor. Monaco: Rocher, 1953.

McCauley, Elizabeth Anne. *A. A. E. Disdéri and the Carte de Visite Portrait Photograph*. New Haven: Yale UP, 1985.

Michaud, Guy. *Mallarmé*. Trans. Marie Collins and Bertha Humez. New York: New York UP, 1965.

Michon, Jacques. *Mallarmé et les mots anglais*. Montreal: Presses de l'Université de Montréal, 1978.

Mondor, Henri. *Vie de Mallarmé*. Paris: Gallimard, 1941.

Motte, Warren F., Jr., ed. and trans. *Oulipo: A Primer of Potential Literature*. Lincoln: U of Nebraska P, 1986.

Mumford, Lewis. *The City in History: Its Origins, Its Transformations, and Its Prospects*. New York: Harcourt, Brace & World, 1961.

————. *The Culture of Cities*. New York: Harcourt, Brace, 1938.

Newman, Caroline. "Cemeteries of Tradition: The Critique of Collection in Heine, Nietzsche, and Benjamin." *Pacific Coast Philology* 19 (1984): 12–21.

Nicolas, Henry. *Mallarmé et le symbolisme*. Paris: Larousse, 1966.

Noulet, Emilie. *Vingt Poèmes de Stéphane Mallarmé*. Geneva: Droz, 1972.

Olds, Marshall C. *Desire Seeking Expression: Mallarmé's "Prose pour des Esseintes."* Lexington, KY: French Forum, 1983.

Oppenheimer, Ernst M. *Goethe's Poetry for Occasions*. Toronto: U of Toronto P, 1974.

Parker, Patricia. "Mallarmé's 'Toast funèbre': Some Contexts and a Reading." *Romanic Review* 71 (1980): 167–82.

Poirier, Richard. "The Difficulties of Modernism and the Modernism of Difficulty." *Humanities in Society* 1.4 (Fall 1978): 271–82.

Porter, Laurence M. "The Disappearing Muse: Erasure of Inspiration in Mallarmé." *Romanic Review* 76.4 (Nov. 1985): 389–404.

Pound, Ezra. *Personae*. New York: New Directions, 1971.

Pratt, Mary Louise. *Toward a Speech Act Theory of Literary Discourse*. Bloomington: Indiana UP, 1976.

Princeton Encyclopedia of Poetry and Poetics. Ed. Alex Preminger, Frank J. Warnke, and O. B. Hardison, Jr. Princeton: Princeton UP, 1974.

Punin, Nikolai. "On Tatlin's Monument to the Third International, 1919." *Form and Function: A Source Book for the History of Architecture and Design 1890–1939*. Ed. Timothy Benton and Charlotte Benton. London: Crosby Lockwood Staples, 1975. 86–87.

————. "Tatlin's Monument, 1922." *Form and Function: A Source Book for the History of Architecture and Design 1890–1939*. Ed. Timothy Benton and Charlotte Benton. London: Crosby Lockwood Staples, 1975. 91.

Rabelais, François. *The Histories of Gargantua and Pantagruel*. Trans. J. M. Cohen. 1955. Harmondsworth: Penguin, 1976.

Richard, Jean-Pierre. *L'Univers imaginaire de Mallarmé*. Paris: Seuil, 1961.

Riffaterre, Michael. "Prosopopoeia." *Yale French Studies* 69 (1985): 107–23.

————. *Semiotics of Poetry*. Bloomington: Indiana UP, 1978.

Royère, Jean. *Mallarmé*. Paris: Albert Messein, 1931.

Ruskin, John. *The Complete Works of John Ruskin*. Vol. 1. New York: Thomas Y. Crowell, n.d.

Said, Edward W. *The World, the Text, and the Critic*. Cambridge: Harvard UP, 1983.

Sanders, Gerald DeWitt, John Herbert Nelson, and M. L. Rosenthal, eds. *Chief Modern Poets of Britain and America*. Vol. 2 of *Poets of America*. London: Macmillan, 1970.

Saporta, Marc. *Composition n° 1*. Paris: Seuil, 1962.

Saunders, J. W. "The Stigma of Print: A Note on the Social Bases of Tudor Poetry." *Essays in Criticism* 1.2 (Apr. 1951): 139–64.

Scherer, Jacques. *L'Expression littéraire dans l'œuvre de Mallarmé*. Geneva: Droz, 1947.

————, ed. *Le "Livre" de Mallarmé*. Paris: Gallimard, 1957.

Scott, David H. T. "Mallarmé and the Octosyllabic Sonnet." *French Studies* 31 (1977): 149–63.

Shakespeare, William. *William Shakespeare: The Complete Works*. Ed. Alfred Harbage. New York: Viking Press, 1969.

Sheavyn, Phoebe. *The Literary Profession in the Elizabethan Age*. Ed. J. W. Saunders. New York: Barnes & Noble, 1967.

Sherwood, Mrs. John (Mary Elizabeth). *Manners and Social Usages*. New York: Harper, 1884.

Sonnenfeld, Albert. "Elaboration secondaire du grimoire: Mallarmé et le poète critique." *Romanic Review* 69 (1978): 72–89.

Soula, Camille. *Gloses sur Mallarmé*. Paris: Diderot, 1946.

Stevens, Wallace. *The Collected Poems*. New York: Vintage, 1954.

Stewart, Susan. *Nonsense: Aspects of Intertextuality in Folklore and Literature*. Baltimore: Johns Hopkins UP, 1978.

Thayer, Terence K. "Klopstock's Occasional Poetry." *Lessing Yearbook*. Vol. 2. Munich: Max Hueber Verlag, 1970. 181–212.

Thompson, Michael. *Rubbish Theory: The Creation and Destruction of Value*. London: Oxford UP, 1979.

Thomson, Patricia. "The Literature of Patronage, 1580–1630." *Essays in Criticism* 2.3 (July 1952): 267–84.

Tompkins, Jane P. "The Reader in History: The Changing Shape of Literary Response." *Reader-Response Criticism: From Formalism to Post-Structuralism*. Ed. Jane P. Tompkins. Baltimore: Johns Hopkins UP, 1980. 201–32.

Ulmer, Gregory L. *Applied Grammatology: Post(e)-Pedagogy from Jacques Derrida to Joseph Beuys*. Baltimore: Johns Hopkins UP, 1985.

———. "The Post-Age." *Diacritics* 11 (1981): 39–56.

Vivier, Robert. "Mallarmé le Parnassien." *Cahiers du Nord* 21 (1948).

Williams, William Carlos. *Paterson*. New York: New Directions, 1946.

Wines, James. "De-Architecturization." *Esthetics Contemporary*. Ed. Richard Kostelanetz. Buffalo: Prometheus, 1978. 266–79.

Wing, Nathaniel. *The Limits of Narrative: Essays on Baudelaire, Flaubert, Rimbaud, and Mallarmé*. New York: Cambridge UP, 1986.

Woolf, Virginia. *To the Lighthouse*. New York: Harcourt, Brace & World, 1927.

Index

In this index an "f" after a number indicates a separate reference on the next page, and an "ff" indicates separate references on the next two pages. A continuous discussion over two or more pages is indicated by a span of page numbers, e.g., "57–59." *Passim* is used for a cluster of references in close but not consecutive sequence.